Nehemiah N. Gore

Rational Refutation of the Hindu Philosophical Systems

Nehemiah N. Gore

Rational Refutation of the Hindu Philosophical Systems

ISBN/EAN: 9783337036171

Printed in Europe, USA, Canada, Australia, Japan

Cover: Foto ©Lupo / pixelio.de

More available books at **www.hansebooks.com**

A RATIONAL REFUTATION

OF THE

HINDU PHILOSOPHICAL SYSTEMS

BY

NEHEMIAH NI'LAKAṆṬHA S'A'STRI' GORE.

TRANSLATED FROM THE ORIGINAL HINDI',

PRINTED AND MANUSCRIPT,

BY

FITZ-EDWARD HALL, D. C. L., Oxon.,
H. M.'s INSPECTOR OF PUBLIC INSTRUCTION FOR THE CENTRAL PROVINCES.

Calcutta:

PRINTED FOR THE CALCUTTA CHRISTIAN TRACT & BOOK SOCIETY.

BISHOP'S COLLEGE PRESS.

1862.

NOTICE.

It is well known that there are material differences in the representations given by some of the profoundest Oriental scholars of the peculiar tenets of the leading schools of Hindu Philosophy—especially those of the Vedanta. The Committee of the Calcutta Christian Tract and Book Society therefore, beg to intimate that their imprimatur can only be understood as bestowed on the contents of this volume generally—and that they must not be regarded as holding themselves responsible for each and all of its particular views or statements. A work of this kind has long been felt to be a desideratum for educated Hindus—many of whom may be better conversant with English than with Sanscrit. And as the work of a learned Christian Brahmin well acquainted with the distinctive doctrines of his ancestral as well as of his adopted faith, the present volume has much to recommend it to the earnest attention of all candid students of Philosophico-theological Hinduism.

Contents.

	Page.
Preface,	vii
List of the Principal Sanskrit Books quoted in this Volume,	281

SECTION I.

Chapter 1.—On the Uses of an Examination of the Hindu Philosophical Systems; with an Enumeration of these Systems, and a Sketch of the Plan to be pursued in the present Treatise, ... 1

„ 2.—Of the Dogmas common to nearly all the Systems; and of the Dogmas peculiar to each of them, the Vedánta excepted, ... 8

„ 3.—Examination of the Sánkhya Doctrines, (1) of the Non-existence of God, as concurrent with the Belief in Virtue, Vice, and their Fruits; and (2) of the Acceptance of the Veda as having had no Conscious Author, and as being irrecusably authoritative, 71

„ 4.—Examination of the Sánkhya Dogma, that Nature is the Material Cause of the World, ... 79

„ 5.—Examination of the Sánkhya Dogma, that Apprehension, Will, Activity, Happiness, Misery, and other Qualities, do not appertain to the Soul, .. 85

„ 6.—Brief Considerations of one Topic of the Mímánsá, with a few Remarks on the Intellectual Peculiarities of the Pandits, and on their Style of Reasoning, .. 103

SECTION II.

Chapter 1.—Briefly prefatory; with an Examination of the Nyáya and Vais'eshika Doctrines touching God, ... 108

„ 2.—Examination of the Nyáya and Vais'eshika Tenets relative to the Soul; namely, that it had no Beginning, that it is All-pervading, and that it takes Birth again and again, ... 118

„ 3.—Examination of the Cause, laid down in the Nyáya, Vais'eshika, and the other Systems, of the Wretchedness of the Soul, that is, its Bondage, and the Means of escaping therefrom; a Succinct Description of the True Nature of Virtue and Vice; and a Criticism of the Views of the Systematists touching Virtue and Vice, their Consequences, &c. : 138

,, 4.—Examination of the Views concerning the State of Emancipation, professed, in common, by the Naiyáyikas and by the Vaiseshikas, ... 152

SECTION III.

Chapter 1.—Description of the Three Sorts of Existence held in the Vedánta: the Key to a Right Understanding of that Scheme of Philosophy, ... 156
,, 2.—Summary of the Vedánta System, ... 174
,, 3.—Examination of the Vedánta Views concerning the Supreme Spirit, ... 196
,, 4.—Proof that the Existence of Brahma cannot be deduced from the Position of the Vedánta, that the Internal Organ requires an Illuminator, ... 212
,, 5.—Argument to show, that the Brahma of the Vedántins, as being quite Void of Qualities, is reduced to nothing, ... 219
,, 6.—Strictures on the Position of the Vedántins, that the World is False; and a Reply to those who suppose, that the Vedántins' Views respecting External Things accord with those of Berkeley, ... 235
,, 7.—The Soul, being subject to Ignorance, cannot, as the Vedántins hold, be One with the Supreme Spirit; a Description of Ignorance; and an Argument to show, that the Denial of the Soul's Identity with Brahma is not set aside by taking the Epithet of False, as applied to Ignorance, in the Acceptation of Perishable, ... 243
,, 8.—Criticism of the Vedánta Tenet of the Falseness of Ignorance, as set forth in Standard Treatises, and as held by well-read Advocates of the Theory, .. 256
,, 9.—Examination of the Tenet of the Vedántins, that there are Three Kinds of Existence. Ignorance cannot be False; and therefore, the Ignorant Soul cannot be one with the Supreme Spirit, ... 263
,, 10.—Examination of the Vedántin's Emancipation; Proof that the Vedánta does not deserve to be called Theistic; and a few Words on the Faculty of Judgment, its Power, and its Use, .. ,. 273

PREFACE.

THIS essay, in its original form, was published at Calcutta during the last year. It consists of two volumes, in the Hindí language, and is entitled *Shaḍ-dars'ana-darpaṇa*, and "Hindu Philosophy examined by a Benares Pandit." Scarcely a page of those volumes, however, is here reproduced without much change. To say nothing of less important alterations, whole chapters have been retrenched, and others have been inserted. The notes, throughout, are new. These, equally with the text, are the work of Pandit Nílakaṇṭha ; a very few excepted, which the nature of their contents will suffice to distinguish.

The *Shaḍ-dars'ana-darpaṇa* was addressed to a section of the author's countrymen. But the pride of the native literati forbids them to have dealings with their vernacular beyond the narrow range of social occasions. Moreover, the technicalities of philosophy, among the Hindus, are as yet drawn solely from the Sanskrit. Only a meagre number of those technicalities are popularly employed; and, of such as are thus employed, not one in ten is fully comprehended by the vulgar. This being the case, the author, as might have been anticipated, discovered, that his Hindí labours had been to little purpose. As for this translation, it was undertaken, at the instance of an estimable missionary, mainly for the use of his fellow-evangelizers, and of Hindu students of English who may wish to acquaint themselves with the abstruser matters of their ancestral religion.

A familiarity with the sketches of Hindu philosophy drawn up by Colebrooke, will be found well-nigh indispensable as a preparation for understanding what is here presented to the reader. Later writers in the same department will, as a rule, be much more likely to mislead than to render any solid assistance. From this stricture a reservation must, however, be made in favour of the Reverend Professor Banerjea, whose *Dialogues on the Hindu Philosophy* are a mine of new and authentic indications. What from the elucidations of that learned gentleman, and those of Pandit Nîlakaṇṭha, it should seem, that, in order really to penetrate the mysteries of Hinduism, we could scarcely do better than commit ourselves to the guidance of Christianized Bráhmans.

There are scores of terms, belonging to the nomenclature of Hindu philosophy, precise equivalents of which have not yet been wrought out for us with the help of the Latin and Greek. Of the terms in question there are not a few which the translator of these pages has been the first to dress in a European garb; and, that he has had other than moderate success, is more than he can venture to suppose. Colebrooke and his successors have, indeed, elaborated many close and felicitous renderings. Still, they have left much unattempted, and something to be amended. Had the translator departed from "na-

PREFACE. ix

ture," as representing *prakriti*,* he would hardly have done amiss. Again, "modification" conveys a very much nearer conception of *vritti*,† —denoting several of the "evolutions" of the "internal organ,"—than is conveyed by "affection." These and many other improvements were thought of when, unfortunately, it was too late, save at the risk of entailing confusion, to introduce them.‡

---

* "Originant" might answer, or "evolvant;" and "originate," or "evolute," for *vikriti*.

"The Greeks agreed with the cosmogonies of the East in deriving all sensible forms from the indistinguishable. The latter we find designated as the τὸ ἄμορφον, the ὕδωρ προκοσμικὸν, the χάος, as the essentially unintelligible, yet necessarily presumed, basis or subposition of all positions. That it is, scientifically considered, an indispensable idea for the human mind, just as the mathematical point, &c. for the geometrician;—of this the various systems of our geologists and cosmogonists, from Burnet to La Place, afford strong presumption. As an idea, it must be interpreted as a striving of the mind to distinguish being from existence,—or potential being, the ground of being containing the possibility of existence, from being actualized." Coleridge's *Notes and Lectures on Shakespeare*, &c, Vol. II., p. 197.

† See pp. 59, 61, and 185, for the characteristics of *vritti*.

‡ A single one was introduced. Between pp. 47 and 111, "sentience" and its conjugates are frequently put for *chaitanya*, &c. See the second note at p. 176. It was Colebrooke, Professor Wilson, and others who herein set the example which the translator for a while unadvisedly followed.

In a considerable number of places, "God" is substituted for I's'wara. On this point, as regards the Sánkhya and the Yoga, see the *Sánkhyasára*,—in the *Bibliotheca Indica*, —Preface, p. 2, foot-note.

"Soul," in an accommodated sense, has been chosen to stand for *jíva* or *jívátman*. See the notes at pp. 2, 210, and 213. In the latter part of III., 5, inadvertently, and yet naturally enough, "soul" will be found used, more than once, for "the unspiritual part of the soul,"—as a Hindu would be compelled to express himself. At p. 234, l. 5, "soul" occurs twice, where "spirit" is intended. In the fourteenth line of the

PREFACE.

A glossary has been omitted solely from want of leisure to prepare one. In fact, the necessity which lay upon the translator, of executing his task against time, if he executed it at all, should excuse many of the defects which will be seen to mark his performance. Pandit Nílakaṇṭha's disquisitions were certainly well worthy of being brought before the public. Even the most advanced of European Sanskrit scholars may therefrom reap instruction. To such, and to many others who will value them, they might have remained unknown for years, or altogether, had not the translator done for them what he has here done to the best of his opportunities.

This work has had the great advantage of being criticized, in its proof-sheets, by the Reverend Dr. Kay, of Bishop's College, Calcutta. By the obliging assistance of the learned and acute Principal, both the author and the translator have profited largely.

CAMP BILAHARI, JUBULPORE DISTRICT:
Christmas, 1861.

---

same page, in place of "I's'wara, no less than the soul," read "I's'wara no less than every other individuated spirit." A few more similar mistakes, the result of unavoidable haste, are noted at the end of the volume.

SECTION I.

CHAPTER 1.

On the Uses of an Examination of the Hindu Philosophical Systems; with an Enumeration of these Systems, and a Sketch of the Plan to be pursued in the present Treatise.

I purpose, in this book, to discuss succinctly the six philosophical Systems (Dars'anas) of the Hindus. The fundamental authorities of the Hindu religion are the Vedas, the Smṛitis,* the Purāṇas, &c.; not the Systems. Of these the staple is argument. But they profess to derive their views from the Veda and other sacred books. Independent authority, as to those views, they disclaim. Hence it might be supposed, that, in examining the Hindu religion, a discussion of the Systems would be quite unnecessary. Such discussion has, however, these advantages :—

1st. The six Systems are not held, by the Hindus, to be the work of ordinary men, but of Ṛishis ;† and they are adjudged

---

* "The laws of the Hindus, civil and religious, are, by them, believed to be alike founded on revelation, a portion of which has been preserved in the very words revealed, and constitutes the Vedas, esteemed, by them, as sacred writ. Another portion has been preserved by inspired writers, who had revelations present to their memory, and who have recorded holy precepts, for which a divine sanction is to be presumed. This is termed Smṛiti, recollection, (remembered law,) in contradistinction to S'ruti, audition, (revealed law)." Colebrooke.

Rather, a code of memorial law is meant by Smṛiti, as in the text. Again, any composition of a man supposed to be inspired may be denominated Smṛiti.

† Primarily, in the Hindu mythology, Ṛishi signifies a holy sage to whom some portion of the Veda is said to have been revealed. In a vague sense, the word denotes an inspired man.

an equality of rank with the Smṛitis, the Purāṇas, &c., which are reputed to have similar authorship. If then, on investigation, errors are proved to exist in the former, doubt must attach to the credit of the latter. When it is shown that the very Ṛishis are wrong, and make gross mistakes in writings by which they undertake to communicate to the world the knowledge of truth and the means of salvation, who can esteem any statement deserving of confidence, simply because it emanated from a Ṛishi?

2ndly. Though vulgar Hindus are indifferent to, and unacquainted with, the dogmas established in the Systems, yet those dogmas are highly considered by the learned. To them those dogmas, concerning God, the world, its origin, the soul,* its bondage, emancipation, and so on, are, as it were, the root and life of the Hindu religion; while the narratives, and tales, and ritual matters of the Vedas, Smṛitis, Purāṇas, &c., may be viewed as its branches. To the learned so excellent do those doctrines appear, and so fully accordant with reason, that they cling to them with the strongest affection; and the cord of this affection holds them fast to the Hindu faith. It is, therefore, my firm conviction, that if they saw those doctrines to be faulty, and discarded them, they would be led to lose all regard for Hinduism. And such a result would, with God's blessing, attend candid enquiry.

3rdly. There is no question that the authors of the systems, and their great expositors, were, in their way, most intelligent and learned men, and acute investigators. But, since, in spite of all the energy they threw into their search after truth they fell into serious errors, it is evident how extremely difficult it is for men to arrive, by their own wisdom, at the true knowledge of God. Add to this, that sages, as in India, so in all other

---

* Throughout these pages, 'soul' is used, in an accommodated sense, to translate *jíva*; a term not applied to the Divine Spirit, while it is employed of men, gods, and all other persons. As these have souls, so, it is thought, have all things animal and vegetable.

countries, have herein failed. Hence, that system, it is established, is divine, which propounds correct views of God and of His right path.

My prayer is, that God may have mercy upon you. Relinquishing partiality, and with a desire for the salvation of your souls, as you would reach the right path, may you ponder what I am about to set forth.

The six Systems are the Nyáya, Vais'eshika, Sánkhya, Yoga, Mímánsá, and Vedánta. They are also called the six S'ástras.* The Sánkhya and the Yoga agree in all essentials; save that the former does not acknowledge God, while the latter does. Hence, occasionally, in Hindu books, both are denominated Sánkhya; the one, atheistic, and the other, theistic. In many places, also, the Mímánsá is styled the prior Mímánsá, and the Vedánta, the latter Mímánsá. The reason of this is, that they are alike concerned with discussing statements of the Veda. The prior Mímánsá pertains to its ritual section; and the latter Mímánsá, to its scientific section. This section, being at the end (anta) of the Veda, is named Vedánta. Thousands of authors, from remote antiquity down to recent times, have written treatises on the six Systems. Among these are some known by the name of Sútras, or Aphorisms, which are reckoned the basis of all the rest, and are referred, by the Hindus, to Rishis. Thus, the Nyáya is ascribed to Gotama, or Akshapáda; the Vais'eshika, to Kaṇáda, or Kaṇabhaksha; the Sánkhya, to Kapila; the Yoga, to Patanjali; the Mímánsá, to Jaimini; and the Vedánta, to Bádaráyaṇa.

The plan which I have resolved upon for criticizing the six Systems is this. In the first place I shall exhibit those doctrines which, with slight deductions, are common to all the Systems; and then those distinctive doctrines of all the

---

* By this word, in its wider acceptation, is denoted a body of teaching, revealed, or of human origin, concerned with any subject whatsoever.

Systems, save the Vedánta, which are especially worthy of examination. In the third section I shall canvass the characteristic doctrines of the Vedánta. The distinctive tenets of the other five Systems I shall deal with in this wise. I have remarked above, that the Sánkhya and the Yoga consent in all important respects but one. On the ground of this general unanimity, I shall treat of their doctrines together. Then I shall speak of one or two articles of the Mimánsá, which are deserving of attention. As for the Nyáya and the Vais'eshika, the learned recognize a close affinity between them. They concede that, for the greater part, nothing found in the one is repugnant to anything occurring in the other, and that, in fact, they supplement each other.* Indeed, Hindus who now-a-days write on the Nyáya, combine the Vais'eshika with it.† The discrepant opinions of these two Systems I shall pass by unnoticed. Their other opinions I shall take account of conjointly. An examination of all the Systems will then follow, in the manner about to be stated.

---

* The seven Vais'eshika predicaments are thus spoken of by Vis'wanátha Panchánana Bhattáchárya: एते च पदार्था वैशेषिकप्रसिद्धा नैयायिकानामप्यविरुद्धाः | *Siddhánta-muktávali* on the first couplet of the *Bháshá-parichchhedu*. "And these categories are well-known in the Vais'eshika, and are not opposed to *the views of* the Naiyáyikas."

† काणादन्यायमतयोर्बालव्युत्पत्तिसिद्धये ।
अन्नम्भट्टेन विदुषा रचितस्तर्कसङ्ग्रहः ॥

"The *Tarka-sangraha*, *i. e.*, *Tract on the Categories*, was composed by the learned Annam Bhatta, with a view to rendering the uninstructed proficients in the doctrines of Kanáda and of the Nyáya."

Thus ends the *Tarka-sangraha*, a Nyáya manual. The couplet has been translated in accordance with Annam Bhatta's explanation of it in his *Tarkadípiká*.

Such books as that just cited, the *Muktávali*, and many more, might fairly —in respect of their subject-matter, and of the fact that they ignore the Nyáya Aphorisms,—be entitled to the appellation of Vais'eshika treatises, were it not that, on topics where the Nyáya and the Vais'eshika deviate, as concerning the kinds of proof, the doctrines of the former are strenuously maintained as against those of the latter.

Many and voluminous are the books concerned with the six Systems; and they handle a large variety of topics. I do not, by any means, undertake to pass all these topics under review, but only such as are most considerable. Many of them are common to all the Systems; while, as to some, the Systems differ among themselves diametrically. Hence, if we investigate any one System thoroughly, our decisions will affect no small portion of the others. To me the Nyáya and the Vais'eshika seem most reasonable of all. Not to mention their claims to preference on other accounts, they acknowledge a God, eternal and omnipotent; and so are superior to the Sánkhya, and to the Mímánsá, which deny God; and to the Vedánta, as well, —which identifies souls with Deity. I shall, therefore, apply a searching scrutiny to the whole of the leading opinions of the Nyáya and Vais'eshika. First of all, however, I shall dispose of a few peculiar doctrines of the Sánkhya and Mímánsá, which call for observation. As was before said, those dogmas of the Yoga, in respect of which it deviates from the Nyáya and Vais'eshika, will be included in treating of the Sánkhya; and I shall dilate on the specialities of the Vedánta in the last section of the volume.

It should be borne in mind that, in this work, I shall present the tenets of the Nyáya and Vais'eshika, not simply as they are expressed in the Aphorisms, but as they have been developed by authors of a later date, both ancient and modern. For, though the Hindus think otherwise, I suspect a difference between the Aphorisms and the treatises founded on them. For instance, these treatises dwell at much length on the subject of God, and adduce numerous arguments in proof of His existence. Indeed, it is ordinarily believed, in the present day, that the capital end of the two Systems in question is, to prove that there is a Deity:* but it is a

---

* In a work of modern date, where an atheist is represented as having put to silence antagonists belonging to divers Hindu persuasions, a Tárkika (or Naiyáyika) is looked to, by the company, as the last refuge in defence of

singular fact that nothing of this transpires in their Aphorisms. In only a single one of the Nyáya Aphorisms do we find God so much as named; and it does not indubitably appear from that, that the author of the Aphorisms believed in Him. In that place, God is declared to be the Maker of the world. But it should be known, that the writer of the *Nyáya-sútra-vṛitti* offers two interpretations of the aphorism referred to, and of the two that succeed it. According to the first of those interpretations, the first of the three aphorisms does not enunciate the view of the author, but is given as the view of an opponent; and the two ensuing aphorisms are for the purpose of refuting it. The expositor, however, understands that his author did not intend to deny the divine origination of the world, but only to assert that God cannot be the Maker of the world, independently of the works of souls. At the same time, the expositor states that, by some, the purport of the three aphorisms is taken otherwise, that is to say, as designed to

the belief in a God. इत्याकर्ण्यं चकिते वेदान्तिनि सर्वे तार्किकमुखम्-
वलोकयन्ति स्म । *Vidwan-moda-tarangiṇí, Ms., fol. 4, verso.* "When the Vedántin, hearing this, was confounded, they all turned their eyes towards the face of the Tárkika."

The following couplet, which has not been traced beyond oral tradition, at once illustrates the irreverence of the Hindu mind, and shows that the Nyáya is prized as the stronghold of theism. The verses are reported—falsely, it is hoped—to have been uttered by Udayana A'chárya, a very celebrated ancient Naiyáyika; in fact, the foremost of Naiyáyika writers after Gotama, the author of the Aphorisms, and Vátsyáyana, his scholiast, both of whom are reputed inspired. It is said that Udayana, after the trouble of a pilgrimage to the temple of Jagannátha at Pooree, found the door shut, on his arrival. Upon this, the impatient logician thus delivered himself, addressing the inhospitable divinity:

ऐश्वर्यमदमत्तोऽसि मामवज्ञाय वर्तसे ।
उपस्थितेषु बौद्धेषु मदधीना तव स्थितिः ॥

"Thou art drunk with the inebriation of majesty: me thou scornest. *But* let the Bauddhas show themselves, and upon me will depend thy *very* existence."

establish God's existence.* In a matter so beset with doubt, it is difficult to arrive at certainty.

---

* The three aphorisms referred to will here be given, with the drift of the commentator's remarks.

The first is: ईश्वरः कारणं पुरुषकर्माफल्यदर्शनात् । "God is the cause, since the works of souls *(purusha)* are found to be ineffectual."

This, in the first place, is assumed to be asserted by an opponent who rejects the dogma—taken for granted, by the commentator, to be held by Gotama—that God and the works of souls are, in concert, the cause of the universe. On one supposition, the opponent is, to all appearance, a Vedántin, whose meaning is, "God is the sole cause," *i. e.,* agreeably to one presumed Vedánta view, "sole and material cause" of the universe, and, agreeably to another view, undoubtedly Vedántic, its "sole and illusory-material cause." "Ineffectual;" *viz.,* on some occasions. "The works of souls are found to be" so. Hence, they are not to be accounted a cause.

But it is to a second interpretation that the commentator evidently accords his preference. This interpretation supposes an objector to urge simply, that God alone, since the works of souls are ineffectual, is the Author of the universe, independently of such works.

Gotama replies: न पुरुषकर्माभावे फलानिष्पत्तेः । "Not so: since, in default of the works of souls, there is no production of effects."

In explication, the commentator argues, resisting the Vedántin, that, inasmuch as God, in his system, is devoid of volition, if He alone were the cause of the universe, everything would be produced at all times, and be uniform in character. The works of souls must, by consequence, be conjoined with God, in order to an origination of the universe.

Anticipating the objection, that, if such weight be attached, as in the last aphorism, to the works of souls, resort must be had to the fiction, that the efforts of souls never miss of their end, the Ṛishi pronounces: तत्कारि- तत्वादहेतुः । *"The efforts of souls are, at times,* no cause *of effects,* because the non-production thereof is caused by that *default of works.*"

That is to say, when a man, for instance, is unsuccessful, his failure is due to want of merit.

In conclusion, the commentator informs us that the construction of the aphorisms, adopted by some, is as follows. Gotama's purpose is to establish God's existence. He begins by laying down that God is Author of the universe; and he repels the notion that souls can be so; as they sometimes fail of bringing their efforts to bear, and thus prove themselves to fall short of omniscience. A Mímánsaka antagonist rejoins, in the second aphorism, that it is not so. But for the works of souls, he contends, effects cannot be produced:

And, again, the name of God nowhere shows itself in the Vais'eshika Aphorisms. In a few of them there is a pronominal prefix—*tad*—which the commentators explain as referring to God.* But I do not mean to enter upon this nice matter. I shall consider the Nyáya and the Vais'eshika doctrines as they are set forth by their expounders, and understood by the Pandits.

CHAPTER 2.

Of the Dogmas common to nearly all the Systems; and of the Dogmas peculiar to each of them, the Vedánta excepted.

I shall first speak of those points on which almost all the Systems are consentaneous.

It appears, even on the most cursory inspection of the Systems, that, the Mímánsá apart, their end is, to inculcate expedients for salvation.†

---

therefore, the good and evil works of souls suffice, through merit and demerit, to account for the universe; and God may be dispensed with. To this the answer of Gotama is, that the works of souls cannot of themselves be the cause of the universe, since they are effectual only under God's directing.

See the *Nyáya-sútra-vritti*, pp 175-177; Book iv, Aphorisms 19, 20, & 21.

* The third aphorism, for one, is as follows: तद्वचनादाम्नाय-प्रामाण्यम् | S'ankara Mis'ra says of this: तदित्यनुप्रक्रान्तमपि प्रसिद्धतयेश्वरं पराम्टशति | "The *tad* refers to God,—though He is not previously mentioned,—because of His being well-known." According to this comment, the aphorism signifies: "The Veda is authoritative, as being God's declaration." But S'ankara, uncertain whether his first exposition be tenable, gives, as a second: यद्वा तदिति सन्निहितं धर्ममेव पराम्टशति | "Or, the *tad* refers to 'virtue'; because juxtaposed." In this case, the meaning is, that the Veda has authority, by reason that it treats of virtue. *Dharma*, 'virtue,' is the last word of the preceding aphorism, the second. *Vais'eshika-sútropaskára*, Ms., fol. 3, recto.

† साङ्ख्यशास्त्रस्य तु पुरुषार्थतत्साधनप्रकृतिपुरुषविवेकावेव मुख्यो विषय: | *Sánkhya-pravachana-bháshya*, p. 5. "But of the Sánkhya

Again, according to all of them alike, ignorance is the chief

system the foremost matters are, the aim of the soul, *viz*, *emancipation*, and the means of compassing it, *i. e.*, the discrimination of soul from nature."

अथ शास्त्रस्य परमं प्रयोजनमपवर्गः । *Nyáya-sútra-vṛitti*, p. 198.
" Now, the paramount purpose of *this* system is emancipation."

अस्याऽनर्थहेतोः प्रहाणाय आत्मैकत्वविद्याप्रतिपत्तये सर्वे वेदान्ता आरभ्यन्ते । S'ankara A'chárya on the *Brahma-sútra: Bibliotheca Indica*, No. 64, p. 22. "For the destruction of this *misconception*, the source of *all* evil, and for the acquisition of the knowledge of the oneness of spirit, are all Vedánta disquisitions taken in hand." The commentator, Rámánanda, observes that the acquisition indicated leads to emancipation.

To anything beyond a very superficial acquaintance with the Mímánsá the author does not pretend : and yet he is not, on this score, at all in arrear of ninety and nine pandits in every hundred. In seven paragraphs, beginning with that to which this note is subjoined, as many articles of belief are reckoned up. So far as he is aware, the last three are held, without any deviation from their general character, in the Mímánsá ; whereas the first four are, he believes, wholly rejected by it. The Mímánsá scheme of philosophy, as laid out by the most accredited writers on it, is not known to deal with emancipation and other high spiritual topics. Only some recent authors, it should seem, hold a different language, and would raise the Mímánsá to a level with the other more conspicuous Systems. Thus, Laugákshi Bháskara, in his *Púrva-mímánsártha-sangraha*, has these words :

ईश्वरार्पणबुद्ध्या क्रियमाणस्तु निःश्रेयसहेतुः । न च तदर्पणबुद्ध्या-
नुष्ठाने प्रमाणाभाव इति वाच्यम् ।

यत् करोषि यदश्नासि यज् जुहोषि ददासि यत् ।
यत् तपस्यसि कौन्तेय तत् कुरुष्व मदर्पणम् ॥

इति भगवद्गीतास्तेरेव प्रमाणत्वात् । "When it, *duty*, is performed with intent of oblation to God, *it becomes* the cause of emancipation. And let it not be said that there is no authority for observance *of duty* with such intent; since there is, as such, in that sacred record the *Bhagavad-gítá*, this precept : ' Whatever thou doest, whatever thou eatest, whatever thou offerest in fire, whatever thou bestowest away, whatever austerity thou practisest, Kaunteya, do it as an oblation to me.' " See the *Bhagavad-gítá*, IX., 27.

How, it is obvious to enquire, since the Mímánsá is atheistic, this can be other than an innovation ?

cause of bondage."   And ignorance is this, that the soul,

---

* विपर्ययाद्तत्ज्ञानादिष्यते बन्धः ।   *Tattwa-kaumudí*, p. 44.
" Bondage is held, *in our system*, to result from the reverse *of knowledge*,
i. e., from ignorance of the *twenty-five* principles."

तत् तस्मादस्य दुःखसामान्यरूपस्य दुःखसमूहस्योत्पत्तेर्बीजं मुख्यं निमित्तकारणमविद्या प्रथमक्लेशः ।   Vijnána Bhikshu's *Pátanjala-bháshya-várttika*, MS., *fol*. 69, *verso* ; on the second quarter of the *Yoga-sútra*.   " 'Hence', therefore, the first affliction, *among five*, is ignorance, the main cause, *i. e.*, the seed that produces, this aggregate of miseries made up of everything perceptible".

दुःखजन्मप्रवृत्तिदोषमिथ्याज्ञानानामुत्तरोत्तरापाये तदनन्तरापायादपवर्गः ।   Second aphorism of the *Nyáya-sútra*.   " Misery, birth, activity, defect, error : when any one of these is removed, all that precede it go with it; and then ensues emancipation."   A beginning can be made, however, with ignorance only.   This is the ground of all, and the cause of misery.

From the third quotation in the last note it is clear that the Vedánta considers misconception, that is to say, misapprehension, to be the great cause of bondage.

By 'ignorance' we are not to understand the absence of knowledge, but erroneous apprehension, misconception.   In the onomastica of Amara and Hemachandra, the synonyme of *ajnána* and *avidyá* is *aham-mati*.   अज्ञानमविद्याऽहम्मतिः ।   *Amara-kośa*.   अविद्याऽहम्मत्यज्ञाने ।   *Haima-kośa*.   Kshíra Swámin says, in his gloss on Amara : " The notion ' I ' *is called aham-mati*, because there is, *in it*, the conceit of that's being soul which is not soul : " *viz.*, the mind, the body, and the like ; as is taught in the Systems.   The Sanskrit runs : अहमित्यस्य मननमहम्मतिरनात्मन्यात्माभिमानात् ।   Clearly, this is not mere want of knowledge or right apprehension, but something positive.   Váchaspati Miśra says : विपर्ययोऽज्ञानमविद्या सा बुद्धिधर्मः ।   *Tattwa-kaumudí*, p. 44.   " Wrong notion is ignorance, nescience, which is a property of the intellect."   In like manner says Vijnána Bhikshu :   अत एव चाविद्या नाभावोऽपि तु विद्याविरोधिज्ञानान्तरमिति योगभाष्ये व्यासदेवैः प्रयत्नेनावधृतम् ।   *Sánkhya-pravachana-bháshya*, p. 38.   " And, for this very reason, nescience is not a negation, but a distinct *sort of* consciousness, opposed to *true* science.   Thus it has been laboriously established, in the *Yoga-bháshya*, by the divine Vyása."   A little before this we read :   न पुनरविवेकोऽज्ञाभावमात्रम् ।

though distinct from the mind,* the senses, and the body, identifies itself with them. From this identification it is

---

"And non-discrimination, in this *system*, is not simply a negation." 'Non-discrimination'—is, on the showing of the context, one with *avidyá*, 'nescience' or 'false knowledge.' The author of the *Nyáya-sútra-vritti* says, at p. 168: विपर्ययो मिथ्याज्ञानमपर्य्यायो ऽयथार्थनिश्चयः। "Wrong notion, equivalent to which is false apprehension, is incorrect conviction." As *mithyá-jnána* is used to signify that special misapprehension which estops release from the world, so, in the Sanskrit vocabularies, *mithyá-mati*, 'false conception', is given to express misapprehension in general. Thus Amara and Hemachandra: भ्रान्तिमिथ्यामतिभ्रमः। In short, whenever the words *ajnána*, *mithyá-jnána*, *avidyá*, &c., occur in the technical use of the Systematists, they must be taken to denote something positive, and not negations. Dr. Ballantyne says: "According to the Naiyáyikas, *ajnána* is merely the privation (*abháva*) of *jnána*." *Christianity contrasted with Hindu Philosophy*, &c., p. xxxiv. That *ajnána* is so, in the language of the Nyáya, when it represents the great impediment to emancipation, is an allegation which requires to be substantiated.

All the Systems hold misapprehension to be the cause of bondage. For the Vedánta view of *ajnána* and *avidyá*, see the third Section.

* It is only to avoid the introduction of a strange Sanskrit word into the text, that I have consented to replace *manas* by 'mind.' The *manas* is averred, in all the six Systems, to be an internal organ, the organ of cognition; as the eye is the organ of sight. It has dimension, but no other quality of matter; and, except in the Nyáya, it is perishable. It must be carefully distinguished from the soul of which it is only an instrument.

Manas, in the Sánkhya, the Yoga, and the Vedánta, is also used in a special sense, for a portion of the internal organ. The other portions are, in the Sánkhya, *buddhi* and *ahankára*, 'intellect' and 'egoism;' in the Yoga and Vedánta, these and *chitta*, 'thinking.' When severally considered, each of them is called an organ. They are not operations. The renderings—and they are the ordinary ones—therefore convey but a very imperfect idea of the original expressions.

Though all the Systems style the *manas* an organ, the Sánkhya, the Yoga, and the Vedánta do not in fact treat it as such: the Nyáya and the Vaiseshika do. No opinion is here pronounced as to the Mímánsá.

Dr. Ballantyne says, for the instruction of the Hindus: "But our opinion is, that there belongs to the human soul a certain natural *incapacity* (*asʼakti*) to grasp cognitions simultaneously; and a soul thus distinguished is spoken of as a mind." *Synopsis of Science*, second edition, p. 6. This he thus puts

that it conceives of some things as its own, and of other things as belonging to others; and that, through the body,

into Sanskrit: अक्षन्मतं तु जीवात्मनो यगपज्ञानाज्ञानधारणे स्वाभाविकी काचिदशक्तिर्विद्यते तद्विशिष्ट व्यात्मा मनःपदेन व्यव-क्रियत इति । 'Mind' is here translated by *manas*: and what must be the Hindu's inference? Is anything correspondent, even by approach, to the *manas* recognized in our metaphysic?

It is taught, in all the Systems, that the soul's identifying itself with the mind, the organs, the body, &c., constitutes that misapprehension which entails bondage. But the Sánkhya, the Yoga, and the Vedánta go further. According to the first two, to regard the soul as one with nature is also a misapprehension bearing the same fruit. This is plain from the subsequent passages: ननु प्रकृतिपुरुषाविवेक एव चेत् संयोगद्वारा बन्धहेतुस्त-योर्विवेक एव च मोच्चहेतुस्तर्हिं देहाद्यभिमानसत्त्वेऽपि मोच्चः स्यात् । तच् च श्रुतिस्मृतिन्यायविरुद्धमिति तत्राऽऽह

प्रधानाविवेकादन्याविवेकस्य तद्गाने हानम् ॥ ५ ७ ॥

पुरुषे प्रधानाविवेकात् कारणाद् योऽन्याविवेको बुद्ध्याद्यविवेको जायते कार्याविवेकस्य कार्यतयाऽनादिकारणाविवेकमूलकत्वात् तस्य प्रधानाविवेकहाने सत्यवश्यं हानमित्यर्थः ।

यथा शरीरादात्मनि विविक्ते शरीरकार्येषु रूपादिष्वविवेको न सम्भवति तथा कूटस्थत्वादिधर्मैः प्रधानात् पुरुषे विविक्ते तत्का-र्येषु परिणामादिधर्मकेषु बुद्ध्यादिष्वभिमानो नोतात्तमुत्सहते तुल्य-न्यायात् कारणानाशाच् चेति भावः। *Sánkhya-pravachana-bháshya*, pp. 40, 41; including the 57th aphorism of the Sánkhya, Book I. "But, *says an objector*, if the mere non-discrimination of nature and soul be, through the conjunction *of intellect and soul*, the cause of bondage, and if the mere discrimination of them be the cause of emancipation, it will follow that, though the conceit of the body and the like *being one with soul* remained, there would be emancipation; and this is opposed to the Veda, the Smṛitis, and reason. To this it is replied, *by an aphorism:* 'Of the non-discrimination *of soul* from other things, which is because of the non-discrimination *of soul* from nature, there is the extinction, on that of the latter.' 'Non-discrimination from other things': the non-discrimination *of soul* from intellect, &c., which results 'from non-discrimination' of soul 'from nature,' as its cause,—non-discrimination from effects being *itself* an effect, and having for

it receives pleasure from this object, and pain from that. Hence there arises, in it, desire for what affords pleasure, and

---

its root eternal non-discrimination *of the soul* from the cause *of that effect, nature,*—is necessarily extinguished, on the extinction of non-discrimination *of soul* from nature. Such is the meaning. As, when soul is discriminated from body, non-discrimination of the effects of the body, colour and so on, *from the soul* is impossible; so, when soul is discriminated, by its unchangeableness, and other properties, from nature, egoism cannot have place, *identifying soul* with intellect, &c., possessing the properties of mutability and the like, which are effects of it, *nature*: there being a parity of reason, and there being extinction of cause. This is the tenor."

अव्यक्तमहदहङ्कारपञ्चतन्मात्रेष्वनात्मखष्वात्मबुद्धिरविद्याऽष्ट- विधं तमः ज्ञानावरकत्वात् । एतास्खेव देहाद्यात्मबुद्धीनामन्तर्भावः देहादीनामेतत्कार्यत्वात् । Vijnána Bhikshu's *Pátanjala-bháshyavárttika*, MS., *fol.* 12, *recto.* "The notion, in *these* eight, which are not soul, viz., in the unmanifested *nature*, in the great *principle*, i. e., *intellect*, in the organ of egoism and in the five tenuous particles, that they are soul, is ignorance: as obscuring right apprehension, it is the eight-fold darkness. In these notions are included those that the body and the rest are soul; since the body and the rest are effects of those eight."

अहङ्कारोऽहमित्यभिमानः स च शरीरादिविषयको मिथ्या- ज्ञानमुच्यते । *Nyáyı-sútra-vritti*, p. 198. "Egoism is the conceit of 'I'; and, when it has for its object the body and the like, it is called false apprehension."

अध्यासो नाम अतस्मिंस्तद्बुद्धिरित्यवोचाम । तद् यथा पुत्र- भार्यादिषु विकलेषु सकलेषु वाहमेव विकलः सकलो वेति बाह्यधर्मानात्मन्यध्यस्यति । तथा देहधर्मान् स्थूलोऽहं कृशोऽहं गौरोऽहं तिष्ठामि गच्छामि लङ्घयामि चेति । तथेन्द्रियधर्मान् मूकः काणो बधिरः काणोऽन्धोऽहमिति । तथाऽन्तःकरणधर्मान् कामसङ्क- ल्पविचिकित्साध्यवसायादीन् । S'ankara A'chárya on the *Brahma-sútra : Bibliotheca Indica*, No. 64, pp. 20, 21. "Misconception, we have said, is the notion that a thing is what it is not. It is when a man, accordingly as his sons, his wife, &c. are in evil case, or in good, by thinking 'I am in evil case,' or 'I am in good case,' imputes properties of things external to himself, *to his own soul.* Thus, *he imputes to his soul* properties of the body, when he thinks 'I am stout,' 'I am spare,' 'I am fair,' 'I stand,' 'I go,' 'I leap.' In

aversion from what produces pain. And, by reason of desire and aversion, it engages in various good and evil works, from like manner *he imputes to his soul* properties of the senses, when he thinks 'I am dumb,' 'I am impotent,' 'I am deaf,' 'I am one-eyed,' 'I am blind.' And *he imputes to his soul* properties of the internal organ, such as desire, resolve, dubiety, and certitude."

But the Vedánta goes beyond anything hitherto adduced, in its view of misapprehension. Witness the next extract, which gives particulars surplus to those in S'ankara A'chárya. It is from the *Vedánta-sára*, p. 15, Calcutta edition of 1829. प्राभाकरतार्किकाव्यो॰त्तरात्माऽऽनन्दमय इत्यादिश्रुतेः बुद्धादीनामज्ञाने लयदर्शनादहमज्ञोऽहं ज्ञानीत्याद्यनुभवाच् चाज्ञानमात्मेति वदतः भाट्टस्तु प्रज्ञानघन एवाऽऽनन्दमय आत्मेत्यादिश्रुतेः सुषुप्तौ प्रकाशाप्रकाशसद्भावान् मामहं न जानामीत्यनुभवाच् चाज्ञानोपहितं चैतन्यमात्मेति वदति। अपरो बौद्ध असदेवेदमय आसीदित्यादिश्रुतेः सुषुप्तौ सर्वाभावाद्धं सुषुप्तौ नाऽऽसमित्युत्थितस्य स्वाभावपरामर्शविषयानुभवाच् च शून्यमात्मेति वदति। "The Prábhákara and the Tárkika argue that ignorance is soul, on the ground of the scripture, 'The other, the inner soul, consisting of bliss,' and so forth; and because we observe intellect and the rest to merge in ignorance; and because of the notions, 'I am ignorant,' 'I possess consciousness,' &c. As for the Bháṭṭa, he asserts that ignorance-enveloped intelligence is soul, since there is the scripture, 'The soul consists of solid knowledge alone, and is bliss itself,' and so on; and because, in deep sleep, there are both the light *of knowledge* and the darkness *of ignorance;* and because of the notions 'Myself I know not,' &c. Another Bauddha, *one additional to several before summoned*, holds that nihility is the soul, by reason of the scripture, 'In the beginning this was a mere nonentity,' and so forth; and because, in deep sleep, there is the negation of everything; and because, in a man who has waked, of the consciousness which has for its object the memory of his non-existence, *the memory*, 'In deep sleep I was not.'"

This is not the place to detail minutely the import of *ajnána*, ignorance, as used in the last extract. A full treatment of the subject will be seen in the third Section.

Among the ignorances, the causes of bondage, is, according to the Sánkhya, the soul's identifying itself with nature, and, according to the Vedánta, its identifying itself with ignorance, &c. &c, as already noted. But who is ever conscious of committing a mistake of this sort? In fact, these hindrances

which accrue to it demerit and merit. Then, to receive requital, it has to pass to Elysium, or to Hell, and repeatedly to be born and to die. Thus it is that ignorance gives rise to bondage.* The soul's identifying itself with the body and

---

to liberation are rarely instanced as samples of misapprehension. What is meant by the soul's identification of itself with the body, and with intellect, can be understood; for, as stoutness and leanness are properties of the body, so, in the Sánkhya and Vedánta, desire, aversion, &c. are properties of the mind. After this explanation, we see at once what is intended by the proposition that the notions expressed by 'I desire,' 'I am lean,' &c., evince ignorance, and that, by these notions, a man confounds his soul with his mind, his body, &c. To these more intelligible species of ignorance, as being those generally referred to by Sanskrit writers, the text restricts its attention.

* अविवेकस्य बन्धजनने द्वारजातं च पिछीकृत्येश्वरगीतायामुक्तम् ।
अनात्मन्यात्मविज्ञानं तस्माद् दुःखं तथेतरत् ।
रागद्वेषादयो दोषाः सर्वे भ्रान्तिनिबन्धनाः ॥
कार्यं ह्यस्य भवेद् दोषः पुण्यापुण्यमिति श्रुतिः ।
तद्दोषादेव सर्वेषां सर्वदेहसमुद्भवः ॥

इति । *Sánkhya-pravachana-bháshya*, p. 39 "The series of media through which non-discrimination produces bondage is *thus* brought together and set forth in the *Iswara-gítá*: 'The conception that what is not soul is soul *is first*: thence come misery, and the other, *happiness*. All the defects *consequential thereon*—desire, aversion, &c.,—are caused, *ultimately*, by misapprehension. The effect of that *assemblage, desire, &c.,* is defect, *i. e.,* merit and demerit, says the Veda. From this defect is the rise of all the bodies of all."

For the Naiyáyika view of the succession here summed up, see the second of Gotama's aphorisms, at the foot of p. 10, *supra*. Misapprehension, as will be noticed, is the root of all ill. From it arises defect, *viz.*, desire, aversion, and the rest. Thence springs activity; thence, birth; and, from it, misery, which is bondage. By activity is meant good and evil acts. Thus the commentator : प्रवृत्तेर्धर्माधर्माधिकायाः । *Nyáya-sútra-vritti*, p. 8. "Of activity, *that is to say*, for virtue and for vice."

In the aphorism with which we are concerned the absence of 'happiness' and 'misery' may have been remarked between 'false apprehension' and 'defect.' They are to be supplied from without; for, as will be manifest from other passages bearing on the subject, defect results immediately from happiness or misery. Nor let the reader be surprised to find misery again at the end of the group,

so forth is the radical ignorance which involves the soul in

The reason is this. In the Hindu Systems, happiness and misery produce defects; these, activity; and this, birth. Then birth anew gives rise to happiness and misery; and so on, in a ceaseless round. And thus it has been from eternity. It was not for Gotama's purpose, which is to show the origin of misery, to mention happiness with it. The unending reproduction just spoken of is the topic of the ensuing extract: आदौ सुखदुःखानुभवेन्-
त्संस्कारप्रयोऽनुद्बुदसंस्कारस्ततः कालादिविशेषेस्तादुद्बोधस्ततः
स्मृतिः ततो रागद्वेषौ तयोश्च प्रवृत्तिस्ततश्च पुनदुःखमिति ।
Pátanjala-bháshya-várttika, MS., *fol.* 67, *verso.* "'First, by experience of happiness and misery *is generated* a fund of impressions,' undeveloped impressions. Then, owing to special causes, such as time, follows their development; next is memory *of the happiness and misery previously experienced;* afterwards are desire and aversion; subsequently is activity; then, again, misery *and happiness.*"

आत्मत्वेन हि शरीरादौ मुह्यन् रञ्जनीयेषु रज्यति कोपनीयेषु
कुप्यति । *Nyáya-sútra-vṛitti*, p. 198. "By mistaking his body, &c. for his soul, a man takes delight in things delightsome, and is vexed by things vexatious."

That happiness and misery are held, in the Nyáya, to be intercalated between false apprehension and defect, comes out from the above. For, where there are delight and vexation, we must presuppose happiness and misery; and antecedent to these is false apprehension.

From the following passages of S'ankara A'chárya it appears that, unless a man identifies himself, misapprehendingly, with his body, &c., all action is impracticable, and of course the consequences thereof. देहेन्द्रियादिष्वह-
म्ममाभिमानरहितस्य प्रमात्वानुपपत्तौ प्रमाणप्रवृत्त्यनुपपत्तेः ।
Commentary on the *Bramha-sútra*: *Bibliotheca Indica*, No. 64, p. 17. "Since he who has not the conceit, regarding his body, senses, &c., of 'I' or 'mine' cannot be a percipient, the instruments of knowledge, *the senses, &c.,* cannot operate *for him.*" Again: न त्वात्मन इष्टानिष्टप्राप्तिपरिहा-
रेकार्यमात्मविषयमज्ञानं कर्तृत्वभोक्तृत्वस्वरूपाभिमानलक्षणं
तद्विपरीतब्रह्मात्मस्वरूपविज्ञानेनापनीतम् । यावद्धि तन् नाप-
नीयते तावदयं कर्मफलरागद्वेषादिदोषाभाविकदोषप्रयुक्तः श्रास्त्रविहि-
तप्रतिषिद्धातिक्रमेणापि प्रवर्तमानो मनोवाक्कायैर्दृष्टादृष्टानिष्टस-

bondage. There are, however, several other species of ignorance, proceeding from this; and they all have the same effect.

धनान्यधर्मसंज्ञकानि कर्माण्युपचिनोति बाहुल्येन स्वाभाविकदोषबलीयस्त्वात् । ततः स्थावरान्ताद् अधोगतिः । कदाचित् शास्त्रकृतसंस्कारबलीयस्त्वम् । ततो मनुष्यादिभिरिष्टसाधनं बाहुल्येनोपचिनोति धर्माख्यम् । तद् द्विविधं ज्ञानपूर्वकं केवलं च । तत्र केवलं पितृलोकादिप्राप्तिफलम् । ज्ञानपूर्वं देवलोकादिब्रह्मलोकान्तप्राप्तिफलम् । तथा च शास्त्रम् । आत्मयाजी श्रेयान् न देवयाजीत्यादि । स्मृतिश्च द्विविधं कर्म वैदिकमित्याद्या । साम्ये च धर्माधर्मयोर्मनुष्यत्वप्राप्तिः । एवं ब्रह्माद्या स्थावरान्ता स्वाभाविकाविद्यादिदोषवतो धर्माधर्मसाधनकृतसंसारगतिः ।

Śankara A'chárya's Commentary on the *Brihad A'ranyaka Upanishad: Bibliotheca Indica*, Vol. II., pp. 10, 11. "But *still* ignorance respecting the soul, *ignorance* characterized by the egoistic notion that *the soul* is a doer and an experiencer, and engendering the wish to secure what is desirable to it, and to obviate what is undesirable, is not eliminated by right apprehension—the reverse of ignorance—of the nature of the soul, one with Brahma. And, so long as that *ignorance* is not eliminated, this one, *viz.*, *a man*, being actuated by natural defects, (namely, desire, aversion, &c., consequences of works,) goes on, infringing the law's injunctions and prohibitions, and, by mind, speech, and person, accumulates, in multiplicity, works, known as sins, sources of seen and unseen evils. For the natural defects are *generally* preponderant. Thence comes degradation as far as things immovable. But sometimes the impressions produced by holy writ are preponderant. Then, by the mind and the rest, he plenteously amasses virtue, as it is called, which is the source of benefit. This *virtue* is of two kinds; accompanied by knowledge, and unaccompanied. The latter has for its fruit the attainment of the Abode of Progenitors, and the like. The former has for its fruit the attainment of the Abode of the gods, as one limit, and the Abode of Brahmá, as the other. And thus *says* the scripture: 'The worshipper of the *Supreme* spirit is to be preferred, not the worshipper of the gods,' &c. The Smriti also *declares*: 'Works ordained by the Veda are of two kinds,' &c. Further, when virtue and sin equilibrato, one inherits humanity. Thus is the course of transmigration—beginning with Brahmá, and ending with things fixed, *as trees*, and occasioned by virtue and sin,—with him who has the defects of natural nescience and such like."

The "worshipper of the *Supreme* spirit" is he who, while engaged in constant ritual observances, beholds Brahma in all. So says A'nanda Giri.

Such, for instance, is the setting store by the things of this world, of Elysium, and of other future abodes.*

By the "worshipper of the gods" is meant one who adores them under the promptings of a hope of requital.

In the second sentence, *karma-phala* has been translated, with some hesitation, "consequences of works;" desire and aversion being so designated. If this seems to contradict the statement that desire and aversion instigate to works, which, then, are themselves consequences, the difficulty is solved by the remarks on the second of Gotama's aphorisms, in the note at p. 15. The eternal revolution of causes and effects is here taken for granted.

It transpires, from this extract, that the egoistic conceit that the soul energizes, enjoys, and suffers, is the foundation of desire, aversion, virtue, sin, exaltation and degradation of birth, transmigration, and, in fine, of all evil. It has, further, been shown, in the extract from S'ankara A'chárya, at p. 13, foot-note, that the egoistic notion under consideration consists in identifying the soul with the mind, the body, &c.

* सङ्कल्पः समीचीनत्वेन भावनं तद्विषयैर्ज्ञाता रूपादयः दोषस्य रागादेर्निमित्तं सुन्दरीयमितिज्ञानन् रज्यति । *Nyáya-sútra-vṛitti,* pp. 198, 199. "'High esteem,' the supposition of excellence. Colour and other things, when made objects thereof, are causes of defect, *viz.*, of desire, &c.; as where, taking a woman to be beautiful, one is pleased *with her.*"

परिष्कारबुद्धिरनुरञ्जनसंज्ञा सा चेया । * * * * अनुरञ्जन-संज्ञा यथा ।

खेलत्खञ्जननयना परिगतबिम्बाधरा पृथुश्रोणी ।
कमलमुकुलस्तनीयं पूर्णेन्दुमुखी सुखाय मे भविता ॥

इति । *Ibid.*, p. 199. "'The notion of embellishment,' the consciousness of *anything* being a source of delight, should be relinquished. The consciousness of *anything* being a source of delight is thus *exemplified*: 'This maid, with eyes restless as a wagtail, with a lower lip like a ripe cherry, wide-hipped, with breasts resembling an opening lotus, and whose face rivals the full moon, will serve to give me solace.'"

विषयेष्वाविशच् चेतः सङ्कल्पयति तद्गुणान् ।
सम्यक्कल्पनात् कामः कामात् पुंसः प्रवर्तनम् ॥
* * * * * * *
सङ्कल्पं वर्जयेत् तस्मात् सर्वानर्थस्य कारणम् ।

इति । *Viveka-chúḍámaṇi,* attributed to S'ankara A'chárya; MS., place not noted. "The mind, betaking itself to objects, conceives esteem for their

SEC. I., CHAP. 2.   19

Again, in the Systems, good works, no less than evil works, contribute to bondage.* The fruit of good works is happiness: and yet they are called a cause of bondage, inasmuch as they preclude the soul from being liberated. For the authors of the Systems regard emancipation as being the release of the soul from the body, the mind, cognition, desire, &c. But good works, for the enjoyment of their desert, compel the soul, until their fruition is consummated, to abide in the body of a god, a man, or some other superior being;†

qualities. From *this* esteem *of them* as good *comes* desire *for them*. From *this* desire *is* man's engaging in action. Let one, therefore, eschew esteem, the origin of all evil."

* Virtuous actions, as well as sinful, are said, below, to be a cause, to the soul,—and also to the intellect,—of bondage. ततोऽपि च कारणो-च्छेदाद् धर्माधर्मरूपाणि बन्धनानि बुद्धिपुरुषयोर्बन्धकारणानि स्वयत्नदृष्टोतादनाच्छमाणि करोति । *Pátanjala-bháshya-várttika*, MS., *fol. 2, verso.* "'And on this,' by extirpation of the cause, viz., ignorance, abstraction of thought *(yoga)* loosens the bonds, *i. e.*, virtuous and sinful actions,—for they bind intellect and soul;—*in other words*, incapacitates them for bringing forth desert."

For the Naiyáyika view, see the second of Gotama's aphorisms, lately remarked on. The root of misery is, there, activity,—the originator, as the commentator has explained, of virtue and vice. Hence, in the Nyáya also, good and bad works alike generate misery, and, by consequence, bondage.

That the same opinion is held by the Vedánta is manifest from S'ankara A'chárya's commentary on the *Brihad A'ranyaka Upanishad*. See the citation at p. 17 *supra*, especially its concluding sentence.

† तदुक्तं याज्ञवल्क्येन ।
सर्वधर्मान् परित्यज्य मोक्षधर्मं समाश्रयेत् ।
सर्वे धर्माः सदोषाः स्युः पुनरावृत्तिकारकाः ॥

इति । *Pátanjala-bháshya-várttika*, MS., *fol. 158, recto*.

"It has been said by Yájnavalkya: 'Putting aside all *other* good works, let a man apply himself to the *one* good work which leads to emancipation; *to wit, the attainment of right apprehension:* for all *other* works are attended by defects, and induce renewal *of mundane existence.*"

That good works, in the Nyáya, are a hindrance to emancipation is evident from the *Nyáya-Sútra-vritti*. The sixty-first aphorism of the fourth book

for of works, good or evil, it is impossible to evade the fruit*.

of the *Nyáya-sútra* implies that a man who has acquired right apprehension may, on becoming an ascetic, relinquish the maintenance of a sacrificial hearth; and it is thus intimated that such maintenance can then no longer act as a bar to his being liberated. Relatively to this, an objection is raised, in the preface to the sixty-second aphorism: नन्वग्निहोत्रस्याऽप्रतिबन्धकत्वे-ऽपि तत्फलस्वर्गे एवाऽपवर्गप्रतिबन्धकः स्यात् । "Though the maintenance of a sacrificial hearth is not *itself* a hindrance to emancipation, yet its fruit, Elysium, must be so." To this it is replied, that the ordinary requital of this meritorious act does not take effect in the case of the rightly apprehending ascetic. For his are not the plenary attributes of one who maintains a sacrificial hearth; those attributes not being rendered complete until after his death, at his incremation. A further difficulty is then raised and solved: अग्निहोत्रफलाभावेऽपि ज्योतिष्टोमगङ्गास्नानादि-हिंसाफलानां प्रतिबन्धकत्वं स्यात् । अतो हेत्वन्तरसमुच्चयाय चकार उपन्यस्तथा च प्रारब्ध्यतिरिक्तकर्मणां ज्ञानादेव च्य इत्याशयः ।
"Though the requital of the maintenance of a sacrificial hearth is not *for that ascetic*, nevertheless, there must be a hindrance *to his emancipation*, in the fruits of the *jyotishtoma* sacrifice, ablution in the Ganges, &c., *good works*, and *in the fruits* of injury *to animals, sin, which he may have done*. Therefore, *it is said, in reply*, to add another reason, an 'and' is exhibited *in the aphorism*; and thus the position is, that mere right apprehension obliterates *all* works but those that have begun to fructify."

Works of this class will be explained a little further on.

How far the force of works, virtuous and vicious, extends, is propounded in the ensuing passage: नन्वेवं स्वर्गिनारकिणां कथं पुनर्जन्मादि स्यात् स्वर्गादिश्ररीरे धर्माद्यनुत्पत्तेः प्राचीनसर्वकर्मणां च तत्रैव समापना-दितिचेन् न स्वर्गादिजनककर्मणामेव ब्राह्मणत्वावरादियोनिलाभ-पर्यन्तत्वश्रवणात् । *Pátanjala-bháshya-várttika*, MS., fol. 63, *verso*. "But, some one may object: How can they who have reached Elysium, or Hell, incur return of birth, and the like? For there is no production of merit and demerit in the body a person there tenants; and, as for *the requital of* all his old works, it is exhausted there. To this I demur; for we have heard that works which consign to Elysium, or to Hell, endure until one is born a Bráhman, a tree, or as the case may be."

* Works of whatever character entail inevitable consequences. The following half-stanza to this effect is on the lips of every pandit; but its authorship has not been discovered.

Nor is the happiness rewarded by such works a thing pre-eminently desirable. Transitory,* and conjoined with divers inconveniences, itself is misery.† To explain this:—to go to Elysium, and to be born of a reputable stock, and to amass wealth, and the like, are the consequences of good works. But these consequences terminate as soon as the fund of merit which earned them is exhausted; and the very privation of them brings sorrow, which is misery. So long as the soul misapprehends, desire and aversion constantly affect it, the doing good and evil are unavoidable to it, and it has no

---

अवश्यमेव भोक्तव्यं कृतं कर्म शुभाशुभम् ।
"Good works, or bad, that are wrought are *all* of necessity fructuous."

* कर्मसाध्यस्य चानित्यत्वे श्रुतिः तद् यथेह कर्मचितो लोकः क्षीयत एवमेवामुत्र पुण्यचितो लोकः क्षीयत इति । *Sánkhya-pravachana-bháshya, p.* 62, "That whatever is obtainable by works is non-eternal there is the scripture : 'As perishes the world here, gained by works, just so perishes the world to come, gained by virtue.' "

क्षयित्वं च स्वर्गादेः सत्त्वे सति कार्यत्वादनुमितमिति । *Tattwa-kaumudí, p.* 4. "The perishableness of Elysium, &c. is inferred from their being originated entities."

For, agreeably to a maxim of all the Systems, every originated entity is non-eternal. Texts from the Nyáya and the Vedánta may, therefore, here be dispensed with.

† तदपि पूर्वसूत्रोक्तं सुखमपि दुःखमिश्रितमित्यतो दुःखक्षोटौ सुखदुःखविवेकिना निःक्षिप्तम् इत्यर्थः । *Sánkhya-pravachana-bháshya,* p 212. "That also, the happiness mentioned in the foregoing aphorism, is mixed with misery. Consequently, those who have a discriminative knowledge of happiness and misery cast *the former* to the side of the latter." सुखं हि तावद् दुःखपक्षे निःक्षिप्तमिति सुखभोगोऽपि दुःखभोग एव । *Ibid.,* p. 232. "Since happiness is thrown to the side of misery, to taste of that is really to taste of this."

स्वर्गादिसुखस्यापि तन्नाशज्ञानेन दुःखसम्बन्धितमध्याहृतमेव ।
From the *Dinakarí;* the MS. not at hand to refer to. "That also the happiness of Elysium and the like, from being known for perishable, is connected with misery, is of course undisputed."

escape from the gyration of births and deaths.* Nor can any

* पुरुषतत्त्वानभिज्ञो हि इष्टापूर्तकारी कामोपहतमना बध्यत
इति | *Tattwa-kaumudí*, p. 44. "One ignorant of the nature of the
soul, performing meritorious observances, and having his mind corrupted by
desire, *thereby* incurs bondage."

In the paragraph to which this note appertains, it has been stated, generally, that good works are a cause of bondage. A few particulars may possess interest to one who would go somewhat further into this topic. Good works may be distinguished, primarily, into incumbent and voluntary. The incumbent may, again, be divided into constant and occasional. The voluntary are acts of supererogation, and may be done from the motive of obtaining a determinate reward.

Incumbent good works, some Hindus hold, do not avail except to atone for past transgressions, and to purify the intellect; they thus conducing to the acquisition of right knowledge. Elevation to Elysium, and the like, are not their requital; and the passages of sacred writings which enunciate that such results are their requital are not to be taken, it is contended, according to the letter, but as eulogistic beyond it. These works, agreeably to the view thus taken of them, do not operate for bondage: and yet more or less of stigma cleaves to them; for defecation of the understanding, and ritual ordinances, however helpful towards the acquisition of right knowledge, are not deemed altogether good things. Vijnána Bhikshu, in answer to the question, how virtuous works, done without desire of reward, can bring about misery, since liberation is promised to them, replies: काम्येऽकाम्ये च कर्मणि दुःखाद् दुःखं भवति । कुतः । साध्यत्वाविशेषात् । कर्म-
साध्यस्य सत्त्वशुद्धिद्वारकज्ञानस्यापि निर्गुणात्मकतया दुःखात्म-
कत्वादित्यर्थः । *Sánkhya-pravachana-bháshya*, p. 63. "In works, whether those done with desire *of reward*, or those done without it, there is misery from misery. Why? Because *their rewards* do not differ in respect that they are *alike* effected *by works*. That is to say, even right apprehension—which, through purification of the intellect, is effected by works,—since it consists of the three *guṇas*, is of the essence of misery. Such is the sense."

As for the Naiyáyikas, it is laid down, by them, that all varieties of knowledge, or apprehension, come under the head of the twenty-one species of misery, which are to be got rid of; this riddance constituting emancipation.

Thus the *Dinakarí:* दुःखानि प्ररीरं षडिन्द्रियाणि षड् विषयाः
षड् बुद्धयः सुखं दुःखं चेत्येकविंशतिकं दुःखम् । "The body, the six

one forbear virtue, a cause of thraldom, and so escape thraldom; for, if, while still in misapprehension, a man, otherwise

senses, *the mind being the sixth, their* six kinds of objects, *their* six kinds of knowledge, happiness, and misery, are the one and twenty miseries."

From this we are to understand, that, though right apprehension is desirable, it is so as the means of salvation, not in itself; for, viewed intrinsically, it is to be accounted misery. As the Hindus express themselves, it is like the toil which a man goes through in cooking his dinner.

But, further, even incumbent good works involve the commission of sin, according to *Váchaspati Miśra:* अविशुद्धिः सोमादियागस्य पशुबीजादिवधसाधनता । *Tattwa-kaumudí*, p. 4. "The impurity of sacrifices, *the sacrifice* of the moon-plant juice, for example, comes from their causing the destruction of beasts, of cereal grains, and the like." Much more, to the same purport, follows the above.

Again : यतो यज्ञमुक्तं पण्वावापगतानामपि हिंसानामनिष्टहेतुत्वम् । *Pátanjala-bháshya-várttika*, MS., *fol.* 103, *recto.* "Therefore it is well said, that even those slayings, *in sacrifice,* which accompany the sowing of virtue are sources of evil." Shortly after this we find a quotation from the *Mokshu-dharma* section of the *Mahábhárata*:

सर्वाणि भूतानि सुखे रमन्ते सर्वाणि दुःखेषु तथोद्विजन्ति ।
तेषां भयोत्पादनजातखेदः कुर्यान् न कर्माणि हि जातवेदः ॥

"All creatures delight in happiness; all likewise are discomforted by misery. Grieved by *the thought of* causing fear to them, Játavedas, one should not engage in works."

Vijnána Bhikshu, to bear out the allegation, that incumbent works oblige to sin, elsewhere says: युधिष्ठिरादीनां स्वधर्मेऽपि युद्धादौ ज्ञातिवधादिप्रत्यवायपरिहाराय प्रायश्चित्तश्रवणाच्च । *Sánkhya-pravachana-bháshya,* p. 14. "And we have heard that Yudhishthira and others, though war and such like were, to them, *incumbent* duties, did penance to expiate the sin of killing their kinsmen and others." The fighting of the Pándavas, here called their duty, was with their own relatives.

So much for one theory touching the effect of incumbent good works. Another, and one more accordant with the usual strain of the sacred books, is as follows. In this theory, incumbent good works have all the virtue ascribed to them in the other, and, over and beyond, have for requital what is there denied them. Truth to tell, it is very latitudinarian exegesis that treats as eulogistic the texts where they are said to be rewarded by migration to Elysium. We read, in an unverified quotation in the *Siddhánta-muktávali*:

than after prescribed rules, relinquishes incumbent good works, constant and occasional, by so doing he commits evil. Such works may be given up only according to the rules of asceticism. And yet asceticism is not permitted to all. Thus, it would be improper in a man newly married to a young wife, and who has as yet no offspring; and to a man who has aged parents to support; &c. But the greatest difficulty is in this, that, though, from having entered upon an ascetic course, a man is dispensed from constant and occasional works, still there are many things which, in his own despite, derive merit to him. Such is contact with the water of the Ganges; the merit communicated by which he reaps,

सन्ध्यामुपासते ये तु सततं संशितव्रताः ।
विधूतपापास्ते यान्ति ब्रह्मलोकमनामयम् ॥

"Men of potent observances, who unintermittedly transact their worship at the turns of the day, their sins removed, pass to the Abode of Brahmá, where no harm enters." See the *Bibliotheca Indica*, Vol. ix. p. 134. I have corrected a typographical error.

Worship at the turns of the day, that is, morning, noon, and evening, is an incumbent or obligatory duty.

The opinion now before us is that of the author of the *Vedánta-sára*, who says, at p. 2: एतेषां नित्यादीनां बुद्धिशुद्धिः परं प्रयोजनम् । उपासनानां तु तदैकाग्र्यं परं प्रयोजनम् । "Of these constant and other *works* purification of intellect is the principal final cause. But concentration thereof, *of intellect*, is the principal final cause of devotions." After citing a couple of passages, the author goes on to declare: नित्यनैमित्तिकयो-रुपासनानां चावान्तरफलं पितृलोकसत्यलोकप्राप्ती । "And the subordinate fruit of constant and occasional *works*, and of devotions, is the gaining the Abode of Progenitors and the Abode of Brahmá."

S'ankara A'chárya is of the same mind, as may be seen in the note at p. 17. He there speaks of two sorts of good works, each of which earns some supernal residence. And it appears, from the language of his commentator, that constant good works are therein embraced; for he says that the "worshipper of the spirit" is one who engages in such works.

In this second theory, then, incumbent good works, no less then voluntary, are a cause of bondage.

whether he will or not.* To free oneself from the fetters of both virtue and vice, right apprehension is the sole remedy.

Things being so, the Systems declare that release from transmigration, and all that it entails, can be achieved only by acquiring right apprehension.† And right apprehension consists in the recognition, by the soul, of itself as distinct from the mind, the senses, the body, and all else.‡ This is the

---

* वस्तुतो विनाऽपीच्छां गङ्गाजलसंयोगादितो धर्मादिसम्भवात्। *Nyáya-sútra-vṛitti*, p. 8. "In fact, even independently of volition, virtue and sin may be produced by touching, for instance, the water of the Ganges."

† The twenty-third aphorism of the *Sánkhya-pravachana*, Book III., is ज्ञानान् मुक्तिः। "From right apprehension is emancipation."

For the Nyáya, see the first aphorism of the *Nyáya-sútra*.

The *Vedánta-paribháshá* has, at p. 48: स च ज्ञानैकसाध्यः। "And that *liberation* is to be obtained by right apprehension alone." The word "liberation" is resumed from the previous context.

‡ परमार्थतत्तु सत्त्वपुरुषान्यताज्ञानादेवाज्ञाननिवृत्त्यादितद्दृष्ट-द्वारा कैवल्यमित्यर्थः। *Pátanjala-bháshya-várttika*, MS., fol. 153, verso, "But, in reality, solely from the knowledge of the soul's alterity from the intellect, through the removal of ignorance, and other evident media, there is isolation, *or emancipation*. Such is the sense."

In the Sánkhya, equally does bondage result from identifying the soul with mind, and from identifying it with nature. Prior to liberation, the soul must be distinguished from nature, the radical material principle, as well as from mind. This is implied in the excerpt from the *Sánkhya-pravachana-bháshya* at p. 8, where it is said that discrimination of soul from nature is the means of attaining the aim of the soul, which is there a technicality equivalent to liberation. At p. 41 of the work just referred to we further read: यच् च बुद्धिपुरुषविवेकादेव मोक्ष इत्यपि क्वचिदुच्यते तत्र स्थूल-सूक्ष्मबुद्धिग्रहणात् प्रकृतेरपि ग्रहणम्। "And, as for that also which is said in some places, that emancipation comes from the discrimination of the soul from intellect alone; gross intellect and subtle being there comprehended, nature is comprehended *in the term intellect*."

तथा च योगसूत्रं योगाङ्गानुष्ठानादशुद्धिक्षये ज्ञानदीप्तिरा-विवेकख्यातेः। तदर्थंश्च योगाङ्गानां यमनियमादीनां अनुष्ठानाच्

principal kind of right apprehension : but several other kinds are also necessary, as, for instance, the disesteeming the things

चित्तस्याऽशुद्धेरविद्यादिरूपस्य क्षये सति ज्ञानस्य दीप्तिः प्रकर्षः । स च विवेकख्यातिपर्यन्तो जायते । सा च सत्त्वपुरुषान्यतासाक्षात्कारोऽस्मन्मते तु देहादिभिन्नात्मसाक्षात्कारः । *Nyáya-sútra-vṛitti*, p. 216. "And so the *Yoga-sútra*: 'When, by attending to the auxiliaries to coercion of thought, *mental* impurities are done away, there is the forth-shining of knowledge until discriminative cognition supervenes.' And the meaning of this is, that, when, by attention to the auxiliaries to coercion of thought, *viz.*, subjugation, normal piety &c., impurity of mind, in the from of nescience and the rest, is done away, the shining forth, or a high degree, of knowledge ensues; and this subsists until one obtains discriminative cognition. And this is immediate apprehension of the difference between *the Sánkhya's* intellect and soul; but, in our system, *it is* immediate apprehension of the soul as distinct from the body and so forth." The aphorism of the Yoga which is introduced is the twenty-eight of the second book.

तथा च श्रवणमनननिदिध्यासनानि तत्त्वज्ञानजनकानीत्युक्तं भवति । अत्र श्रुतितः ज्ञातात्मनः श्रवणस्य मनने ऽधिकारः । मननं चाऽऽत्मन इतरभिन्नत्वेनाऽनुमानम् । तच् च भेदप्रतियोगितरज्ञानसाधनम् । तथा चेतर एव के तदर्थं पदार्थनिरूपणम् ।
Jagadíśa Tarkálankára Bhaṭṭáchárya's *Tarkámṛita*, a Naiyáyika treatise, MS. *ad init.* "And thus it is expressed, that hearing *about spirit from sacred books*, and consideration and meditation *thereon*, are originative of a knowledge of the true nature *of the soul*. One who has heard about soul from scripture is qualified for consideration ; which consists in inferring that soul is different from other things. And this *deduction* depends on acquaintance with those other things from which it, *soul*, differs. Thus, then, the categories are described in order to show what those other things are."

Hence it is evident, that, where the first aphorism of the Nyáya makes liberation to result from a knowledge of the truth regarding sixteen things enumerated, we are to understand, that the consequence follows from one's being enabled, by that knowledge, to discriminate soul from what is not soul.

S'ankara A'chárya, after dilating on the topic of mistaking soul for other things, and other things for soul, which is called misapprehension, or ignorance, says : तद्विवेकेन च वस्तुस्वरूपावधारणं विद्यामाहुः । *Bibliotheca Indica*, No. 64, p. 16. "And the ascertainment of the nature of reality, through discrimination of those, *soul and not soul*, they call *true science*."

of this world and of the next, and so on.* To gain right apprehension, one must study the S'ástras; and to this study clearness of intellect and heart is indispensable. To this end good works are recommended, such as sacrifice, alms, pilgri-

---

* ते रूपादयो हेयत्वेन भावनीयाः प्रथमंततः शरीरात्मविवेकः ।

Nyáya-sútra-vritti, p. 199. "Those *things*, colour and the rest, should first be meditated on as deserving to be rejected: subsequently is discrimination of soul from body." Shortly after this we read : दोषदर्शनमशुभ-संज्ञा सा भावनीयेति । "Recognition' as ill is intuition of defects : *and* it is to be practised." The following couplet is subjoined, by the author, as a sample of the sort of thoughts to be called up, by an aspirant after emancipation, when his eyes fall on a woman :

चर्मनिर्मितपात्रीयं मांसाशृक्पूयपूरिता ।
अस्यां रज्यति यो मूढः पिशाचः कस्ततोऽधिकः ॥

"As for this bag of hide, charged with flesh, blood, and feculency, who is a greater ghoul than the fool that fancies her ?"

Further, it is prescribed : स्वशरीरादावप्यशुभसंज्ञैव भावनीया ।

"Also as concerns one's own body and the like should recognition as ill be put in practice."

The feelings of an ignorant man towards his enemy are exemplified as follows :

मां द्वेष्ट्यसौ दुराचार इत्यादिषु यथेष्टतः ।
कराठपीठं कुठारेण छित्वाऽस्य स्यां सुखी कदा ॥

"This wretch hates me most cordially for *all* my felicities. When shall I have the gratification of cutting his throat with a hatchet ?"

On the other hand, a right-minded person is said to reflect on his enemy after this fashion :

मांसाशृक्कीकसमयो देहः किं मेऽपराध्यति ।
एतस्मादपरः कर्ता कर्तनीयः कथं मया ॥

"What offence to me does *his* body, made up of flesh, blood, and bones? The *real doer of the offence, that is, the offender's soul,* which is other than this body, how can I injure that ?"

A strange way this may seem of reasoning oneself out of an intention to be revenged. But an endeavour must be made to dismiss the sentiment of vindictiveness as well,—say the Hindus,—and also all affections, whether of aversion or of desire, before a man is in a condition to be liberated.

mage, repetition of sacred words, austerities, and the like; but to be performed without desire of Elysium and other lower rewards. Therefrom comes the clearness just spoken of, which is of the greatest assistance towards the attainment of right apprehension.* This apprehension the enquirer obtains from the Sástras, and from the tuition of preceptors. And then, for some time, he ponders and reflects on it, and so obtains immediate cognition of his own soul.† On his mastering this

---

* See, for the Sánkhya, the extract from the *Sánkhya-pravachana-bháshya* at p. 22.

For the Nyáya, see the passage of the *Nyáya-sútra-vṛitti* cited at pp. 25, 26. The subjugation and normal piety, spoken of at that place, are just before elucidated in these words: यमानाह् योगसूचं अहिंसा-सत्यास्तेयब्रह्मचर्यापरिग्रहा यमाः । नियमानाह् शौचसन्तोषतपः-स्वाध्यायेश्वरप्रणिधानानि नियमाः । स्वाध्यायः स्वाभिमतम-ब्रजपः । निषिद्धानाचरणात्तदाश्रमविहिताचरणे यमनियमा इत्यन्ये ।
"The *Yoga-sútra* thus specifies *acts of* subjugation: 'Not killing, truthfulness, not stealing, chastity, and self-denial, are *acts of* subjugation.' Thus it specifies normal piety: 'Purification, serenity, austerity, inaudible repetition, and devotion to God, are normal piety.' 'Inaudible repetition', is reiterating, unheard, a favourite holy text. Others aver, that the forbearing what is forbidden is *yama*, and that the doing what is prescribed to each several religious stage is *niyama*."

A Bráhman's life is divided, with reference to religion, into four stages. अस्मिन् जन्मनि जन्मान्तरे वा काम्यनिषिद्धवर्जनपुरःसरं नित्यनैमि-त्तिकप्रायश्चित्तोपासनानुष्ठानेन निरस्तनिखिलकल्मषतया नितान्त-निर्मलखान्तः । *Vedánta-sára*, pp. 1 and 2. "Since a man, by abstaining, in this birth, or in a former birth, from things done with desire of reward and things forbidden, and by engaging in constant and occasional *works*, in penance, and in devotion, is *thereby* purged of all sin, has his mind thoroughly cleansed," &c.

This is only a member of a long sentence, not necessary to be given in its entirety.

† अत्रापि विवेकेऽपि * * * * श्रवणमनननिदिध्या-सनरूपमेव कारणम् । *Sánkhya-pravachana-bháshya*, p. 215. "'Here also,' *i. e.*, as regards discrimination also, hearing *about soul from scrip-*

cognition, though desire and aversion do not on that account altogether take their departure, yet their strength is materially abated: for, however perfect his right apprehension becomes, nevertheless, since he is still connected, through the body, with external objects, it follows, that some traces of desire and aversion manifest themselves so long as the soul tenants the body.* When the soul leaves it, those affections disappear entirely. Further, so long as the man of right apprehension has a body, he does more or less of good and evil. Only these do not ripen, in him, into merit and demerit; and, consequently, they do not entail on him the necessity of visiting Elysium, or Hell, and of

---

ture, and consideration and meditation *thereon*, are *its* cause." Also:

उत्तरूपप्रकारतत्त्वविषयज्ञानाभ्यासादादरनैरन्तर्यदीर्घकालसेवितात् सत्त्वपुरुषान्यतासाक्षात्कारि ज्ञानमुत्पद्यते । *Tattwa-kaumudi*, p. 55.

" By cultivating, in the manner laid down, an acquaintance with the principles,—by pursuing it with due heed, continuously, and protractedly,— knowledge, *or right apprehension*, is generated, immediately perceptive of the difference between intellect and soul."

For the Nyáya, see the *Tarkámṛita*, cited at p. 27.

एवं स्वरूपचैतन्यसाक्षात्कारपर्यन्तं श्रवणमनननिदिध्यासनसमाध्यनुष्ठानस्यापेक्षितत्वात् । *Vedánta-sára*, p. 23. " Till *he attains to* immediate cognition, thus *described*, of that Intelligence which is his own very essence, there being need of the practice of hearing *holy writ*, consideration, meditation, and coercion of thought," &c. &c.

* यद्यपि ज्ञानिनोऽपि रागादयस्तिष्ठन्ति तथाप्युत्कटरागाद्भावे तात्पर्यम् । *Nyáya-sútra-vṛitti*, p. 8. " It is meant, that, though even in the possessor of right apprehension desire, &c. continue, yet they are not excessive."

No manuscript is accessible to the writer, by which to verify the annexed couplet. It is said to be from the *Jívan-mukti-viveka*, a Vedánta work by Mádhava A'chárya:

उत्पद्यमाना रागाद्या विवेकज्ञानवह्निना ।
तदा तदैव दह्यन्ते कुतस्तेषां परोद्गमम् ॥

" Desire and so forth, as fast as they arise, are at once consumed by the fire of discriminative knowledge. How, *then*, can they grow ?"

being born again. And right apprehension has this efficacy, that all good and evil—fructescent works excepted,—which the soul did previously to acquiring it, is thereby obliterated. Works are of three descriptions, technically designated as accumulated, current, and fructescent.* Accumulated works are such, among those done in former lives, as have not yet borne fruit: by the acquisition of right apprehension, these are burnt, or rendered ineffectual. Current works are those which are done in the present life: these have no effect on the possessor of right apprehension. Fructescent works are such as were done in former lives, and gave origin to the body now inhabited, determining its duration, and everything appertaining to the present state of existence. These three sorts of works resemble three kinds of seed-grain. The seed-grain of works which a man, like a husbandman, has stored in his garner, is 'accumulated'; and right apprehension burns it. Again, the seed-grain of works which he is sowing in this life is 'current'; and it is scorched by right apprehension, so that it brings forth no fruit. Once more, the seed-grain which he sowed in a former birth, and which has already begun to bear, is known as 'fructescent'. Now, these fructescent works cannot be made void by right apprehension.† It is to receive the requital of

---

* *Prárabdha*, the word thus rendered, is defined " which has begun to bear fruit." No single English term, in past or present use, being found that conveys this idea, I have taken the liberty of coining one.

'Accumulated' and 'current' translate, respectively, *sanchita* and *kriyamáṇa*. A very rare substitute for the latter is *ágámin*, 'eventual.' I have doubts about it. See my edition of the *Tattwa-bodha*, p. 8.

† ज्ञानस्य हि व्यापारद्वयं क्षयाख्यहेतुत्वेन कर्मानुत्पादः प्राचीनकर्मणां दाहश्च न तु कर्मणाः प्रारब्धकर्मणोऽपि नाशप्रसङ्गात् ।

Pátanjala-bháshya-várttika, MS., *fol.* 62. *recto*. "For the function of right apprehension is two-fold, hindrance to the production of works causative *of happiness and misery,* called affliction, and the combustion of past, *i. e., accumulated,* works; but *its function* is not destruction of works *generally:* for, *if it were so,* fructescent works would perish with the rest."

Frequently, as in several instances in the foregoing passage, the term *kar-*

them that the man of right apprehension has to remain in
the body, and to experience divers joys and griefs.* But,
this experience ended, he quits the body, and is absolved from
the recurrence of birth :† for works are no more his; and

---

man, literally, 'works,' is unquestionably put for the merit or demerit accruing
from them.

Refer, for the Nyáya, to the second citation in the note at p. 20.

उत्पादितकार्यकर्मव्यतिरिक्तानां सञ्चितकर्मणामेव ज्ञानविनाश्य-
त्वावगमात् ।   *Vedánta-paribháshá*, p. 52. "Those accumulated works
alone which are distinct from such as have produced their effects, *i. e*, *distinct
from fructescent works*, are understood to be effaceable by right apprehension."

That coercion of mind in which all thoughts are suppressed is, Vij-
ńáua Bhikshu holds, of greater efficacy than right apprehension even,
in that it, and it alone, is able to neutralize the effect of works that have
begun to bear fruit. The words are: असम्प्रज्ञातयोगेनाऽखिलसंस्का र-
दाहकेन   प्रारब्धकर्माऽप्यतिक्रम्यत इति ज्ञानाद् विशेषः ।
Pátanjala-bháshya-várttika, MS., *fol.* 3, *verso*. "By mental coercion to
the suppressing of every thought, all germs being consumed, even fructescent
works are got over. Thus there is a superiority, *in such coercion*, over right
apprehension."

* एवं ज्ञानोत्तरं कर्मानुत्पत्तावपि प्रारब्धकर्मवेगेन चेष्टमानं
शरीरं धृत्वा जीवन्मुक्तस्तिष्ठतीत्यर्थः ।   *Sánkhya-pravachana-bháshya*
p. 158. "Thus, though there is no production of works after right apprehension, he that is liberated and is still living continues to hold a body,
which is swayed by the impulse of fructescent works. This is the sense." It is
also said: जीवन्मुक्तस्य भोगाभास एव ।   *Pátanjala-bháshya-várttí-
ka*, MS., *fol.* 76, *recto*. "The experience *of happiness and misery* of him
who lives on after emancipation is just a plausible fallacy."

† आत्मानात्मविवेकसाद्यात्कारात् कर्तेत्याद्यखिलाभिमानिवृत्त्या
तत्कार्यरागद्वेषधर्माधर्माद्यनुत्पादात् पूर्वोत्पन्नकर्मणां चाविद्यारा-
गादिसहकार्य्य च्छेदरूपदाहेन विपाकानारम्भकत्वात् प्रारब्धसमाप्य-
नन्तरं पुनर्जन्माभावेन त्रिविधदुःखात्यन्तनिवृत्तिरूपो मोक्षो भवती-
तिश्रुतिस्मृतिसिद्धिक्रमः । *Sánkhya-sára*, MS., *fol.* 1, *verso*. "When there
is discriminative immediate cognition of soul from what is not soul; and

birth is only for the purpose of receiving the recompence of hence removal of all conceit of agency and the like; and hence surcease of the production of the effects of that *conceit*, *viz.*, desire, aversion, virtue, vice, and the like; and when past works are burnt, that is to say, when their auxiliaries, nescience, desire, and so on are extirpated, and therefore cannot begin to bear fruit; and when fructescent *works* have been reaped in experience; birth no longer awaiting, there is liberation, entire cessation of threefold misery. Such is the *proclamation by* drum of the Veda and Smṛitis."

स्वयोपदिष्टयोगविधिना निदिध्यासने कृते तदनन्तरं देहादि-विलक्षणात्मसाक्षात्कारे सति देहादावहमभिमानरूपमिथ्याज्ञान-नाशे सति दोषाभावात् प्रवृत्यभावे धर्माधर्मयोरभावाज् जन्म-भावे पूर्वधर्माधर्मयोरनुभवेन नाशे चरमदुःखध्वंसलक्षणो मोक्षो जायते । *Tarka-dípiká*, MS., *fol.* 30, *verso*. "When meditation has been performed according to the rules for coërcion of thought enjoined by the Veda; and when there has resulted immediate cognition of the soul as distinct from the body and so forth; and when abolition has ensued of the erroneous apprehension, the conceit, that I am body and the like; defects no longer having place; nor, thereafter, activity; nor, then, virtue and vice; nor, then, birth; past virtue and vice being cancelled by right apprehension, *i. e., by the immediate cognition aforesaid;* emancipation is reached, which is the annulment of the last subsisting misery."

The man who has secured emancipation and is still in life, and his plenitude of emancipation after parting from the body, are described, by Vedánta writers, in the next two passages: जीवन्मुक्तो नाम स्वस्वरूपाखण्डशुद्धब्रह्म-ज्ञानेन तद्ज्ञानबाधनद्वारा स्वस्वरूपाखण्डब्रह्मणि साक्षात्कृते सत्य-ज्ञानत्वार्थसञ्चितकर्मसंशयविपर्ययादीनामपि बाधितत्वादखिलबन्ध-रहितो ब्रह्मनिष्ठः । *Vedánta-sára*, p. 27. "The 'liberated, but still living,' is he who—by knowledge of pure Brahma, who is his own essence and indivisible, through removal of ignorance concerning him, *Brahma*, having obtained immediate cognition of Brahma, who is himself and indivisible; whence is riddance of ignorance, and of its effects, which are accumulated works, doubt, misconception, &c.,—set free from all fetters, abides in Brahma, *conscious of being identical therewith.*" अयं देह्यज्ञानमात्रार्थ-मिथ्यानिच्छापरेच्छाप्रापितानि सुखदुःखलक्षान्यारब्धफलान्यनुभव-न्नन्तःकरणाभासादीनामवभासकः सन् तदवसाने प्रत्यगानन्द-

past works.* Thus, after death, the man of right apprehension, being divested of not only his body, but likewise of his mind, and of cognition, and of his sense of all things, remains like a stone,† and is forever exempt from the distresses of

---

परब्रह्मणि प्राणे लीने सत्यज्ञानतत्कार्यसंस्काराणामपि विनाशात् परमकैवल्यमानन्देकरसमखिलभेदप्रतिभासरहितमखण्डं ब्रह्मा ऽवति-ष्ठते । *Ibid.*, p. 28. "This one, *who is liberated, but is still living*,—experiencing, merely for the sustentation of his body, happiness and misery, which are brought *to him* by his own will, or without it, or by the will of others, and which are the effects of fructescent works ; he being the illuminator of the reflexion *of his own soul* in his internal organ, &c. : when it, *the requital of fructescent works*, comes to an end, and his vital breath is merged in the supreme Brahma, one with inward joy ; ignorance and its germinal effects being destroyed,—remains Brahma, who is absolute isolation, unadulterate bliss, pure of all notion of alterity, individual."

* तदभावस्याऽपवर्गै । तस्य शरीरादेरभावः तदारम्भकधर्माध-र्मविरहादिति भावः । *Nyáya-sútra-vṛitti*, p. 215. "And in liberation *there is* the non-existence of that.' 'Non-existence of that,' of body and so forth ; because of the absence of virtue and of vice, originary thereof. Such is the import." The aphorism brought in is the one hundred and tenth of the fourth Book of the *Nyáya-sútra*.

† समाधिसुषुप्तिमोक्षेषु ब्रह्मरूपता । *Sánkhya-pravachana-bháshya*, p. 204. "In coercion of thought, in profound sleep, and in emancipation, oneness with Brahma *is realized*." These words form an aphorism, the one hundred and sixteenth of the fifth Book of the *Sánkhya-pravachana*. The rendering may seem to be free ; but it is implied in the original. Again :

सुषुप्तादौ यो ब्रह्मभावस्त्यागश्चित्तगतात् रागादिदोषवशादेव भवति । स चेद् दोषो ज्ञानेन नाश्रितस्तर्हि सुषुप्त्यादिसदृश्येवाऽवस्था स्थिरा भवति सैव मोच्य इति । *Ibid.*, p. 206. "The being one with Brahma in deep sleep, &c., is intermitted solely by reason of the defects, desire and the like, which belong to the mind. When those defects are destroyed by right apprehension, a permanent state takes place, resembling precisely that of deep sleep. The same is emancipation."

Near the passage from the *Dípakari*, cited at p. 22, it is said, that, in emancipation, the mind and all species of knowledge are done away with. But the mind, in the Nyáya, is imperishable. The sense in which it is said to be

this world. Such is the Systematists' view of emancipation and of the supreme aim of man. From this it is clear, that, agreeably to their tenets, emancipation is simply immunity from misery, and is not a source of any happiness whatsoever.*

---

done away with will appear from the annexed extract, from the work just named : एवमात्ममनःसंयोगरूपव्यापारविशिष्टस्यैव मनसो ज्ञानद्वारा दुःखरूपतया व्यापारनाशेन तद्विशिष्टमनोरूपदुःख-नाशसम्भवादिति । "Likewise, since the mind, when possessing the function of conjoining itself with the soul, is, through *its product*, knowledge, a misery; on the destruction of *that* function, *that* misery, which is the mind as possessing that *function*, may be considered as destroyed."
The purport of this is, that the mind, though it cannot perish, does so virtually, when its functions are definitively discontinued.
That knowledge, with any propriety so called, is not allowed, by the Vedántins, to Brahma, will be shown in the third section of this volume. Emancipation, in their opinion, as in that of the other Systematists, since it is the being identified with Brahma, is, therefore, equally a condition of insensibility.

* ननु एवमानन्दरूपतास्रुतेः का गतिः । तत्राह । दुःखनिवृत्ते-र्गौणः । दुःखनिवृत्त्यात्मनि श्रौत आनन्दशब्दो गौण इत्यर्थः । *Sánkhya-pravachana-bháshya*, p. 189. "But what, in that case, becomes of the scripture which lays down *that the soul is* happiness? The answer is: 'Because of *there being* cessation of misery, *only* in a loose acceptation *does the term happiness denote soul.*'" Repetition has been avoided in the translation. Again : गौणप्रयोगे बीजमाह । विमुक्तिप्रशंसा मन्दा-नाम् । मन्दान्प्रति दुःखनिवृत्तिरूपमात्मस्वरूपमुक्तिं सुखत्वेन श्रुतिः स्तौति प्ररोचनार्थमित्यर्थः । *Ibid.* "The reason of the lax employment *of the aforesaid term* is stated : '*It is in* eulogy of emancipation, for behoof of the dull.' To move ambition in the dull, or ignorant, the emancipated state, which *really* is stoppage of misery, soul itself, is lauded to them by the Veda, as happiness." In these two extracts the sixty-seventh and sixty-eighth aphorisms of the fifth Book of the *Sánkhya-pravachana* are comprehended.

Both pleasure and pain are absent in emancipation, according to the Nyáya also. See the passage from the *Dinakarí*, at p. 22.

Again, the Systematists all maintain, that the soul has existed from everlasting, and that it is exempt from liability to extinction.*

Furthermore, they all hold that the soul is again and again invested with a corporeal form. Death and birth have, for every soul, always existed. When the soul of a man takes on the body of a beast, it becomes a beast; and, when the soul of a beast takes on the body of a man, it becomes a man. The soul may soar to become a divinity; and it may descend to inform a tree.†

In the Vedánta, to realize oneness with Brahma is to be liberated; and Brahma, in that system, as having no proper knowledge, can have no proper happiness. This will be shown in the third section.

* धीरनादिरतोऽस्याश्च सिद्धा भोक्तृरनादिता ।

Sánkhya-sára, MS., *fol.* 16 *verso.* "Intellect is without beginning. And therefore its employer, *soul*, is established to be so."

इत्थं च संसारस्याऽनादितयाऽऽत्मनोऽप्यनादित्वसिद्धावनादिभा-
वस्य नाशासम्भवात् नित्यत्वं सिद्ध्यतीति बोध्यम् । *Siddhánta-muktá-valí: Bibliotheca Indica*, Vol. IX., p. 38. "And thus, by the unbeginningness of transmigration, that of soul being proved, and since an unbeginning entity cannot be destroyed, the eternalness *of soul* is demonstrated. So it is to be understood."

As regards the Vedánta, the ensuing couplet is in the mouth of every well-read Vedántin; but it has not been traced beyond the *Siddhánta-ratnamálá*, a book which the translator has not seen with his own eyes:

जीव ईशो विशुद्धा चित् विभागश्च तयोर्द्वयोः ।
अविद्या तच्चितोर्योगः षडस्माकमनादयः ॥

"The soul, Iśa, pure intelligence, *i. e.*, *Brahma*, the distinctness of the *first* two, nescience, and its connexion with intelligence; *these* our six *are held to be* without beginning."

Consequently—since all the Systems are agreed as to the maxim, that "what had no beginning can never have end,"—the Vedánta also holds, that soul is immortal.

† A late miscellanist, more celebrated for versatility and self-confidence than for exactness, has thus expressed himself, in a paper on the Traditions of the Rabbins: " By a singular improvement on the pagan doctrine of the metempsychosis, there is also a *reverse* change of bodies; and the spirit

Another opinion* common to all the Systems is, that the

which had inhabited the form of a wild beast becomes occasionally the inhabitant of the human shape." *Selections Grave and Gay*, Vol. XIV., p. 238.

Mr. De Quincey had forgotten, while writing this, what Herodotus—*Euterpe*, 123—says of the Egyptians; and his researches on "the pagan doctrine of the metempsychosis" had not extended to India.

The translator avails himself of this opportunity to state, for the information of such as have passed over his preface, that only in a most trifling proportion are the notes of the present volume his own. The few which have suggested themselves to him are sufficiently recognizable, as to their proprietorship, by difference of manner and subject-matter, or by the use of the pronoun of the first person.

* भोक्ता नित्यत्वदर्थंत्वात् तत्कर्मात्यादितत्त्वतः ।
महदादिविकाराणां सर्वेषामविशेषतः ॥

Sánkhya-sára, MS., *fol.* 16, *verso*. "The experiencer *and user, viz.*, *soul*, is eternal, since the great *principle, viz., intellect*, and all the evolutions *from nature*, without reservation, are for its sake, and are produced by its works."

यतः कर्माऽनाद्यतः कर्मभिराकर्षादपि प्रधानस्याऽवश्यकी व्यवस्थिता च प्रवृत्तिरित्यर्थः । *Sánkhya-pravachana-bháshya*, p. 152.

"Since works had no beginning, therefore, by influence from these also, the chief, *i. e., nature*, energizes—necessarily and with regularity."

Other effects besides the fluxional creation of the world are referred to works: यद्यपि सर्गादौ हिरण्यगर्भोपाधिरूपमेकमेव लिङ्गं तथाऽपि तस्य पश्चाद् व्यक्तिभेदो व्यक्तिरूपेभ्यांऽग्रतो नानात्वमपि भवति यथेदानीमेकस्य पितृलिङ्गदेहस्य नानात्वमग्रतो भवति पुत्रकन्यादिलिङ्गदेहरूपेण । तत्र कारणमाह (कर्मविशेषादिति । जीवान्तराणां भोगहेतुकर्मादेरित्यर्थं । *Ibid.*, p. 133. "Though, at the beginning of a world-renovation, but a single subtle body exists, the appurtenance of Hiraṇyagarbha, still there takes place, at an after-period, its 'distribution into individuals,' *i. e.*, also manifoldness, by partition, in the form of individuals; as, in these times, there is manifoldness, by partition, of the one subtle body of a father, in the form of the subtile bodies of sons, daughters, and so on. The cause of this is exhibited: 'From special works;' from the works of other souls, *which works are* causes of *their* experience *of happiness and misery*, and from other things." An aphorism, the tenth of the *Sánkhya-pravachana*, Book the third, is expounded in the preceding extract.

formation of the world, and all effects wrought therein, by

व्याद्विपति । भूतेभ्यो मूर्त्युपादानवत् तदुपादानम् । भूतेभ्य इति सावधारणम् । तथाचाऽदृष्टनिरपेक्षेभ्यो भूतेभ्यः परमाणुभ्यो मूर्तेर्ह्रदादेरुपादानमारम्भो यथा तथैव तस्य शरीरस्योपादानमारम्भः परमाणुभ्योऽदृष्टनिरपेक्षेभ्य इत्यर्थः । समाधत्ते । न साध्यसमत्वात् । नोक्तं युक्तं दृष्टान्तस्य साध्यसमत्वात् पक्षसमत्वात् मृदादेरप्यदृष्टसापेक्षपरमाणुभ्य एवोत्पत्तेरुपगमात् तदजन्यत्वस्य तत्राऽसिद्धेरिति भावः । *Nyáya-sútra-vṛitti*, p. 160. "It is objected: 'Its, *the body's*, origination is, like that of *other* gross material aggregates, from the elements.' The phrase 'gross material aggregates' is for the exclusion *of other causes*. So, then, as the origination, or derivation, of *other* gross material aggregates, constituted of clay and the like, is from the elements, from atoms, irrespectively of desert; after even the same manner, the origination, or derivation, of that, *the animated* body, is from atoms, desert apart. This is intended. The solution is: 'Not so; since *the example is* like what is to be ascertained.' What has been alleged is inadmissible; for the example *brought forward as analogous* is *circumstanced* like what is to be ascertained, *or*, rather, is *circumstanced* like the minor premiss. It being held, *by us*, that also the production of clay and such like is precisely from atoms in dependence on desert *of souls*, unproducedness thereby does not belong to them. Such is the import." This extract takes in the one hundred and thirty-third and one hundred and thirty-fourth aphorisms of the *Nyáya-sútra*, Book III.

Even the production of a jar—to exemplify trifling effects—is ascribed, in the Nyáya, to the works of souls: व्यापकानिमित्ते घटे परमाणुरूपान्तरोत्पत्तौ श्यामघटनाशे पुनर्द्व्यणुकादिक्रमेण रक्तघटोत्पत्तिः । तत्र परमाणवः समवायिकारणं तेजःसंयोगोऽसमवायिकारणमदृष्टादिकं निमित्तकारणम् । *Tarka-dípiká*, MS., fol. 10, *recto*. "In the case of a jar placed in the kiln, when its atoms assume a new hue, the dark-coloured jar is destroyed, and then a red jar is produced, in the order of two atoms *combining at first*, and then more. Of this *red jar* atoms are the material cause; contact with fire, the incidental cause; and the desert *of souls*, and the like, are its *impelling* cause." The souls meant are those destined to be in any wise aided or harmed by the jar.

The objection is supposed, in the *Brahma-sútra*, that, if I's'wara had made the world, he would be liable to the imputation of unequal dealing and

which souls are in any wise affected, are the result of good and evil works done by souls. In the Nyáya and Vais'eshika,

cruelty: and disparity is everywhere and at all times before us. In reply, there is the aphorism: वैषम्यनैर्घृण्ये न सापेक्षत्वात् तथाहि दर्शयति ।
"*There is* no unequal dealing and cruelty *in him;* because of reference. Thus it is shown." S'ankara A'chárya comments on this as follows:

वैषम्यनैर्घृण्ये नेश्वरस्य प्रसज्येते । कस्मात् । सापेक्षत्वात् । यदि हि निरपेक्षः केवल ईश्वरो विषमां सृष्टिं निर्मिमीत स्यातामेतौ दोषौ वैषम्यं नैर्घृण्यं च । न तु निरपेक्षस्य निर्मातृत्वमस्ति सापेक्षो हीश्वरो विषमां सृष्टिं निर्मिमीते । किमपेक्षत इति चेद् धर्माधर्मावपेक्षत इति वदामः । अतः सृज्यमानप्राणिधर्माधर्मापेक्षा विषमा सृष्टिरिति नायमीश्वरस्यापराधः ।

"Unequal dealing and cruelty do not attach to I'swara. Why? Because of relativity. If, indeed, I's'wara had independently made this world of inequalities, without reference *to the works of souls*, those faults would have been *predicable of him*. He does not, however, so make it, but with reference, *as just mentioned*. If it be asked what he has reference to, we reply, to merit and to demerit. Therefore, this world of inequalities is owing to the merit and demerit of the living creatures that are produced; and so that fault, viz., *of making a world of inequalities*, is not chargeable upon I's'wara."
The MS. from which this passage was taken,—occurring in the first quarter of the second book of S'ankara's *Brahma-sútra-bháshya*,—is not at present accessible to the translator.

All changes passing on in the world, in fact, are set to the account of the works of souls. Thus: एतेन जागरितं ब्रह्मणि कल्पितमुक्तं । तदेव स्वप्नकल्पनां दर्शयति । पुनरपीति । जाग्रद्धेतुधर्माधर्मक्षयानन्तर्यं पुनःशब्दार्थः । स्वप्नहेतुकर्मोद्भवे च सतीत्यपि नोच्यते ।

A'nandajnánn's gloss on S'ankara A'chárya's commentary on the *Mándúkya Upanishad: Bibliotheca Indica*, Vol. VIII., p. 327. "By this it is expressed, that what is beheld in the waking state, *i. e., all that is perceived*, is imagined in Brahma. That what is seen in dreams is imagined in the same is *next* declared: 'Again, also,' &c. By the word 'again' is intended 'after the exhaustion *of a given quantity* of merit and demerit, the cause *of a given measure* of what is allotted to the waking state.' 'Also' indicates 'when the works which are the cause of dreams present themselves *for requital*.'"

What is meant by "imagined in Brahma" will be seen early in the third section.

every effect is such a result.* Be it ever so trivial or insignificant, it obeys the general law. Let an atom start up in the air, and travel a distance of no more than four fingers: so far as we can perceive, it works no advantage or prejudice to any one; and yet, either directly or indirectly, some soul or other will, without fail, be affected thereby, for good or for evil, in a greater or in a lesser degree. And so it cannot but be acknowledged, that even this slight circumstance had place in consequence of the acts of souls.

That the world originated from a material cause, is likewise a doctrine of all the Systems.† That, out of which anything is

---

* कार्यमात्रं प्रति साधारणकारणानि ईश्वरतज्ज्ञानेच्छातयः प्रागभावकालदिगदृष्टानि | *Tarkámṛita*, MS., *fol.* 3, *recto.* "Causes common to all effects are God, His knowledge, will, and activity, antecedent non-existence, time, space, and desert *of souls.*"

Whether the following words of Vijnána Bhikshu deliver a tenet held by any philosophy but the Yoga, is a point to be decided by further enquiry than is now practicable. किञ्चाऽस्कामे द्रव्याणामनारम्भिकाप्यनुच्छामणूनां क्रिया सर्वसम्मता न च तत्र धर्मोऽधर्मो वा कारणं कस्याऽपि भोगाहेतुत्वात् | नाऽपि तन्नेश्वरसङ्कल्पादिः कारणं गौरवात् | अतो निरन्तराणुक्रियाऽपपत्तये लाघवेन गुणत्वेनैव सामान्यतः प्रवृत्तिकारणत्वात् प्रवृत्तिखातन्त्र्यं सिद्धम् | *Pátanjala-bháshya-várttika*, MS., *fol.* 152 *verso* and 153 *recto.* "Moreover, it is acknowledged on all hands, that, though not productive of substances, the motion of atoms is going on every moment in the ether: and merit or demerit is not the cause thereof; for it does not give rise to any one's experiencing *happiness* or *misery.* Nor are Íswara's will and the like *to be held* causative of it; since such an hypothesis is superfluous. Hence, to account, consonantly to the law of parsimony, for the incessant motion of atoms, &c., if the *three guṇas* in general alone are *postulated as* originating activity, it is made out, that nature, *the complex of the three guṇas*, is independent."

† In the Sánkhya, nature is so; in the Nyáya, atoms; and, in the Vedánta, ignorance, or illusion.

The appellations given, in various Systems, to the material cause of the universe are rehearsed in this couplet:

made, or from which any thing proceeds, is called its material cause. Clay is such a cause of a jar; and gold, of a golden ornament. As every effect must have a material cause, the Systematists deem the ultimate material cause of all effects to be without a beginning.*

Since, then, souls are considered to be without beginning, and so the ultimate material cause of the world; and since birth and death, and the doing good and evil works, and the arranging and disarranging of the multitudinous constituents of the world, in order that those works may reap their fruit, have been going on from eternity; it is patent, that the maintainers of the six Systems regard the world as having always had existence. To be sure, during its history, it has, from time to time, been resolved into its elements, and then evolved again; the gross world being sublimated, on the occurrence of this resolution, into its subtile material cause:† but, as those muta-

---

नामरूपविनिर्मुक्तं यस्मिन् सन्तिष्ठते जगत् ।
तमाङ्गः प्रकृतिं केचिन् मायामन्ये परेऽणून् ॥

इति । Cited, as from the *Bṛihád-vásishṭha*, in the *Pátanjala-bháshya-várttika*, MS., fol. 74, recto. "That in which the world resides, when divested of name and form, some call nature; others, illusion; others, atoms."

But it must not be supposed, from this, that the different Systematists consent in respect of the nature of the world's material cause.

* That this is the opinion of the Sánkhyas and Naiyáyikas is too well known to require citations in proof. For the Vedánta, see the passage at p. 35, where ignorance is reckoned as one of six eternals.

† Speaking of the consummation of all things, Vijnána Bhikshu says:

यस्य विकारजातस्य खखकारणेषु प्रकृत्यादिषु संसर्गाद्विभागा-
ख्यात् कार्यस्य सौक्ष्म्यमव्यक्तता तस्माच् चास्यानुपलब्धिः ।

Pátanjala-bháshya-várttika, MS., fol. 115, verso. "When all these evolutions *from nature* have commingled, or united, severally, with their causes, nature and the rest, the effect becomes subtile *i. e.*, undiscernible; and, therefore, it is not to be discovered."

tions have always been taking place, the stream of the world has been flowing on from eternity.*

---

* अनादिर्भगवान् कालो नास्तोऽस्य द्विज विद्यते ।
अव्युच्छिन्नास्ततस्त्वेते सर्गस्थित्यन्तसंयमाः ॥
इत्यादिवाक्यशतेभ्यः दृष्टिप्रवाहस्यानादित्ववदनन्तत्वस्यापि सिद्धेः
* * * * * * भूयश्चान्ते विश्वमायानिवृत्तिरिति श्रुतिश्च माया-
ख्यप्रहृतेः प्रलये व्यापारोपरमाख्यां निवृत्तिमेव वदति । *Pátanjala-*
bháshya-várttika, MS., fol. 176, *verso.* "'Adorable time is beginningless, and there is no end of it, O twice-born. These, consequently, are unintermitted, *namely,* the creation, continuance, termination, and quiescence *of the world.'* Since, by hundreds of such statements, it is settled, that, as the on-flowing of the world had no beginning, so it has no end, * * * * *. Moreover, the scripture 'And further, *there is,* at last, the surcease of all illusion,' speaks of that surcease only which is known as the ceasing of the operation, in the universal dissolution *of the world,* of nature, called, *in the words cited,* illusion."

In the aphorism which occurs before the extract from the *Brahma-sútra-bháshya,* given at p. 38, it is asserted, that Iśwara makes this world of inequalities with reference to the works of souls. What follows, derived from the same work, puts forward an objection, and rebuts it in the very next aphorism; the commentator elucidating the whole: न कर्मा़विभा-
गादितिचेन् नानादित्वात् । सदेव सौम्येदमग्र आसीदेकमेवा-
द्वितीयमिति प्राक् सृष्टेरविभागावधारणान् नास्ति कर्म य-
दपेक्षा विषमा सृष्टिः स्यात् सृष्ट्युत्तरकाले हि शरीरादिवि-
भागापेक्षं कर्म कर्मापेक्षश्च शरीरादिविभाग इतीतरेतराश्रयः
प्रसज्येत । अतो विभागादूर्ध्वं कर्मापेक्ष ईश्वरः प्रवर्ततां नाम ।
प्राक् विभागाद् वैचित्र्यनिमित्तस्य कर्मणोऽभावात् तुल्ये वाऽद्या
सृष्टिः प्राप्नोतीति चेन् नैष दोषोऽनादित्वात् संसारस्य । भवेदेष
दोषो यद्यादिमान् संसारः स्यात् । अनादौ तु संसारे बीजा-
ङ्कुरवदेतुहेतुमद्भावेन कर्मणः सर्गवैषम्यस्य च प्रवर्त्तनं विद्यते ।

Once more, all the Systematists receive the words of the Veda as unquestionable authority; and they also accept, as warrants, the Smṛitis, the Purúṇas, &c., the work of Ṛishis, when those books do not thwart with the Veda.

The foregoing are the leading dogmas of the Systems; and, with trifling modifications, all the Systems hold them.

An examination of these dogmas is fraught with very great benefit; for one gains, by it, an acquaintance with the general bias of the minds of the pandits.

I now proceed to sketch the more important doctrines among those which characterize the Systems severally, the Vedánta excepted.

The tenets of the Sánkhya and Yoga are these. Nature and soul are the ultimate bases of all existent things. Souls are eternal and many. Nature is unintelligent substance, and is the material cause of the world. It consists of goodness, passion, and darkness, in equal proportions.* And here it

---

* "'If it be said, that there are no works, for that there is no diverseness, it is denied; because of unbeginningness.' The absence of diverseness, *i. e.*, *of the diversified developement of things*, prior to creation being certified by these utterances, "Meek one, this was, at first, merely existent,' and "One only, without a second,' there are *then* no works, with reference to which a creation of inequalities could originate : and, *if works were supposed to have p!ace subsequently to creation*, mutual dependence would be the result; that is to say, works must require diversified developement *of things*, bodies, &c., and the diversified developement *of things*, bodies, &c., must require works. Let it be, therefore, that I'śwara acts in dependence on works, after the diversified developement *of things*. There being, before such developement, no works causative of inequalities, it follows, that the first creation ought to be one of uniform equalities. The answer to this is, that it, *the argument*, is of no weight, 'because of the unbeginningness' of the course of the world. It would have weight, if the course of the world had a beginning. But the continuous operation, in the beginningless conrse of the world, of works and of inequalities of creation, as *mutual* causes and effects, after the manner of the seed and the sprout, is not incompatible."

* गुणा एव प्रकृतिशब्दवाच्याः न तु तदतिरिक्ता प्रकृतिरस्ती-त्यवधारयति । एते गुणा इति । एते सत्त्वादयो गुणा एव प्रकृ-

should be borne in mind, that it is not the goodness, passion, and darkness, popularly reckoned qualities or particular states of the soul, that are intended in the Sánkhya. In it they are unintelligent substances.* Otherwise, how could they be

---

* तिष्छब्दवाच्या भवन्ति । *Pátanjala-bháshya-várttika*, MS., *fol.* 73, *verso.* "The *guṇas* themselves are denoted by the word nature; and nature does not differ from them. Thus is *this* pronounced: 'These *guṇas*,' &c.; these self-same *guṇas*, goodness and the rest, are what is signified by the term nature."

In the sixty-first aphorism of the *Sánkhya-pravachana*, Book I., nature is said to be the equilibrium of goodness, passion, and darkness. On this declaration Vijnána Bhikshu remarks: तेषां सत्त्वादिद्रव्याणां या साम्यावस्थाऽन्यूनानतिरिक्तावस्था न्यूनाधिकभावेनासंहननावस्थेति यावत् । अकार्यावस्थेति निष्कर्षः । अकार्यावस्थोपलचितं गुणसामान्यं प्रकृतिरित्यर्थः । *Sánkhya-pravachana-bháshya*, p. 45, "The 'equilibrium' of those substances, 'goodness' and so forth, *i. e.*, a state in which none is less or more; in short, a state in which there is not aggregation of less and more. The extractive import is, the state of not being an effect. The *guṇas*, taken collectively, when characterized by the condition of not being effects, make up nature. Such is the sense."

Nature is not, then, a substrate of the *guṇas*, but the very *guṇas* in a certain state, that of equivalence.

* सत्त्वादीनि द्रव्याणि न वैधर्म्यविका गुणाः संयोगविभागवत्त्वात् लघुत्वचलत्वगुरुत्वादिधर्मकत्वाच् च । *Ibid.* "Goodness and the rest are substances, not specific qualities; for they *themselves* possess qualities, those of contact and separation, and also have the properties of levity, mobility, gravity, &c."

For the specific qualities, see the *Bháshá-parichchheda*, ninetieth stanza.

It is a maxim of the Hindus, that endowment with quality is a token of substance alone. There cannot be quality of a quality.

The reason why goodness, passion, and darkness are called *guṇas* is supposed, by expounders of the Sánkhya, to be as follows: तेष्वन शास्त्रादौ च गुणशब्दः पुरुषोपकरणात्वात् पुरुषपशुबन्धकत्रिगुणात्मकमहदादिरज्जुनिर्माणत्वाच् च प्रयुज्यते । *Ibid.* "The term *guṇa* is applied, in this system, and also in the Veda and elsewhere, to these, *goodness, passion, and darkness*, because they are appliances of the soul, and because

the material cause of earth and like gross things. From nature arise effects, to requite the good and evil works of souls.* First, among these effects, arises the great principle, or intellect; and, from it, the organ of egoism: and these, too, are unintelligent substances.† From the organ of egoism proceed eleven instruments and five rudiments. The latter are tenuous sources of the gross elements, earth and the rest. The eleven instruments derived from the organ of egoism are the senses of sight, hearing, smell, taste, and touch, with the tongue, hands, feet, anal orifice, organ of generation, and mind. Intellect, the organ of egoism, and mind, are all termed internal organs, or, collectively, the internal organ.‡ Cer-

---

they form the triple-stranded rope, *i. e.*, the great *principle, viz., intellect* and the rest, which binds the soul a beast, *as it were.*"

Guṇa, it must be observed, signifies rope, or cord; and, likewise, quality; but not here, as we have seen.

* In the Sánkhya, it is not only the works of souls that move nature to bring about reward of good and evil, in the developement of the world, &c.; but nature has itself an intrinsic power of acting on behalf of the soul.

† अहङ्कारस्याभिमानवृत्तिकमन्तःकरणद्रव्यं न त्वभिमानमात्रम्।
Sánkhya-pravachana-bháshya, p. 49. "And the egoizer is a substantial internal organ, having self-consciousness for its affection. It is not self-consciousness alone, *but inclusive thereof.*"

All the principles of the Sánkhya—intellect, the organ of egoism, and mind, being, of course, among them,—are said to be substances: अयं च पञ्चविंशतिको गणो द्रव्यरूप एव। *Ibid.*, p. 46. "And this group of twenty-five *principles* is substantial."

Dr. J. R. Ballantyne has strangely written: "Souls alone are, in the Sánkhya, regarded as substances." *Christianity contrasted with Hindu Philosophy*, p. xxvii.

‡ It seems, oftentimes, as if there were not three organs, so much as one tripartite organ. Each is, however, frequently found styled an organ. यतः:- करणमेकमेव बीजाङ्कुरमहदादिवदवस्थानयमात्रभेदात् कार्य-कारणभावमापद्यत इति च प्रागेवोक्तम्। अतएव वायुमात्रायोः।

titude is the distinguishing property of intellect; to evolve self-consciousness, that of the organ of egoism; and to cognize discriminatively that of mind.*

मनो महान् मतिर्ब्रह्मा पूर्बुद्धिः ख्यातिरीश्वरः ।
इति मनोबुद्ध्योरेकपर्यायत्वमुक्तमिति । *Ibid.*, p. 117. "The internal organ, though single, comes to be, *in itself, partly* cause and *partly* effect, by virtue merely of its distinction into three states, *those of intellect, egoizer, and mind;* like the seed, the germ, and the full-grown tree; as has been said higher up. For this same reason, in the verse of the Váyu and Mátsya, *two of the Puránas,* 'Mind, the great *principle,* understanding, Brahmá, city, intellect, knowledge, and I'swara,' mind and intellect are exhibited as synonymes."

चित्तमन्तःकरणसामान्यमेकस्यैवान्तःकरणस्य वृत्तिभेदमात्रेण चतुर्धाऽन्न दर्शने विभागात् । *Pátanjala-bháshya-várttika,* MS., *fol.* 4 *recto.* "'The thinker,' the internal organ in general; since, in this system, that organ, which is one only, has, simply on account of its possessing a variety of affections, a fourfold division."

Thus, while, in the Sánkhya, the internal organ has three members, in the Yoga it has four. The Vedánta herein agrees with the Yoga.

* अध्यवसायो बुद्धिः । "Intellect is certitude." So runs the thirteenth aphorism of the *Sánkhya-pravachana,* Book II. Vijnána Bhikshu remarks on it: महत्तत्त्वस्य पर्यायो बुद्धिरिति । अध्यवसायश्च निश्चयाख्यस्तस्याऽसाधारणी वृत्तिरित्यर्थः । अभेदनिर्देशस्तु धर्म-धर्म्यभेदात् । *Sánkhya-pravachana-bháshya,* p. 115. "Intellect is a synonyme of the great principle. And its distinguishing affection is certitude, or assurance. As for the enunciation *of them* as identical, it is because of the indifference between a property and that to which it belongs."

In definition of egoism, it is said: अभिमानोऽहङ्कारः । अहङ्करोतीत्यहङ्कारः कुम्भकारवदन्तःकरणद्रव्यं स च धर्मधर्म्यभेदादभिमान इत्युक्तः । *Ibid.,* p. 117. "The egoizer is egoism. It makes *(karoti)* I *(aham)*: hence *it is termed* egoizer. Compare *kumbhakára, maker of jars,* or *potter. It is* a substantial internal organ; and it is called egoism, because of the indifference between a property and that to which it belongs."

Strictly speaking, then, egoism is the property of the organ of egoism.

Soul, say the Sánkhyas, is sheer knowledge.* But, on examination, it turns out to be, with them, only nominally so. For, in all knowledge, properly so called, there is apprehension, or cognition, of some object; as, this is a jar, this is cloth,

---

Mind is thus characterized by Váchaspati Miśra; तदसाधारणेन रूपेण लक्ष्यति सङ्कल्पकमनमनः । सङ्कल्पेन रूपेण मनो लक्ष्यते । आलोचितमिन्द्रियेण वस्त्विदमिति समुग्धमिदमेवं नैवमिति सम्यक् कल्पयति । *Tattwa-kaumudí,* p. 34. "That, *mind*, is defined by *a statement of its* distinguishing nature: 'Mind, here, is a cognizer discriminatively.'' Mind is defined by its characteristic, cognizing discriminatively. A thing *is, at first,* indistinctly perceived, by the senses, in *the notion* 'This *is something. Then the mind* thoroughly settles, 'It *is* of this sort, not of that.'"

The translator has conformed, in the English of the body of the page, to this explanation of *sankalpa.*

Vijnána Bhikshu dissents from the foregoing view, and assigns to the mind a function in addition to *sankalpa:* तथा च बुद्धितत्त्वेऽध्यवसायोऽभिमानोऽहङ्कारस्य सङ्कल्पविकल्पौ मनस इत्यायातम् । सङ्कल्पस्य कीर्षं सङ्कल्पः कर्ममानसमित्यनुशासनात् । विकल्पस्य संशयो योगोक्तभ्रमविशेषो वा न तु विशिष्टज्ञानं तस्य बुद्धितत्त्वादिति । *Sánkhya-pravachana-bháshya,* p. 122. " And thus it follows, that the *chief* affection of intellect is certitude ; that of the egoizer, egoism ; and that those of the mind are resolution *(sankalpa)* and irresolution *(vikalpa).* Resolution is the willing to do; agreeably to the canon 'Resolution *is* the mental act.' Irresolution is either indecision, or a specific kind of misapprehension spoken of in the Yoga. It is not the cognizing *a thing* together with *its* properties ; for this, *viz., thus to cognize,* is an affection of intellect."

* ज्ञानं नैवाऽऽत्मनो धर्मो न गुणो वा कथञ्चन ।
ज्ञानस्वरूप एवाऽऽत्मा नित्यः पूर्णः सदाशिवः ॥

इति । Cited in the *Sánkhya-pravachana-bháshya,* p 96. "Knowledge is not at all a property of the soul; nor is it, in any way, a quality *of it.* The soul is knowledge itself, and is eternal, full, or *self-sufficing,* and ever-happy."

Vijnána professes to have taken this couplet from a Smṛiti ; but he does not designate the Smṛiti by name.

&c. In the Sánkhya, however, it is not this apprehension, or cognition, that is soul, or even a quality thereof: this apprehension being an evolution from the internal organ.* This

---

* Several of the notes next after the excursus which here begins would have been divorced from the pages to which they severally belong, had this excursus been subjoined—as else it would have been—to the end of the paragraph of the text, on the insentience of the soul and the sentience of the internal organ.

To any tyro in the Sánkhya and Vedánta it is notorious, that cognition is an affection of the internal organ. Here is, however, a passage in proof of the assertion: अध्यवसायस्य बुद्धिव्यापारो ज्ञानम्। उपात्तविषयाणा-मिन्द्रियाणां वृत्तौ सत्यां बुद्धेस्तमोऽभिभवे सति यः सत्त्वसमुद्रेकः सोऽध्यवसाय इति च वृत्तिरिति च ज्ञानमिति चाऽऽख्यायते ।
Tattwa-kaumudí, p. 8. "And certitude is the operancy of intellect; *it is* cognition. An affection having taken place of *any one of* the senses, after they have apprehended their *respective* objects, the intellect's darkness being overpowered, *the intellect's* preponderance of goodness is called certitude, and affection, and cognition."

As nature, the great root, is compounded of three substances, goodness, passion, and darkness, so are all its derivates, intellect, &c. &c.; the constituent parts being variously proportioned for each. Intellect, when darkness overweighs in it, is torpid; and, when goodness does so, is vivid, and cognizes.

It is not tropically, but literally, that the affection of the internal organ is said to be cognition. It is not an instrument of cognition, but cognition itself. This is evident from the ensuing words: ताश्च बुद्धिवृत्तयो नाऽज्ञा-तास्तिष्ठन्ति ज्ञानेच्छासुखादीनामज्ञातसत्ताऽस्वीकारे तेष्वपि घटा-दाविव संशयादिप्रसङ्गादहं जानामि न वा सुखी न वेत्यादिरूपेण ।
Sánkhya-pravachana-bháshya, p. 210. "And those affections of intellect are never unrecognized. If an unrecognized existence of cognition, desire, happiness, &c., were granted, it must follow, that, just as *men are sometimes doubtful* about a jar, or the like, *whether it be existent*, or *non-existent*, they would have doubt about them; *this doubt* taking the form of 'Do I cognize, or not?' 'Am I happy, or not?'"

This language, it is palpable, is relevant only as regards veritable cognition, that which the Naiyáyikas thus denominate.

Cognition, as being an affection of the internal organ, is, therefore, seen to be a thing not belonging to the soul.

organ, it is averred, assumes the form of a jar, of cloth, &c. &c.;

A reflexion of the affection cognition, it is moreover maintained, is cast on the soul. But what is this? Is it a matter of which any of us are conscious? According to the Sánkhya, it is a cognition of the affection cognition just spoken of. Thus: यच्च चैतन्ये बुद्धेः प्रतिबिम्बः स चास्तूढविषयैः सह बुद्धेर्भानार्थमिष्यते । *Ibid.*, p. 73. "And the reflexion, in intelligence, *or the soul*, of intellect is held in order to *account for the soul's* cognition of intellect, along with the objects borne *by it.*"

Again: यच् चैतच् चैतन्ये बुद्धिवृत्तिसारूप्यमुक्तं चैतन्यस्य बुद्धिवृत्त्याकारताऽरूपमिदमेव चैतन्यस्यार्थेपरक्तवृत्तिभानम् ।
Pátanjala-bháshya-várttika, MS., fol. 8, verso. "And this forementioned assimilation of intelligence to the affection of intellect, its becoming of like aspect thereto, this very thing is the cognition, by intelligence, *or soul*, of the affection *of intellect* which has taken the shape of the object *cognized*."

The Naiyáyikas hold four species of right notion *(pramá)*, to each of which corresponds an instrument suited to it *(pramána)*; but, in the Sánkhya, these four species become three, by the inclusion in inference *(anumiti)*, of cognition from recognizing similarity *(upamiti)*. These species of right notion become, however, in the Sánkhya, instruments of other right notions lying beyond,—reflexions, in the soul, of the former,—they at the same time retaining their character of right notions as regards their instruments, the senses, &c. The Sánkhya has, therefore, two sets of species of right notion, and as many of instruments adapted to them. Vijnána Bhikshu says:

सा च द्वयोर्बुद्धिपुरुषयोरेव धर्मो भवतु किंवैकतरमात्रस्य ।
Sánkhya-pravachana-bháshya, p. 64. "And whether it, *right notion*, be a property of both intellect and soul, or of but one of the two," &c.

By "property of intellect" is meant affection of intellect; and, by "property of soul," reflexion, in the soul, of that affection.

In the same page with the Sanskrit last cited we read: अत्र यदि प्रमारूपं फलं पुरुषनिष्ठमात्रमुच्यते तदा बुद्धिवृत्तिरेव प्रमाणम् । यदि च बुद्धिनिष्ठमात्रमुच्यते तदेन्द्रियसन्निकर्षादिरेव प्रमाणम् । पुरुषस्तु प्रमासाक्षेव न प्रमातेति । यदि च पौरुषेयबोधो बुद्धिवृत्तिस्तोभयमपि प्रमोच्यते तदा तुल्लमुभयमेव प्रमाभेदेन प्रमाणं भवति ।
"Here, if the fruit right notion is supposed to reside in soul alone, the affection of intellect exclusively is an instrument of right notion; and, if in intellect alone, the contact of a sense, &c. are exclusively such an instrument.

and this evolution is called an affection. Thus, the cognition

---

As for the soul, it is only the witness of right notions, not the subject of them. And, if the soul's apprehension and the intellectual affection are equally reckoned right notions, both the aforesaid, viz., *the affection of intellect and the contact of a sense, &c.*, are instruments of right notion relatively to those notions respectively."

But the soul's apprehension is considered, by the Sánkhyas, as the principal sort of right notion: पातञ्जलभाष्ये तु व्यासदेवैः पुरुषनिष्ठबोधः प्रमेत्युक्तः । पुरुषार्थमेव करणानां प्रवृत्त्या फलस्य पुरुषनिष्ठताया एवौचित्यात् । अतोऽत्रापि स एव मुख्यः सिद्धान्तः । *Ibid.*, p. 65. "But, in the commentary on Patanjali, Vyása says, that apprehension resident in the soul is right notion. For it is fitting, that the fruit should reside in the soul only, inasmuch as the operation of instruments is for it. Therefore, in this *Sánkhya system* likewise, the same, *the position that the soul's apprehension is right notion*, is the foremost opinion *among the three enumerated.*"

It has been stated, that the reflexion, in the soul, of the internal organ's affection is the cognition of that affection, itself a cognition. But this cognition of cognition is not analogous to that which, in the Nyáya, is styled supervenient apprehension *(anuvyavasáya)*, or consciousness of cognizing. In this system, primary apprehension *(vyavasáya)* is in the form, for example, of "This is a jar;" and the relative supervenient apprehension is, "I cognize the jar." This primary apprehension is, as we know, in the Sánkhya, an affection of the internal organ, exemplified by "This is a jar," &c.; and the reflexion, in the soul, of such primary apprehension, to which the Sánkhyas give the name of psychic apprehension, agrees with it in form. That is to say, it is "This is a jar," not "I cognize the jar." To show this, a passage lately given is here repeated, with its continuation: यच् चैतच् चैतन्यं बुद्धिवृत्तिसारूप्यमुक्तं चैतन्यस्य बुद्धिवृत्त्याकारतरूपमिदमेव चैतन्यस्यार्थोपरक्तवृत्तिभानम् । तस्य चाऽहंकारोऽयं घट इत्यादिरूप त्वादन्यथा वृत्तिसारूप्यानुपपत्तेः । न तु वृत्तिबोधस्य एथगाकारोऽस्ति । "And this forementioned assimilation of intelligence to the affection of intellect, its becoming of like aspect thereto, this very thing is the cognition, by intelligence, *or soul*, of the affection *of intellect* which has taken the shape of the object *cognized*. And the form of this *psychic cognition* is precisely such as 'This is a jar,' &c. Else, the *aforesaid assimilation of intelligence* to the affection *of intellect* could not be established.

H

"This is a jar," or "This is cloth," is an affection of the in-

---

The form of the cognition of the affection is not different *from that of the affection itself.*"

The writer goes on to say, that a cognition in the form of "I cognize the jar," which the Naiyáyikas call a supervenient apprehension, is only another affection of the internal organ : घटमहं जानामि दुःखितोऽहमित्या-दिकं तु बुद्धेरेवाऽऽकारान्तरम् । पुरुषस्यापरिणामिवादभ्रान्त-त्वाच् चेति । "As for *the cognition* ' I cognize the jar,' ' I am miserable,' or the like, it is merely another form of intellect. For the soul is immutable, and unobnoxious to error."

For the soul to acquire cognitions would presuppose it exposed to mutability, argue the Sánkhyas. They further maintain, that, in all cognitions, such as "I know," &c. &c., there is something of erroneousness; for any notion implicating "I" unifies the soul with the internal organ. To keep good the ground, that the soul never changes, nor errs, the theory was set on foot, that all cognitions arise in the mind, and that only their reflexions touch the soul,—and yet without at all affecting its essence.

But the doctrine, alike of the Sánkhya and of the Nyáya, that cognition and the consciousness of cognition are separate in fact, is inadmissible. When I cognize a jar, simultaneously I become conscious that I do so. What the Naiyáyikas term supervenient apprehension, arising after the primary, cannot be cognition : it is remembrance. The Sánkhyas' reflexion, in the soul, of the primary cognition,—their affection of intellect,—is not, however, thought, by them, to present itself subsequently, but at the same time. Still, in postulating that reflexion as a cognition of the primary cognition, and as separate in fact, they also mistake. This kind of cognition of a cognition is not a thing of which any of us are cognizant; and it is to be rejected as a figment.

As is primary cognition, so likewise the cognition of it, a reflexion of it, is an evolution from the internal organ. For all reflexions, as that of the sun in water, are, agreeably to the Sánkhya, evolutions of intellect. Near the extracts recently made from the *Pátanjala-bháshya-várttika*, we are told : एतेन नीरूप-त्वाद् बुद्धिपुरुषयोरन्योन्यप्रतिबिम्बं न सम्भवतीत्यपास्तम् । उभय-नोभयाकारबुद्धिपरिणामस्यैव प्रतिबिम्बशब्देनाऽत्र विवक्षितत्वात् । जलादावपि सूर्याद्याकारबुद्धिपरिणामस्यैव सूर्यादिप्रतिबिम्बत्वाच् च ।
" By this is repelled *the objection*, that, since intellect and soul are colourless, there can be no reflexion of them in each other. For, by the vocable ' reflexion' is here intended an evolution from intellect, in the likeness of each, *cast* upon each ; *i. e., in soul, in the similitude of intellect, and, in intellect, in*

ternal organ. But, in consequence of the proximity to each

the similitude of soul: and also because the reflexion of the sun, &c., in water, &c., is nothing but an evolution from intellect, in the likeness of the sun, &c."

We thus see, that the Sánkhyas consider not only primary cognition, but their secondary cognition also, fictitious as it is, to be merely an evolution from the internal organ, and no quality or true affection of the soul. The relation of such secondary cognitions to the soul is no more intimate than that of a bird to the branch on which it perches.

The psychic apprehension of the Sánkhyas, the reader should rest assured, is the very reflexion of the internal organ's affection, and not something produced, by that reflexion, in the soul's nature. From the passage of the *Pátanjala-bháshya-várttika,* at p. 49, it is manifest, that the soul's cognition of an intellectual affection is identically the reflexion of it, there spoken of as the assimilation of intelligence to that affection. Further proofs of this are as follows:

प्रमाता चेतनः शुद्धः प्रमाणं दृष्टिरेव नः ।
प्रमाऽर्थाकारवृत्तीनां चेतने प्रतिबिम्बनम् ॥

इति । *Sánkhya-pravachana-bháshya,* p 67. "With us, the possessor of right notion is the pure intelligent one, *soul;* and the instrument of right notion is affection *of the internal organ.* Right notion is reflexion, in the intelligent one, of the affections *aforesaid,* which have assumed the forms of the objects *cognized by* those affections."

Of the three opinions touching right notion, its instruments, and its subject, mentioned at pp. 48, 49, the one there designated as most eminent is adopted above.

Vyása's commentary on the Yoga Aphorisms states, that intellect notifies things to the soul. This notification is explained by the annotator:

निवेदनं च स्वार्थविषयस्य प्रतिबिम्बरूपेण चित्याधानम् ।

Pátanjala-bháshya-várttika, MS., fol. 7, *recto.* "And notification is *intellect's* depositing in intelligence, *or soul,* objects borne by itself, in the shape of reflexions."

एतदुक्तं भवति । यद्यपि पुरुषश्चिन्मात्रोऽविकारी तथापि बुद्धेर्विषयाकारवृत्तीनां पुरुषे यानि प्रतिबिम्बानि तान्येव पुरुषस्य वृत्तयः । न च ताभिरवस्तुभूताभिः परिणामित्वम् । *Ibid.* "The drift is this: though the soul is sheer intelligence, and unalterable, still the reflexions, in the soul, of the affections of intellect, which have taken on the forms of the objects *cognized,* are the soul's affections. And there cannot be, in consequence of these unreal *affections,* any alteration *in the soul.*"

other of the internal organ and the soul, each is reflected in

Hence we are to understand, that the reflexions themselves, in the soul, of the internal organ's affections, which may be cognition, will, activity, happiness, or misery, are the soul's cognition or knowing, and the soul's experience of will, activity, &c. &c. They are designated as false, in the Sánkhya, not because they are nonentities, but because they are not what they seem to be; that is to say, however they may appear to be affections of the soul, they are not so in reality, and work no change of any sort in its nature. Consistently enough, the Sánkhyas apply the epithet "unreal" to the reflexion of a rose in crystal. Here, again, according to them, the reflexion is not non-existent. Only it does not belong inherently to the crystal, to which it seems so to belong.

सोऽयं बुद्धितत्त्ववर्तिना ज्ञानसुखादिना तत्प्रतिबिम्बितत्त्वच्छाया-पत्त्या ज्ञानसुखादिमानिव भवतीति चेतनोऽनुगृह्यते । *Tattwa-kaumudí*, p. 8. "This, *soul,*—by reason of the cognition, the happiness, &c., which *actually* reside in the principle intellect,—from receiving their reflexions, and from being assimilated thereto, as it were becomes possessed of cognition, happiness, and the rest. In this wise is the intelligent one, *soul*, benefited by them, *those reflexions.*"

Vijnána Bhikshu, speaking of the soul, which is named, in the text he is scholiazing, by a word of the feminine gender, says: विशेषगुणानि विशेषगुणा वैशेषिकशास्त्रोक्तास्तैः कालत्रयेऽप्यसम्बद्धा इत्यर्थः । तेन संयोगसंख्यापरिमाणादिसत्त्वेऽप्यवृत्तिः । *Pátanjala-bháshya-várttika*, MS., *fol.* 84, *verso.* "''Properties,' the specific qualities recited in the Vaiseshika system. With these *qualities soul* is unconnected throughout threefold time, *viz., time past, present, and future*. Such is the sense. Therefore, *i. e., on this interpretation of 'properties'*, for all that *the common qualities*, contact, number, dimension, &c., appertain *to the soul*, it matters not."

The specific qualities which the Vaiseshikas refer to the soul are cognition, will, and happiness, among others. These, as we perceive, the Sánkhyas altogether deny to the soul.

किञ्च बुद्धितिरिक्तेभ्य आत्मविवेकस्य न्यायवैशेषिकाभ्यामेव सिद्धत्वेन बुद्धितो विवेक एव सांख्ययोगयोः साधारणं कृत्यम् । *Ibid., fol.* 86, *recto.* "Moreover, since the discrimination of the soul from other things than intellect may be acquired even from the Nyáya and Vaiseshika, the *peculiar* office of the Sánkhya and Yoga, *and* common *to them*, is the discrimination *of soul* from intellect."

the other. Hence, the affections of the internal organ, in the

---

It is because the Nyáya and Vaiseshika describe soul so as to make it one with the Sánkhya "intellect," that Vijnána Bhikshu reputes those doctrines inadequate to communicate, in its integrity, a correct knowledge of discrimination.

The origination, in the soul, of cognitions would betoken the soul to be changeable: and it is argued, by the Sánkhyas, that it is unchangeable.

सामान्यगुणातिरिक्तधर्मात्यञ्चैव परिणामित्वव्यवहारात् । *Sánkhya-pravachana-bháshya,* p. 22. "Because, solely on account of the rise of properties other than the common qualities, a thing is said to have undergone a change."

Those other properties are the specific qualities lately referred to. They include cognition, will, colour, taste, &c.

अर्थाकारस्यैवार्थग्रहणशब्दार्थत्वाच् चेति । स चार्थाकारः पुंसि परिणामो न सम्भवतीत्यर्थात् प्रतिबिम्बरूप एव पर्यवस्यतीति दिक् । *Ibid.,* p. 73. "And also because by the expression 'cognizing an object' is meant simply assimilation to an object. And that assimilation to an object cannot be, in the case of the soul, *from* alteration ; *as happens in the case of the internal organ.* By consequence, it turns out to be exclusively in the form of reflexion. Such is the direction *indicated.*"

ननु निर्गुणत्व एव का युक्तिरिति चेदुच्यते । पुंसस्येच्छाद्यास्तावन् नित्या न सम्भवन्ति जन्यताप्रत्ययात् । जन्यगुणाङ्गीकारे परिणामित्वापत्तिः । *Ibid,* p. 96. "But, if the ground of *the soul's* being *thought* void of qualities be enquired, the reply is, that the soul's will, &c. cannot be eternal; for *their* originatedness is evidenced by consciousness. If originated qualities *of soul* were admitted, it would be incident to mutation."

Cognition is here denoted by the suppletive expression after "will."

ननु पुंसस्याप्यपरिणामित्वव्यवस्थापने किमिति साङ्ख्ययोगयोराग्रह इति चेत् गृह्या । यदि हि पुंसस्य ज्ञानादिलक्ष्यधर्मः कश्चन मोचे नश्येत् तद्दोषेण तदा दारिद्र्यवन् मोचो न परमपुरुषार्थः स्यादिति । *Pátanjala-bháshya-várttika,* MS., *fol.* 164, *verso.* "But, should it be asked, why the Sánkhya and Yoga are so eager to establish that soul is immutable, hearken. If, in *the state of* emancipation, any property of the soul, such as cognition and the like, were to perish, then, owing to

shape of a jar, of cloth, &c., are reflected in the soul. Conse-

---

this defect of loss, emancipation could not, any more than penury, be the supreme aim of the soul."

The meaning is, that such evanescent things as cognition, will, and so forth, cannot have existence in the state of liberation. If they were the soul's qualities, the soul would lose something by being liberated. Hence, to save it from liability to loss, they are represented as having never belonged to the soul.

न नित्यस्याऽनित्यज्ञानसम्भव इति ।   *Sánkhya-pravachana-bháshya* p. 96. "Non-eternal cognition cannot appertain to the eternal *soul.*"

Attention should be paid to the circumstance, that, in the Sánkhya, the term "cognition" *(jnána)* denotes two distinct things. One of them is that which we all so denominate. This is really the apprehending of objects; and, to us, this alone deserves the name it bears. This cognition is that on which we have hitherto been dwelling. But, again, the Sánkhyas apply the appellation of cognition to the soul itself, which they also style intelligence, the intelligent one, &c. Here, however, cognition is so but nominally; as it is not one with apprehension of objects. Cognition as denoting soul, it is laid down, is eternal. तस्मान् नित्यात्मनो ज्ञानं नित्यं *Sánkhya-sára,* MS., *fol.* 17, *recto.* "Therefore, the cognition of soul, *which soul itself is* eternal, is eternal."

That this cognition, by which the soul itself is intended, is cognition only in name, is thus shown: न प्रेत्य संज्ञाऽस्तीति पूर्ववाक्ये याज्ञवल्क्येन मोक्षकाले ज्ञानस्वरूपोऽपि पुरुषो न जानातीत्युक्तमखिलदुःखभोगनिवृत्तिरूपं परमपुरुषार्थं मोक्षे प्रदर्शयितुम् । *Pátanjala- bháshya-várttika,* MS., *fol.* 136, *verso.* "In the foregoing sentence, Yájnavalkya,—for the purpose of setting forth, that, in liberation there is *the attainment of* the soul's supreme aim, which is the removal of the experience of all misery,—has, by the words 'After departure there is no consciousness,' expressed, that the soul, though essentially cognition, knows nothing throughout the duration of liberation."

Thus, even when liberated, the soul continues to be cognition. If this cognition were that which apprehends objects, the soul would be cognizant. Yet it does not possess, when emancipated, any more sentience than a stone.

The cognition just spoken of, that which does not apprehend, is eternal The other, which apprehends, and which resides in the soul, as a reflexion, is non-eternal.

चेत्योपरागरूपत्वात् सञ्चिताऽप्यभुवा चितः ।

quently, the reflexion, in the soul, of the affection apprehension

इति | *Sánkhya-sára*, MS., *fol.* 26, *recto*. "Also the intelligent one's witnessing is impermanent ; it being the reflexion of objects."

Since it is but a reflexion, it lasts only during the presence of that which is reflected.

It has been abundantly made clear, that the cognition in question is not intrinsic to the soul. Nevertheless, the Sánkhyas are wont to use language from which it seems as if they believed, that the soul itself, as reflected into, were this cognition. वस्तुतो वृत्तिबोधोऽहम् | *Ibid., fol.* 28, *recto*. " In truth, I, *soul,* am the cognition of affections *of the internal organ.*"

But this is deceptive. The explanation is thus. Just as crystal which is receiving the reflexion of a rose is said to be red, so the soul, from receiving the reflexion of intellectual affections, is said to be cognition. In the first case, it is, really, the reflexion of the rose that is red ; and, in the second case, it is the reflexion of the affections, not soul, that is cognition.

Though the Sánkhyas contend strenuously, that the soul is incognitive, still, with an uneasy consciousness that their view in this behalf is not entirely correct, they compound the matter by giving to the soul the titles of cognition, knowledge, intelligence, &c., and yet refuse to accept the legitimate consequences of such a procedure. And this fact will assist us to understand a singularity connected with the Sánkhya system. All such cognitions as "I will," "I am happy," &c. &c., say its advocates, are erroneous ; since qualities which are not proper to the soul are, thereby, attributed to it. Less erroneous, according to those philosophers, and erroneous on a different ground, is the cognition "I know." Here, they say, there is not the attribution to soul of a property alien to it, but, rather, the supposing that cognition is a property of the soul, whereas it is its essence. The untenableness of this is obvious. For it is not that cognition, falsely so called by the Sánkhyas, namely, the essence of the soul, that is cognized in the consciousness "I know," but that cognition which is truly the apprehension of objects. And this latter cognition is neither the soul itself, nor a property of it. No more, on account of this cognition, is the soul real cognition, than it is a real experiencer of happiness and misery, by reason of the reflexions of them. For, in the Sánkhya, happiness, misery, will, and activity, no less than cognition, are evolutions from, and affections of, the internal organ. Their reflexions, not themselves, come in contact with the soul.

To recapitulate : the Sánkhya holds, that all true cognitions are evolutions from the internal organ. A primary cognition, as "This is a jar," is an affection of that organ, and also an evolution from it ; and its reflexion falls upon the soul. This reflexion is psychic, or secondary, apprehension ; and it likewise is an evolution from the internal organ.

is the soul's apprehension. In the Sánkhya doctrine, then, whether apprehension be considered as an affection of the internal organ, or as a reflexion, in soul, of that affection, it does not appertain to soul, or is not intrinsic to it.

Similarly, will and activity also are affections of the internal organ.* Soul, by reason of receiving their reflexions, ac-

---

Furthermore, also the cognition "I cognize the jar" is an affection of the internal organ. Its history is this. The soul, along with a reflexion of the affection of the internal organ, such as "This is a jar," is reflected into the internal organ. This second reflexion is the affection of the internal organ in the form "I cognize the jar;" and, like all reflexions, it is an evolution from the internal organ. बुद्धौ चैतन्यप्रतिबिम्बचैतन्यदर्शनार्थं कल्प्यते । *Sánkhya-pravachana-bháshya.* p. 73. "The reflexion of intelligence into intellect is supposed with a view to *account for* the perception of intelligence." It is meant, that the soul, when it has received the reflexion of an affection of the internal organ, to the end that it may behold itself possessed of that reflexion, must be reflected back into that organ; just as a man's face must be reflected into a mirror, in order that he may see himself. The reflexion into the internal organ must be reflected back into the soul; and this is the soul's self-inspection. प्रमाणख्यत्याहृतं प्रकृतिपुरुषादिकं प्रमेयं दृष्ट्वासत् पुरुषे प्रतिबिम्बितं सद् भासते । *Ibid.,* p. 76. "Objects of right notion, *viz.,* nature, soul, &c., are perceived, when borne by the affection known as instrument of right notion, and when, in conjunction with that affection, reflected in the soul."

The notion "I" is an affection of the internal organ; but the object of that notion is soul : for the affection "I" is nothing but the soul reflected into the internal organ. Hence, the notions, or affections, of that organ, in the form "I cognize", or "I am happy", and so forth, mean, that the soul cognizes, or is happy, &c.

* शब्दादिनिश्चयरूपस्य परिणामस्य बुद्धौ सिद्धेव तत्कार्याणामिच्छाकृतिसुखदुःखादृष्टसंस्कारादीनां बुद्धिधर्मत्वेनैव सिद्धेः ।
Pátanjala-bháshya-várttika, MS., *fol.* 85, *verso.* "That evolution which is certitude about, *i. e., cognition of,* sound and other *objects* being established *to belong* to the intellect, its, *that evolution's,* effects, *viz.,* will, activity, happiness, misery, desert, impression *(sanskára),* &c., are established to be properties of the intellect solely."

अहङ्कारः कर्ता न पुरुषः ॥ ५७ ॥ अभिमानवृत्तिकमन्त:-

counts itself, from ignorance, a willer and a doer; and, of course, it befals it to experience happiness, misery, Elysium, Hell, birth, death, &c., the fruits of good and evil works. For, since the soul, though not actually a doer, misapprehendingly thinks itself one, it is brought into the bondage of experiencing those fruits.* This is what it is for the soul to be bound.

By the statement, that the soul, on admitting the reflexions of will, activity, and other qualities of intellect, misapprehendingly looks upon itself as an agent, &c., we are to under-

---

कर्त्तामहङ्कारः स एव कृतिमान् । *Sánkhya-pravachana-bháshya*, p. 226. "'The egoizer, not the soul, is the agent.' That internal organ which has egoism for its *characteristic* affection is the egoizer. It alone is endowed with activity."

The fifty-fourth aphorism of the *Sánkhya-pravachana*, Book VI., is included above.

Since the Sánkhyas consider the internal organ to be the real agent, or doer of works, the virtue and vice arising from the works are supposed to be that organ's properties,—or evolutions from it, as they are styled,—and not properties of the soul. Hence, in the penultimate passage of Sanskrit, desert is comprehended among the properties of the internal organ. Desert denotes both merit and demerit.

प्रकृतिः कुरुते कर्म शुभाशुभफलात्मकम् ।
प्रकृतिश्च तदश्नाति त्रिषु लोकेषु कामगा ॥

इति । *Ibid.*, p. 35. "Nature executes works, which have fruits, good and evil. Moreover, nature, ranging the three worlds at will, eats those *works, in the fruit.*"

Not nature itself, but nature in its evolution the internal organ, is here spoken of as executing works and eating their fruit.

* अहं कर्त्तेत्याद्यभिमानस्यैव धर्म्माधर्म्मोत्पत्तिद्वाराखिलजगद्धेतु-
त्वात् । *Pátanjala-bháshya-várttika*, MS., *fol. 57, recto.* "For the egoistic notions 'I do', and the like, are, through *their* production of merit and demerit, the cause of the entire universe."

It is meant, that, when a man thinks "I am a doer," he incurs vice or virtue from his doings. To the end that their fruit may be reaped, it is that the world is produced.

stand it to be meant, that the soul does not really so look upon itself: for, as we have remarked, in the Sánkhya system, it has, in truth, no apprehension; both this and misapprehension being affections proper to the internal organ.* The soul's being misapprehensive is nothing else but its receiving the reflexion of this misapprehension,† an affection of intellect. In fact, neither does it at all misapprehend, nor does it at all apprehend.

On this topic the followers of the Sánkhya allow themselves in singular theories, intelligible only at the cost of close attention. That the soul should be made out destitute of all specific qualities,‡ such as apprehension, will, &c., is most material to their views; and hence they altogether refuse to it the possession of apprehension. Now, misapprehension itself is a species of apprehension, mistaken apprehension;§ as the taking nacre to be silver. Thus they are driven to regard both sorts of apprehension, the true and the false, as affections of the internal organ, or reflexions, in the soul, of those affections.

The precise mind of the advocates of the Sánkhya, when

---

* दुःखाज्ञानमया धर्माः प्रकृतेस्ते तु नाऽऽत्मनः ।
इति । *Ibid., fol.* 8, *recto.* This is an isolated verse, of unknown paternity.

"The properties misery and ignorance are nature's, not soul's."

After quoting as above, Vijnána Bhikshu observes, that this and similar passages deny ignorance to the soul.

See also the second passage from the *Tattwa-kaumudí*, given at p. 10.

† अयं चाऽविवेकोत्तिरूपः प्रतिबिम्बात्मना पुरुषधर्म इव भवति ।
Sánkhya-pravachana-bháshya, p. 214. "And this non-discrimination, an affection *of the internal organ,* becomes, in the shape of reflexion, as it were a property of soul."

‡ अत आत्मा निर्गुणः । *Ibid.,* p. 96. "Therefore the soul is without qualities."

But compare what is said at the foot of pp. 52, 53.

§ See the note at p. 10.

they call activity an affection of the internal organ, and say, that only from misapprehension does the soul esteem itself an agent, will now become clear to the reader. As is the case with apprehension, will, and activity, so is it with happiness and misery. That is to say, they are all evolutions from the internal organ;* and their reflexions in the soul are the soul's becoming happy or miserable.† Again, either a fresh affec-

---

* सुखदुःखादिगुणानां चित्तधमंत्वेऽपि तत्राऽऽत्मनि सिद्धिः प्रतिबिम्बरूपेणाऽवस्थितिरविवेकान् निमित्तात् । *Sánkhya-pravachanu-bháshya,* p. 113. "Though the qualities happiness, misery, &c. are properties of the internal organ, 'there,' *viz.,* in the soul, is *their* ' residence,' or abiding, in the form of reflexions, ' owing to non-discrimination,' as a cause."

The aphorism elucidated in the eleventh of the sixth Book.

Happiness, misery, merit, and demerit are all called evolutions from the internal organ ; and the first two are likewise termed affections of that organ. All affections of the internal organ are held to be objects of consciousness. Cognition, will, activity, happiness, misery, and aversion, being objects of this sort, are affections ; but merit, demerit, and impression, not being objects of consciousness, are not viewed as affections.

† A distinction is groundlessly taken, by the Sánkhyas, between happiness and misery and the experience thereof. Happiness and misery, they say, reside in the internal organ ; and the reflexions of them, cast on the soul, are the soul's experience of them. Hence it is, that they call the soul the experiencer,—of happiness and of misery, to-wit. But that experience, since it is only a reflexion, and therefore an evolution from the internal organ, and not intrinsic to the soul, is considered to be false.

कूटस्थासङ्गचिद्योऽन्ति धीदुःखप्रतिबिम्बनम् ।
योऽन्यो बन्धो भोगरूपः सोऽपि चिद्दर्पणे मृषा ॥

इति । *Sánkhya-sára,* MS., *fol.* 30, *recto.* "Another bondage is the reflexion, in intelligence,—immutable, unaffected, etherlike,—of the intellect's misery; *and it is the soul's* experience *of misery.* This too is false in the mirror of intelligence, *or soul.*"

It is observable, that, though the Sánkhyas distinguish between happiness and misery and the experience of them,—taking the former to be affections of the internal organ, and the latter to be reflexions of those affections, lying on the soul,—still they give to these latter as well, the name

tion of the internal organ, cognizing the soul, when happiness or misery is reflected therein, or the reflexion, in the soul, of such an affection, is the soul's cognizing itself as happy or miserable;* and in this consist all its bondage and wretchedness. To escape from this wretchedness, he who listens to the Sánkhya, and ponders and revolves it, and derives from it this discriminative knowledge, that to do and to experience are qualities of nature alone,—for the internal organ is an affection of nature; and the soul is in every way distinct from nature, and is, in reality, neither doer nor experiencer of happiness or of misery,‡ and is unchangeable,—is released from the captivity of nature. For it is a dogma of the Sánkhya, that, for shamefastness, nothing surpasses nature. So long as soul does not detect her, she spreads her toils; but,

---

of happiness and misery. प्रतिबिम्बरूपेण पुरुषेऽपि सुखदुःखे स्तः ।
Sánkhya-pravachana-bháshya, p. 10. "Happiness and misery reside in the soul likewise, in the form of reflexions."

* The reflexions, in the soul, of the internal organ's affections happiness and misery are the soul's happiness and misery. Then the soul, together with those reflexions, is reflected into the internal organ: and thus is constituted that organ's affection in the form of "I am happy" or "I am miserable." Afterwards, the reflexion of those reflexiform affections is cast upon the soul; and this is its psychic apprehension of them: in other words, it is the soul's cognition "I am happy" or "I am miserable."

अहं सुखीत्यादिविशिष्टज्ञानार्थं बुद्धेस्तत्रैव तादृग्राकारत्वम् । पुरुषे वृत्तिसारूप्यमात्रस्वीकारेण इच्याकारातिरिक्ताकारानभ्युपगमात् खत्वाकारेण परिणामायत्तेरिति । *Ibid.*, p. 99. "In order to account for the complex cognition 'I am happy,' or the like, *we believe, that* the very affection of intellect takes on a similar form. Acknowledging that there is only the assimilation of the soul to *that* affection, *viz., by the soul's receiving its reflexion*, we do not hold that there is, *in the soul*, any form but that of *such* affection *received by the soul as a reflexion*. For, if we held an independent form *in the soul*, it would follow, that it, *the soul*, is changeable."

Compare what is said at the foot of p. 56, about the affection of the internal organ, in the form of "I cognize the jar," and its reflexion in the soul.

‡ See the passage from the *Sánkhya-sára*, given at p. 59.

directly when her delusive play is noticed, she flees, in confusion, from soul, and her face is never beheld again.*
Accordingly, when the soul has acquired right apprehension, accumulated works, are, by its efficacy, done away. And, inasmuch as it no longer deems itself a doer, its current works, or those which it does day by day, do not devolve upon it, either merit or demerit. Only to exhaust the experience of fructescent works, has it to remain in its body; and, when these works shall have received their full requital, it will relinquish the body, and there will be no more fear, for it, of Elysium, or of Hell, or of metempsychosis: since then no works will appertain to it, the experience of which will oblige it to tenant a corporeal frame.

In connexion with this subject, what I have said above should be kept in remembrance; that, agreeably to the Sánkhya, neither apprehension nor misapprehension actually belongs to soul, both being qualities of the internal organ.†

---

* प्रकृतेः सुकुमारतरं न किंचिदस्तीति मे मतिर्भवति ।
या दृष्टास्मीति पुनर्नं दर्शनमुपैति पुरुषस्य ॥

इति । Sixty-first stanza of the *Sánkhya-káriká*. "My opinion is, that nothing is more coy than nature; which, on finding herself beheld by the soul, does not again come in sight *of him.*"

पुरुषेण परिदृष्टामिलदुःखात्मकत्वादिदोषदर्शनादपि लज्जितायाः प्रकृतेः पुनर्नं पुरुषं प्रत्युपसर्पणं कुलवधूवत् । *Sánkhya-pravachana-bháshya*, p. 154. "Nature, also when her defects, *viz.*, changeableness, the being filled with misery, &c., have been observed by the soul, abashed, never again approaches him; like as a woman of good family."

Such is the description found of nature, though, in the contemplation of the Sánkhya and Yoga systems, it is an insentient principle.

† वृत्तिरूपौ च विवेकाविवेको चित्तस्यैव । *Ibid.*, p. 43. "And discrimination and non-discrimination, *both which are* affections, belong to the mind alone."

The discrimination spoken of, that is to say, between soul and nature, is the right apprehension mentioned in the text, which is to be acquired before emancipation can be realized.

Therefore, the cognition "I am distinct from nature, and am unchangeable" is an affection of the internal organ: and this organ is an evolution from nature. So it is to be understood, that, as nature, by means of its evolution misapprehension, binds the soul, so, no less, through its evolution right apprehension, does it set the soul free. Hence nature is both the captivator and the emancipator of the soul.* According to the Sánkhya doctors, the entire office of nature is to bring about the experience and the liberation of the soul.† Nay, these autho-

---

* एवं यस्मै पुरुषाय प्रकृतिर्विवेकेनाऽऽत्मानं दर्शितवती तदासनावज्ञात् तमेव संयोगद्वारा बध्नाति नान्यम् । तथा यस्मै विवेकेनाऽऽत्मानं दर्शितवती तमेव स्ववियोगद्वारा मोचयति वासनोच्छेदादिति । *Ibid.,* "Thus, to whatever soul nature shows itself, as not discriminated therefrom, that very soul, and no other, does it hold captive, through junction, by force of the impression of that *non-discrimination.* In like manner, to whatever *soul* it shows itself, as discriminated therefrom, that very soul it releases, through disjunction from itself, by the destruction of the impression *aforesaid.*"

† स्वभावतो दुःखबन्धात् विमुक्तस्य पुरुषस्य प्रतिबिम्बरूपदुःखमोच्चार्थं प्रतिबिम्बसम्बन्धेन दुःखमोच्चार्थं वा प्रधानस्य जगत्कर्तृत्वम् । अथवा स्वार्थं खस्य पारमार्थिकदुःखमोच्चार्थमित्यर्थः । यद्यपि मोचवद् भोगोऽपि दृष्टः प्रयोजनं तथापि मुख्यत्वान् मोच एवोक्तः । *Ibid.,* pp. 110, 111. "Nature's fabricating the world is for the purpose of liberating the soul—naturally freed from the bondage of misery—from the misery *which is in it,* in the form of reflexions, or from that misery *which is an affection of the internal organ, and is connected with the soul* through the relation of reflexion. Or *nature's fabricating the world is* for its own behoof, i. e., to deliver itself from veritable misery. Though the aim, in creation, is experience, as well as emancipation, the latter alone is specified, because it holds the chief place."

The first aphorism of the *Sánkhya-pravachana,* Book II., is here commented on. It is cited in short in the next extract.

By nature's creation for itself we are to understand, that it creates inclusively for itself, while officially creating for soul. The words subjoined make this evident: ननु विमुक्तमोच्चार्थं स्वार्थं वेत्यनेन स्वार्थोऽपि

rities even declare, that, in truth, the soul is neither bound nor freed, but that bondage and freedom both appertain to nature; as is distinctly set forth in the sixty-second stanza of the *Sánkhya-káriká*.*

दृष्टिरक्तोति चेत् सत्यम् । तथापि पुरुषार्थेतां विना स्वार्थ-
तापि न सिद्ध्यति । स्वार्थे हि प्रधानस्य कृतभोगापवर्गात्
पुरुषादात्मविमोचनमिति । *Ibid.*, p. 151. "But, if it be said, that creation, *by nature*, is laid down—in *the sentence* 'For the liberation of the *already* liberated *soul*, or for itself'—to be for its own, *i. e.*, *for nature's*, sake also; it is admitted. Still, abstractedly from service of the soul, there cannot be *nature's* service of itself. For the good *to be done* for itself, by nature, is the deliverance of itself from the soul, whose experience and emancipation it has brought to effect."

But how, it may be asked, does nature free the soul by forming the world? The ensuing extract will disclose the singular view which the advocates of the Sánkhya cherish on this point: लिङ्गसंहतितो जन्मद्वारा विवेकसा-
त्कारात्तस्मान् मुक्तिरूपः पुरुषार्थो भवतीत्यर्थः । *Ibid.*, p. 138.
'By transmigration of the subtile *body*, through birth, *is gained* immediate discrimination. From this comes the soul's aim, emancipation. Such is the meaning."

We are now enabled to see in what sense it is understood, that nature aims to liberate the soul by creating the world. In furnishing the soul with a body, mind, senses, &c., it capacitates the soul to obtain knowledge, which likewise it brings into existence; and by this knowledge the soul becomes unfettered.

* तस्मान् न बध्यतेऽद्धा न मुच्यते नापि संसरति कश्चित् ।
संसरति बध्यते मुच्यते च नानाश्रया प्रकृतिः ॥

"Therefore, in reality, not any *soul* is bound, or freed, or transmigrates: *it is* nature, in relation to various *souls*, *that* transmigrates, is bound, and is freed."
प्रकृतेरेव तत्त्वतो दुःखेन बन्धमोक्षौ । *Sánkhya-pravachana-bháshya*, p. 155. "Bondage and release belong to nature alone; *because to it*, in truth, belongs misery."

Respecting the bondage of soul, the same author says: प्रतिबिंबरूपदुः-
खयोगस्य पारमार्थिको बन्ध इति भावः । *Ibid.*, p. 20. "The bondage *of the soul, consisting in* its connexion with misery, which is reflexional, is unreal. This is the import."

Such are the chief doctrines of the Sánkhya and Yoga. But, as I have already remarked, there is this great distinction between these systems, that the latter recognizes God, while the former denies Him.*

The Sánkhyas hold, that the Veda had no author. Yet they do not, like the Mímánsakas, contend, that it has existed from eternity. They say, that, at the beginning of each renovation of the universe, it has issued from the mouth of Brahmá. He was no conscious composer of it, however: it simply escaped from him like an expiration. Thus the Sánkhyas, though maintaining that the Veda originated from Brahmá, would have it to be authorless. And they further declare, that, often as the universe has been redintegrated, the Veda has as often been produced without the

---

* The ninety-second aphorism of the *Sánkhya-pravachana*, Book I., is ईश्वरासिद्धेः | "Since *the being of* I'swara is not proved."

आरम्भः सर्गः प्रकृत्यैव कुतो नेश्वरेण *Tattwa-kaumudí*, p. 51. "'Commencement,' *i. e.*, creation, is executed by nature exclusively, not by I'swara."

Long arguments are entered into by the commentators who wrote the *Sánkhya-pravachana-bháshya* and the *Tattwa-kaumudí*, to disprove God's existence. At the same time, neither Vijnána Bhikshu nor Váchaspati Misra was a thoroughgoing Sánkhya. This is shown, as to the former, by the fact that he strives strenuously to excuse the one error, as he rates it, of the system he so largely endorses.

The Yoga, avowedly indeed, is theistic ; but, on near scrutiny, we find this claim to be futile. The god of the Yoga differs in no respect, psychically, from its man or beast. His soul is as incognitive as a clod ; and his internal organ, which creates the world, and which is omniscient and omnipotent, is an evolution from nature. In the matter of omnipresence,—or, rather, all-pervadingness,—he possesses it, indeed ; but so does every other soul, down to that of a tree.

परमेश्वरस्य सर्वज्ञत्वादिव्यवहारस्तु लोकव्यवहारादिति | *Pátan-jala-bháshya-várttika*, MS. *fol.* 87, *recto.* "As for the custom, *in Yoga treatises,* of saying, that the supreme I'swara is omniscient, &c., it is in compliance with popular usage."

least variation whatever, and thus has retained the same form from all duration of time.*

Strange indeed are the tenets that have been enumerated. Great labour, as we see, has been expended for the one end

---

* न नित्यत्वं वेदानां कार्यत्वश्रुतेः ॥ ४५ ॥ स तपोऽतप्यत तस्मात् तपस्तेपानात् त्रयो वेदा अजायन्तेत्यादि श्रुतेर्वेदानां न नित्यत्व-मित्यर्थः । *Sánkhya-pravachana-bháshya*, pp. 181, 182 "'The Vedas are not eternal, since there is scripture for *their* originatedness.' There being the scripture 'He, *Brahmá*, performed austerity, *and* from him, so doing, the three Vedas were produced,' the Vedas are not from eternity. This is the sense."

The forty-fifth aphorism of the *Sánkhya-pravachana*, Book V., is herein included.

Still the Sánkhyas do not acknowledge, that the Vedas were composed by Brahmá. न पुरुषोच्चरितत्वमात्रेण पौरुषेयत्वं श्वासप्रश्वासयोः सुषुप्तिकालीनयोः पौरुषेयत्वव्यवहाराभावात् किन्तु बुद्धिपूर्वकत्वेन । वेदास्तु निःश्वासवदेवादृष्टवशादबुद्धिपूर्वका एव स्वयम्भुवः सकाशात् स्वयं भवन्ति । अतो न ते पौरुषेयाः । तथा च श्रुतिः । तस्यैतस्य महतो भूतस्य निःश्वसितमेतद् यद्‌ऋग्वेद इत्यादीति । *Ibid*, pp. 182, 183. "Not from the mere fact of *its* being uttered by a person, *can one say there is* producedness *of a thing* by *that* person ; since it is not the wont to speak of the respiration of deep sleep as the production of a person : but, by *reason of its* production consciously, *a thing is said to be produced by a person*. The Vedas, however, just like an expiration, and by virtue of desert *of souls*, issue, spontaneously, from Brahmá, without ever being consciously produced *by him*. Hence they are not productions of a person. And thus the scripture : 'This, which is the *Ŗig-veda*, is the efflation of that great being.' "

The last extract, if fully given, would be seen to recite the other divisions of Veda, the *Yajush*, &c.

In proof of the assertion in the last sentence of the paragraph to which this note is attached, we read : वेदनित्यतावाक्यानि च सजातीयानुपूर्वीप्रवाचनानुच्छेदपराणि । *Ibid*, p. 182. "And the texts *of scripture* declaratory of the eternalness of the Vedas signify, that the course of *their* uniform verbal collocation has never been departed from, *at the times of the several renovations of the universe*."

of proving, that the soul must be regarded as devoid of apprehension, will, activity, happiness, misery, and all other qualities. For it is asked, if apprehension, will, and the like, be allowed to soul, and so these qualities be proved natural to it, what is to transform its nature, and how will its liberation be effected? For, in all the Systems, the absence of apprehension, will, &c. is held to be necessary to the state of emancipation; the dread of apprehension, will, &c. being such, that all manner of wretchedness is believed to ensue, where they subsist. To be released from misery is, of course, necessary to emancipation. Hence all the Systematists, with a view to liberate the soul from every sort of wretchedness, aim at devising some scheme for its getting rid of apprehension, will, and the rest; and each of them frames a project after his own principles. As for the upholders of the Sánkhya, to their mind, nothing can be done, unless the soul be demonstrated to have been devoid of apprehension, will, and all other qualities, from all time.* We have seen what extraordinary

---

* बन्धोऽत्र दुःखयोग एव । तस्य बन्धस्य पुरुषे न स्वाभाविकत्वं वच्यमाणलच्यमस्ति यतो न स्वभावतो बद्धस्य मोचाय साधनोपदेशस्य श्रौतस्य विधिरनुष्ठानं नियोज्यानां घटते न ह्यग्नेः स्वाभाविकादौष्ण्यान् मोचः सम्भवति । *Ibid.*, pp. 14, 15. "Bondage, in this *system*, is connexion with misery. This bondage is not natural to the soul, in the way about to be explained; since it cannot reasonably be supposed, that they who are directed can carry out, or perform, the instructions of the Veda regarding means for the emancipation of that which is naturally bound. For fire cannot be set free from the heat that is natural to it."

These words expound the seventh aphorism of the *Sánkhya-pravachana*, Book I.

What is meant by the term "natural" will be made manifest by these words, which are put into the mouth of an objector: ननु स्वाभाविकस्याप्यपायो दृश्यते । यथा मुक्तपटस्य स्वाभाविकी शौक्र्यं रागेणापनीयते । यथा च बीजस्य स्वाभाविकाप्यङ्कुरशक्तिरग्निनाऽपनीयते । *Ibid.*, p. 16. "But we see the elimination even of that which is

things they have enunciated. It is a long way that they have wandered beyond the limits of common sense, after having once over-leapt them.

It is not the design of the Mímánsá, as it is of the other Systems, to consider bondage and emancipation, and soul and what is not soul; but simply to treat of the precepts of the Veda, and of its cultus: and I do not purpose to examine it as touching these heads. Its points which are here especially deserving of mention are as follows. First, it repudiates the idea of God; and, in the second place, it contends, that the Veda was originated by no one, but has always existed. The injunctions, inhibitions, and good and evil fruits of works rehearsed in it, are held, indeed, to be true. But the accounts of the divinities, given in the Veda, are reputed to be false,*

---

natural. For instance, the natural whiteness of white cloth is removed by dyeing; or, again, the germinative power of a seed, though natural, is destroyed by fire."

As whiteness, a quality of white cloth, is here said to be natural to such cloth; so, if cognition, will, happiness, misery, &c. were supposed to be qualities of the soul,—as the Naiyáyikas assert they are, – they would be called natural to it, in the terminology of the Sánkhya. On this point the Sánkhyas assail the Naiyáyikas; as might be shown by adduction of texts, if it were necessary to adduce them.

Just as, in complete liberation, there must be dismissal of misery, so must there be of cognition likewise; it being itself a misery, and compounded of the three *guṇas*. See the note at p. 22; and a passage cited at p. 53, which implies that, if cognition were reckoned a quality of the soul, a loss would be sustained in liberation,—when it must be parted with,—and liberation would be no supreme aim of the soul. Will and other qualities obey the same law as cognition. See, further, what is said at p. 33, on the notion of liberation common to all the Systems.

* यतः कथमपि न विग्रहादिस्वीकारः किन्तु शब्दमात्रं देवता। अर्थं तु प्रातिपदिकानुरोधाच् चेतनोऽचेतनो वा कश्चित् क्रीह्निय-ते न तु विग्रहादिमान्। उपासनादौ परं ध्यानमात्रमाश्रयं तस्येति जैमिनिमतनिष्कर्षः। मम लैवं वदतोऽपि वाक्यो दुष्यतीति तत्र हरिस्मरणमेव शरणम्। *Bháṭṭa-dípiká*, MS., ninth chapter, second

and to have been written solely for the purpose of magnifying works. With regard to this matter, the surprising notions about to be noted are professed. It is recorded, in the Veda, that Elysium is obtained by sacrifice. And a sacrificial observance consists in offering, in fire, clarified butter, flesh, &c., to Indra, Varuṇa, Agni, and other divinities; with the recitation and intonation of hymns of praise from the Veda, and laudation of the exploits and virtues of the aforesaid divinities. Now, the Mímánsakas assert, that Indra and those other divinities have no existence whatever, and that the prowess ascribed to them is entirely fictitious. Nevertheless, there is such a wonderful potency in the falling of offerings into the fire, in their name, after the manner prescribed by the Veda, and in uttering the syllables of the songs that hymn them, as to ensure attainment of the celestial abodes.

The Naiyáyikas and Vais'eshikas hold, for their foremost doctrines, as follows.* They believe in a God, described as one,

---

quarter, topic of *Devatá*. " Therefore it is not, by any means, to be acknowledged, that a god is an embodied form, and so forth ; but *he is to be regarded as* a mere verbal expression *of the Veda*. As for the thing signified *by that expression*, it is held to be, according to the expression, some sentient being, or insentient object,—not endowed, however, with a figure, &c., *i. e.*, *purely notional*. But, in devotion and so forth, mere meditation on him, in picturing to oneself the unreal as real, *is to be observed*. Such is the gist of the doctrine of Jaimini, *here considered*. But, by the very repetition of this *blasphemy*, my tongue contracts defilement,—from which the remembrance of Hari is the only safeguard."

The functions discharged by a god, in virtue of his possessing "an embodied form and so forth," are indicated as follows : देवता विग्रहवती प्रति- गृह्य भक्षां हृप्यति प्रसीदति च । *S'ástra-dipiká ;* the manuscript not at hand for reference. " A god, incorporate, accepting and consuming a *sacrifice*, is satisfied and becomes auspicious."

Consonantly to the Mímánsá theory, works are instinct with an inherent potency for desert ; and, though the devotee may be convinced, that the gods are purely chimerical, Mímánsakas believe, that he derives virtue, as it were magically, from adoring them.

* Almost all the statements of this paragraph may be verified by a heedful

eternal, immutable, without form, pervading everything, all-powerful, omniscient, framer of the universe, lord of all, and bestower of the consequences of the good and evil works of souls, which souls have always existed. In order towards this bestowal, He fashions the world out of its material cause, and preserves the world, governs it, and brings it to a termination. The followers of the two systems just named maintain, that some of the constituents of the world had no beginning, and that others among them had. Of the former category are the originary atoms of earth, water, fire, and air, as well as ether, time, space, mind, and soul. An atom is the minutest portion of earth, or the like; invisible to the eye, intangible to the hand, in short, inappreciable by any of the senses; and it is incapable of further division. It is supposed to have existed, spontaneously, from eternity. From the aggregation of atoms results whatever is visible, tangible, &c., earth and water, for example; and hence such things had a beginning, and are also liable to destruction. To souls belong apprehension, will, activity, happiness, misery, virtue, vice, and other qualities; and they are eternal and innumerable, and distinct from the body, the senses, and the mind. Further, they are all-pervading. It is only so much of the soul as dwells in the body, that can see, hear, apprehend, will, &c.; and yet the psychical essence is not limited by the body, but is diffused everywhere.* Moreover, like the other Systematists, the Naiyáyikas and Vais'eshikas allege, that the soul misapprehen-

---

perusal of the *Bhásha-parichchheda*. It has been translated into English by Dr. Röer, in the ninth volume of the *Bibliotheca Indica*. The reader may profitably compare with it Dr. J. R. Ballantyne's translation of the *Tarka-sangraha*, as far as it goes. But both these works must be used critically.

* No one of the Six Systems entertains correct ideas of spiritual substance. Material properties are attributed to it by all of them. For instance, they ascribe dimension to the soul; and they further speak of it as actually touching matter. Again, though they hold the soul to be indiscerptible, they use such language as that, though diffused everywhere, it is in contact with a jar in the place where the jar is, and not elsewhere.

sively identifies itself with the body, &c., and that, consequently, to it all wretchedness adheres, and that solely through right apprehension can it escape therefrom, and attain emancipation. In the two systems under notice, the Veda is believed to have God for its author.

Such are the distinctive doctrines of the several Systems, the Vedánta excepted, which possess the greatest importance. There are many distinctive doctrines, in them, of lesser moment, which demand no mention on the present occasion.

Now, any man of the least discrimination, if he has not girded his loins pertinaciously to withstand the truth, can readily discern, that, since these systems disagree among themselves, they cannot all be true. When one man calls a thing black, and another man calls it white, it is clear, that one or other of them is in the wrong. There are some people who labour hard to make out, that there is no discordancy among the Six Systems. Let them only look into the fundamental aphorisms of those systems, and they will see, that the views laid down in one set are, in another set, repeatedly brought forward and refuted. S'ankara A'chárya and others even go the length of reviling those who deviate from themselves in doctrine. For instance, S'ankara stigmatizes a Naiyáyika as a bull, sans horns and tail.*

---

* In his commentary on the *Brihad A'ranyaka Upanishad.*

Vijnána Bhikshu writes thus, of the Vedántins: व्याधुनिकानां वेदान्तिब्रुवाणां प्रपञ्चासत्यत्वरूपया अपसिद्धान्ता नास्तिकमतानुसारिणो मुमुक्षुभिर्दूरतः परिहार्यांः । *Pátanjala-bháshya-várttika*, MS., *fol.* 80, *verso.* "The false doctrines of the modern Vedántins, so self-styled, *maintaining* that the world is unreal, as being in accord with the views of the infidels, should be avoided afar by aspirants after emancipation."

Vijnána, who lived centuries ago, meant, by "modern Vedántins, so self-styled," S'ankara A'chárya and his school. These he looked upon as innovators with respect to the Vedánta notions he himself professed; which, aright or amiss, he considered as much more ancient, and as alone genuine.

Pray, is this a token of unanimity? Even without separate consideration of the tenets of the several Systems, it becomes manifest, that they contain errors, and, by consequence, that their authors, the Ṛishis, like ourselves, were not infallible. When, however, each of these systems is examined by itself, as concerns its dogmas, these conclusions are rendered indubitable.

CHAPTER 3.

An Examination of the Sánkhya Doctrines (1) of the Non-existence of God, as concurrent with the Belief in Virtue, Vice, and their Fruits; and (2) of the Acceptance of the Veda as having had no Conscious Author, and as being irrecusably authoritative.

How great is the error of the Sánkhya in denying the existence of God! On all sides of us, in this Kosmos, countless and

---

The same writer again says: किञ्च मिथ्याबुद्धिर्नास्तिकतेत्यनुशासनाद् धर्मादिषु खापवन् मिथ्यादृष्टयो बौद्धप्रभेदा एव । सांक्तिकशब्देन प्रपञ्चस्यास्सविद्यकतायाश्च तैरभ्युपगमात् । *Sánkhya-pravachana-bháshya*, p. 107. "For the rest, by the canon 'The idea of the falsity *of all* is infidelity,' they who account virtue &c. to be false, like a dream, are, verily, a sect of Bauddhas. For these also, by the term 'illusory,' argue the world to be sprung from nescience."

It is the *Amara-kosa* which Vijnána here quotes from.

S'ankara A'chárya, moreover, owns, that the founders of the philosophies were not at unity among themselves: प्रसिद्धमाहात्म्याभिमतानामपि तीर्थकराणां कपिलकणभुक्प्रभृतीनां परस्परविप्रतिपत्तिदर्शनात् ।
"For mutual opposition is seen between Kapila, Kaṇabhuk, and other authors of systems, whose greatness is conceded to be notorious."

This passage, which occurs in S'ankara's commentary on the *Brahma-sútra*, is cited by the Reverend Professor Banerjea, in his valuable *Dialogues on the Hindu Philosophy*, p. 18.

Very different, in their sentiments, were the Hindu philosophical writers of bygone days from those of recent times, with their nugatory endeavours to reconcile the irreconcilable.

manifest are the tokens, from which it is certain, that some most mighty and ineffable Intelligence framed the world with design.* Any effort directed to an end has, self-evidently, mind for its author; for only he who knows that a particular end will be accomplished by a given act, will engage in such an act with a view to such an end. We are, therefore, sure, that he who does this act possesses consciousness; and such a one is called an intelligent being. Now, when, after contemplating a thing, we are certified that it is intended for a certain end, there is no room for doubt that an intelligent being has had to do with it. To give an example: I find, somewhere, a pile of wood sufficient to cook a meal for four men, and as much as they would require of pulse, rice, meal, ghee, vegetables, and so forth, disposed in separate vessels, and a fireplace, and the ground clean round about. Would any sceptic, I demand, in all the earth, doubt whether the requisites aforesaid were prepared by some one for culinary purposes, or whether they collected together spontaneously and fortuitously. Just so is it with a clock. No one, on examining the arrangement of its wheels, will ever entertain a misgiving as to whether it was made by some one, and in order to measure time. Similarly, I maintain, that this world is full of innumerable things, analogous in character to those above mentioned, on scrutinizing which it becomes certain, that they were made for such and such ends.

And here it is to be noticed, that, as regards a single thing,—that is, not an aggregate made up of many and heterogeneous parts, jointly indicating a distinct final cause,—though it be ca-

---

* The dominant argument urged, in defence of the existence of God, by the theistical schools of Hindu philosophy, is, that the earth, the sprout, &c. must be referred to an agent, inasmuch as they are effects; according to the maxim, that " every effect implies an agent, as a jar, for instance." Those schools, and likewise the generality of Hindus, are, however, but little conversant with the teleological argument, the subject of a portion of the present chapter.

pable of producing a certain end, still the doubt may arise, concerning it, whether that end was contemplated, or whether it be governed by pure chance. For instance, I come upon one or two sticks. They may serve for cooking; and yet I do not know, for certain, whether they were meant for that purpose. It may be, that they dropped accidentally from off somebody's head. As they would answer for cooking, so they would answer for other ends as well. I might drive off a dog with them; or I might turn them to account as stakes. No one can say, with perfect positiveness, for what particular end, out of these and others, those sticks were designed. But, when I see together a fagot, and water, and pulse, and meal, &c. &c., no hesitation possesses me, but certainty, that those appliances are for cooking. And the ground of this certainty is, that each of them bears a share in cooking: and it is out of question, that all those heterogeneous articles, concurring to one end, could never have come together casually, each in its due measure and appropriate place, but must have been assembled by an intelligent being, and with design. Now, there are, in this world, unnumbered things which, not being single and incomposite, accomplish fixed ends. Had they been isolated, it would have been hard to say whether their ends were not the result of mere chance. But these things are compounded of numerous constituents, gross and subtile; each of which is necessary, in its proportion, to bring about the end, and is also of due dimension, is adjusted to a fit position, and is constituted of proper material: as, in a watch, the parts that should be made of iron are of iron; and it is similar as to those that should be of brass, of porcelain, and of glass.

Although there are many wonderful things in this world, which we of India did not heretofore thoroughly understand, yet the learned of Europe, with their subtle ingenuity, deep investigation, persistent industry, and the help of various instruments, have so explored the fabric of the body and of vegetable products, the earth, the celestial system, and the nature, varieties, and properties of water, air, light, &c. &c., that he who reads the books written by those men, gains an almost supernatural faculty of vision, and beholds on every hand innumerable evidences of the inscrutable power and exquisite skill of God. Even in the human eye we perceive an amazing and indescribable workmanship. Between the structure of the eye and that of the telescope there is some resemblance; only that the telescope is far inferior to the eye in nicety. Opticians have demonstrated, that everything seen by the eye must have its image reflected on the retina; and, with a view to this end, the skill which the eye reveals in its formation is such as to strike the mind with astonishment. Part of the eye consists of lenses; and these are so disposed, and are made of such substance, as that the desired end should be accomplished. Again, the eye has several internal departments; and so minute are some of them, as to be invisible, save with the assistance of the microscope. But all these constituent portions are constructed, and adjusted, and proportioned, agreeably to a fixed rule. As for the marvellous contrivances of the eye, adapted for looking at objects distant and near, and as the light is more or less; and the peculiar conformation of that organ in birds, fishes, and other animals, fitted to enable them to see objects according to their several circumstances; and many other particulars relating to the eye; if I were to treat of these topics exhaustively, I should be compelled to devote a large book to them. And now I would ask, if, on seeing preparations for cooking, or on inspecting a watch, we have no doubt of there being an agent in connexion with them, why should we harbour doubt, after looking upon natural objects such as have been spoken of, that they had a Maker? For, the same reasons that conclude an agent in the former case, present themselves in the latter. If any one says, that, in the alleged instance of culinary ingredients, he has assurance of an agent, whereas he has none as regards the Maker of the world, I reply, that the reason is simply this: because of pride, he dislikes that the existence of God should be proved; and, consequently, he does not earnestly apply his mind to deliberate on the subject, and so he arrives at no conviction of the truth.

Some men, too indolent to think, rashly argue as follows:* With respect to cooking materials, and with respect to a watch, and so forth, we acknowledge an agent, on the ground that we have seen people making watches: but we have never seen any one making the world: and therefore we do not own that it has a Maker. My reply is: let a man of this country never have seen any one making a watch, and let it be, that no one here could make one: nevertheless, if a watch were to be shown to him, and if he were to reflect on the arrangement of all its parts, and on the end of each, would he not confess it to be the mechanism of some very ingenious artificer? Know, that the reason for acknowledging an agent is not the seeing one engaged in action, but, what I have stated before, namely, the perceiving that so many things, in due quantities and in fitting positions, have been collected together, every one of which, in its proportion, is indispensable to a certain end. For reason teaches, that it is impossible they could have been got together so systematically, but for the intervention of an intelligent agent.

The word "nature,"† with some unthinking people, is regarded as so potent a charm, that the bare utterance of it is sufficient to dissipate every doubt. It is because of nature, they say, that a human body arises from human seed; as

---

* What is objected, in this and the next paragraph, may be thought almost too frivolous to merit refutation. At the same time, it correctly represents the crudities which one daily hears from the lips of young Hindus who have acquired a smattering of English, and have learnt, that there has been a single white man, "one Hume," who rejected Christianity. The North-Western Provinces and the West of India are here especially referred to.

† This is not the Sánkhya "nature," *prakṛiti*, but our own polysemantic "nature," so very imperfectly apprehended by the sciolists spoken of in the last note.

wheat grows from wheat. To such persons I address a question: This "nature" not being an intelligent thing, endowed with understanding, will, and other qualities, how can it effect that in which tokens of the operation of understanding and design are distinctly manifest? Those who talk thus about nature plainly give proof, that they have not caught sight of the strong point of my argument, which is in this, that, on examining a body, or other similar thing, it clearly appears, that it was made for certain ends, and that it exhibits, as contributing thereto, an adjustment indicative of great skill and forethought. Further, it is indubitable, that, to devise anything for an end, and to construct it after an exact consideration of many components befitting it, is impossible but to an intelligent being. An intelligent Maker is, therefore, established. And how can this be refuted by speaking of nature? Can nature resolve on a particular act, and is it conscious that, by doing so and so, a certain end will be brought about? If it can do thus, it is proved to be God; and then I and my opponent differ only about names. If, on the other hand, it cannot do so, but is a thing inanimate and devoid of understanding, it cannot produce the effects which my opponent attributes to it. For, if he reflects a little closely, he will see, that, though we may allow air to possess the nature of raising dust from one spot and depositing it in another, yet it would never enter the mind, that the air should of itself rear a sumptuous house, or that fire should of itself cook pulse, bread, and vegetables.

Now, observe the extraordinary position of the Sánkhyas. They allege, that nature, for the sake of soul, engages in various works; and, by way of proving this point, they adduce the example of milk, which, though inanimate, with a view to the sustenance of the calf, secretes itself, they say, in the udder of the cow.* But this is bringing forward one

---

* दृष्टमचेतनमपि प्रयोजने प्रवर्तमानं यथा वत्सविवृद्ध्यर्थं क्षीर-

thing insusceptible of proof in order to ratify another thing of the same character. For, as I have before shown, the doing anything for an end can be predicated of none but an intelligent being. When a man hardens his heart, and determines to uphold atheism, how blind he grows! The Sánkhyas, for instance, have converted into instruments for disproving the existence of God, that very thing which is an irrefragable testimony to the contrary. For the fact of milk being produced in the cow's udder for the sake of the calf, and countless other such things, go to prove, that God exists, and that all these are His works: but the Sánkhyas use them to prove, that the whole world, every constituent part of which is for an end, has for its author that which possesses no sentience, —nature.

Again, a most egregious error of the Sánkhyas is seen in this, that, although they deny God, yet they believe in virtue, vice, and their fruits, and impose upon men's shoulders the yoke of multifarious ceremonies, repetition of sacred words, austerities, meditation, &c. &c.† One would indeed suppose that God must be the root, and the chief and first thing, in all religions. Except for God, who is there to enact commands and prohibitions? And how can there be an Elysium, or a Hell? For who is there to award the meed of good works, or the penalty of evil? The truth is, that all the originators of S'ástras, in this country, mistake in common

---

मचेतनं प्रवर्तते | *Tattwa-kaumudí*, p. 52. "An insentient thing also is seen acting for an end. For example, insentient milk exerts itself for the nurture of the calf."

Váchaspati Mis'ra thus writes in his annotations on the fifty-seventh couplet of the *Sánkhya-káriká*.

† स्वकर्म स्वाश्रमविहितकर्मानुष्ठानम् | Thirty-fifth aphorism of the *Sánkhya-pravachana*, Book III.; in the *Sánkhya-pravachana-bháshya*, p. 142. "One's duty is performance of the works enjoined for one's stage of life."

See the note at the foot of p. 28.

in this, that, while dwelling on the consideration of virtue and vice, and their issues, they have forgotten, that the good and evil requital of virtue and vice is in this wise alone:— God has enjoined virtue, and forbidden vice; and hence, being pleased with the obedient, He confers happiness upon them, and, by reason of His equity, visits punishment upon such as disobey His laws. Oblivious of this, the authors of the Systems by degrees came to regard works, like seed, for instance, as possessing a natural power of bringing forth fruit. This error is not so patent in the Naiyáyikas and some others; but it is most conspicuous in the Sánkhya and Mimánsá schemes, which even go the length of inculcating, that works can, of themselves, account for the production of the universe, and that there is, therefore, no need of supposing an intelligent Author of it.* To this momentous defect I shall return in the sequel.

How strange, once more, is the view of the Sánkhyas concerning the Veda! At the beginning of each universal renovation, it is emitted, they say, from the mouth of Brahmá. But he is not its composer; for he does not consciously frame it: it only proceeds from his throat, like an expira-

---

* Vijnána Bhikshu thus introduces the second aphorism of the *Sánkhya-pravachana*, Book V.: ईश्वरासिद्धेरिति. यदुक्तं तन् नोपपद्यते कर्मफलदातृतया तत्सिद्धेरिति ये पूर्वमाविख्यातान् निराकरोति । *Sánkhya-pravachana-bháshya*, p. 170. "That which was asserted, *viz.*, that I'swara cannot be proved *to exist*, will not stand; since he is proved *to exist*, by *the fact*, that there must be a giver of the fruit of works. They who object as above are refuted *in what follows*."

The aphorism pointed to is thus elucidated: ईश्वराधिष्ठिते कार्ये कर्मफलरूपपरिणामस्य निष्पत्तिनं युक्ता । आवश्यकेन कर्मणैव फलनिष्पत्तिसम्भवादित्यर्थः । *Ibid.*, pp. 170, 171. "It is not proper *to say*, that, in a cause superintended by I'swara, there takes place an evolution which is the fruit of works; since the production of fruit may be *accounted for*, *without the superintendence of I'swara*, by works alone, *which are granted, in all the Systems, to be* necessary *for the production of effects*. Such is the sense."

tion. Against this I have to say, that no book can be originated that is not made knowingly. In establishing the existence of God, I have said, that, on seeing materials for cooking, we are clear, that all the various articles are for the end of cooking; and it is, further, certain, that they were accumulated by some one. Just so, on observing, in a book, the apt ordonnance of its sentences, words, and letters, and its orderly construction, it becomes certain, that this ordonnance and this construction have, for their end, the expression of certain ideas, and, hence, that some one wittingly assembled, as we find them, the letters, words, and sentences adverted to. For they unquestionably betoken a desire to give expression to certain ideas. But it is manifest, that this desire, and the collocation in fitting order, with a view to such expression, are not the work of inert elements of language: since none but a conscious agent could design, and no other could determine, such an arrangement as I have spoken of. If the Veda was not devised by a conscious agent, how can it lay down injunctions and prohibitions? And how can it inform us touching the fruit of good and evil works? Even a child can understand, that, to give an order, or to notify a fact, implies mind, and not that which is destitute of it. Therefore, for letters, words, and sentences, things insentient, to come together of their own accord, and to command, or the like, is impossible.

CHAPTER 4.

Examination of the Sánkhya Dogma, that Nature is the Material Cause of the World.

The Sánkhya doctrine of nature likewise seems to me altogether unreasonable. Preferable, by much, is the doctrine of atoms maintained in the Nyáya and the Vais'eshika. I do not mean, that these systems are right in arguing, that the world is composed of eternal atoms: for I do not hold, that anything, God excepted, is eternal; and I do hold, that, quite irrelatively to any material cause, God created all things by His inscrutable might. What I here intend is, that, if one does not accept the belief, that the world was originated without a material cause, there is, to my thinking, no view left for him, more congruous with reason, than that which deduces the world from atoms. But what argument of reason is there for the proof of nature, and the great principle, and the organ of self-consciousness,&c.? The Sánkhyas assert, that happiness, misery, and insensibility inhere in everything* in the universe; and that, therefore, one is constrained to believe the material cause of the world to be that which possesses those qualities: and such is nature.† But this is not correct:

---

* घटरूपमितिप्रत्ययवत् स्त्रीसुखं चन्दनसुखमित्यादिप्रत्ययादपि विषये सुखाद्युचितम् । *Sánkhya-sára*, MS., *fol.* 11, *recto*. "Since, in like manner as we are wont to speak of jar-colour, so, also, we are wont to speak of woman-pleasure, sandal-pleasure, &c., it is proper *to suppose*, that pleasure and the like *inhere* in objects."

Vijnána is here a victim to phraseology on which, plainly enough, he did not reflect with sufficient attention. For "jar-colour" means "the colour of a jar;" whereas "sandal-pleasure" means "the pleasure derived from the use of sandal." Such fallacies are far from uncommon among the pandits.

The English rendering of the Sanskrit is just a trifle *ad synesim*.

सुखादिकं च घटादेरपि रूपादिवदेव धर्मान्तःकरणोपादानत्वादन्यकार्यत्वाणामित्युक्तम् । *Sánkhya-pravachana-báshya*, p. 88. "And it has been said, that happiness and so forth, just like colour, &c., are properties of a jar and the like, also; since the internal organ, *which has happiness*, *misery*, *&c., for properties*, is the material cause of *all* other effects."

† कार्यं हि कारणगुणात्मकं दृष्टं यथा तन्त्वादिगुणात्मकं पटादि । तथा महदादिलक्ष्णेनापि कार्येण सुखदुःखमोहरूपेण स्वकारणतत्सुखदुःखमोहात्मना भवितव्यम् । तथा च तत्कारणं सुखदुःखमोहात्मकं प्रधानमथ्वतां सिद्धं भवति । *Tattwa-kaumudí,* p. 24. "An effect is seen to be made up of the qualities of *its* cause. For instance, cloth

for happiness, misery, and insensibility do not inhere in external things, but are qualities of an intelligent being, and reside in it alone; as I shall prove presently. The truth is, that external objects may become the cause, to an intelligent being, of happiness, misery, and so forth; as fire, on being touched, produces pain. Fire is not, however, the site of pain, but only the cause thereof, to him who touches it. It is a surprizing error of the Sánkhyas, that they assign to the outward material world such things as apprehension, will, happiness, misery, and so forth,—which are qualities of the soul, and reside in it alone, and have no independent existence,—and further allege, that, as is the world, so must be its material cause, namely, nature. In this way they make the soul to be insentient, and the world and its material cause to be intelligent. And, while they make the latter to be intelligent, they say, that nature, the great principle, and so on, are nothing but insentient substances.* Such strange entities as these can never be established by any ratiocination.

---

and the like are made up of *their* qualities, thread, &c. In like sort, also such an effect as the great *principle, i. e., intellect,* composed of happiness, misery, and insensibility, should be *considered as* made up of happiness, misery, and insensibility, appurtenances of its cause. And thus a cause made up of happiness, misery, and insensibility, *namely,* nature, the unmanifested, is established for them, *viz., for intellect, &c.*"

Váchaspati Mis'ra's language, throughout this passage, is somewhat lax. To exemplify: instead of saying, that an effect is made up of the qualities of its cause, he ought, in strictness of Hindu terminology, to have said, that an effect is beholden, for its own qualities, to those of its cause. So, again, it is a loose mode of expression, to speak of nature as being made up of happiness, misery, and insensibility ; since these, in philosophical rigour, are laid down as constituting nature's qualities, or properties. This latter assertion is shown by what follows : सुखात्मकता तु गुणानां मनसः सङ्कल्पात्मकतावत् धर्माधर्म्यभेदादेवोपपद्यते । *Sánkhya-pravachana-bháshya*, pp. 88, 89. " As for *the phraseology,* that the *guṇas, or components of nature,* are made up of happiness, &c., it is accountable for only by the identity, *under one aspect,* of a property and that which is propertied ; as *we hear it said, that* mind is one with resolve."

* सर्वं एव प्रधानबद्ध्याद्योऽचेतनाः । *Tattwa-kaumudí*, p. 20. "The whole, nature, intellect, and so on, are insentient."

Let the terms *prakṛiti, sattwa, rajas, tamas, buddhi,* and *ahankára* be taken otherwise than as they are taken in the Sánkhya, and the result will be very different. Goodness, passion, and darkness, a Naiyáyika might argue, may be conditions of soul, and therefore may be alleged, to belong to its nature: for "nature," in such a sense, or *swabháva,* is one of the classical acceptations of the multivocal *prakṛiti.* When the apprehensive faculties of the soul are in their full vigour, and when the soul is calm and unperturbed, it may be said to be in a state of goodness; when agitated, and greatly drawn towards external objects, we may speak of it as being in a state of passion; and, when it is stupefied, one may call it dark.* Again, intellect is a quality of soul; and to soul appertains egoism† also. If we understand, in some such way, the words selected, in the Sánkhya, as fundamental technicalities, the things denoted by them can be proved to have existence; but not otherwise.

I am unable to say, with certainty, how the Sánkhyas came to entertain such strange ideas on the subject under discussion. Nevertheless, considering the intellectual peculiarities of the pandits, and their method of argumentation, I hazard this conjecture. There is no question, that the atheistic Sánkhya system was not primeval in India; for, though the *Manu-sanhitá, the Gítá,* and other books, in describing the generation of the world, &c., countenance the tenets of the Sánkhya, yet God likewise is there acknowledged to be the Author of the world. Hence, it seems to me, that the theistic Sánkhya was first elaborated, and the atheistic, by little and little, at an after-period. The germ of the former

---

* The words goodness, passion, and darkness, with their conjugates, as here employed, and elsewhere, must be understood to be technical, and as inexpressive substitutes, at best, for the *sattwa, rajas, tamas,* &c. of the Sanskrit.

† In the Sánkhya, *buddhi,* intellect, is the organ of cognition; *ahankára,* that of egoism: but, in this place, the Nyáya view is adopted, that is to say, that intellect itself is cognition, and that *ahankára* itself is egoism.

may have been as follows. It is written in the Veda, with reference to God, that, at the time the world was made, "He saw," and that he said "I am one: I would become many." By these words, perception and self-consciousness are implied to have arisen, in God, at the beginning of the universe: and perception is intellect; and the notion denoted by "I" is egoism. From this the ancients may have concluded, that God, in order to the construction of the world, assumed intellect and egoism;* and thus they may have been induced to regard His intellect and egoism as the causes of the world. One will here ask: Though they thus accounted intellect and egoism the causes of the world, still these are only its instrumental causes; and why do you suppose that they are held, in the Sánkhya, to be material causes? The answer is, that the pandits have come, in process of time, to forget the true character of several things which they have been accustomed to treat about. Thus, in many cases, as concerns qualities, which are inseparable from things qualified, they have brought themselves to think of them as independent things possessing qualities. The founders of the Sánkhya system, having long

---

* This conjecture proves to be corroborated by the ensuing words of Vijuána Bhikshu: श्रुतावपि स ईच्चाचक्रे तदैच्चतेत्यादौ सगांद्यृत्पन्नबुद्धित एव तदिनराखिलष्टिरवगम्यते । *Sánkhya-pravachana-bháshya*, p. 50. "Also in the Veda, by *the texts* 'He beheld,' 'He saw,' &c., we learn, that, from intellect itself, produced at the outset of creation, was the creation of all besides itself."

अच चाऽयमनुकूलस्तर्कः । बहु स्यां प्रजायेयेत्यादिश्रुतिस्मृतिभ्यस्तावद् भूतादिष्ट्रेरभिमानपूर्वकत्वाद् बुद्धिष्टिपूर्वकष्टो कारणतयाऽभिमानः सिद्धः । *Ibid*, p. 49. "And this is an expedient argument on this behalf. Since, in *passages of* the Veda and of the Smṛitis, such as 'May I become many,' 'May I be produced,' &c., *it is set forth, that* the creation of the elements and the like is preceded by egoism *as a cause*, egoism is made out to be the *immediate* cause of the creation, which *creation* has an affection of intellect for its *mediate* cause."

been used to call intellect and egoism the instrumental causes of the world, passed on to view them as independent objects, and have ended in making them the material causes of the world. In attributing to qualities the nature of independent objects, nay, in ascribing to them personality, the Hindus, in other instances as well, are seen to go amiss. For example, we find, in the Puráṇas and other books, accounts of the generation of love, wrath, serenity, content, and such like qualities, taken by themselves, and stories of their nuptials and so forth. The general error here animadverted on is not, however, peculiar to the Hindus. The old inhabitants of other countries than India were not clear of it. In the second and following centuries of the Christian era, Valentinus, Basilides, and other heretics, as is evidenced by their writings, made intellect, will, and other qualities to possess personality; and they regarded them as makers of the world. The progress in error of the Sánkhyas was, it appears to me, somewhat similar to that of the Gnostics. It is evident, that, when the people of former ages had quite forgotten the reason which first led them to account intellect and egoism to be the causes of the world, and began to consider them as, in another way, the causes of the world, they likewise changed their ideas of the things denoted by the terms intellect and egoism, began to look upon them as organs of cognition and egoism, respectively, and as unintelligent substances, and, imagining a subtile source from which intellect could be evolved, gave that source the appellation of nature. Their reason for making nature to consist of goodness, passion, and darkness, was, perhaps, that intellect is sometimes in a state of goodness, sometimes in a state of passion, and sometimes in a state of darkness; and hence its cause, nature, must be constituted of three ingredients. When, subsequently, they saw, that the whole world might be derived from this nature, they concluded, that there was no need of a God. It is thus, on conjecture, that the more recent Sánkhya system sprang up; the doctrines of which, on all points, have, it may be, gradually undergone so much of alteration, that there is now not a vestige of similarity between it and the scheme from which it descended.

CHAPTER 5.

Examination of the Sánkhya Dogma, that Apprehension, Will, Activity, Happiness, Misery, and other Qualities, do not appertain to the Soul.

To deny that cognition, will, activity, happiness, and misery are qualities of the soul, and to hold them to be affections of the internal organ, is utterly at issue with reason.* I maintain, that apprehending, willing, doing, &c. are qualities of intelligence. That in which these qualities reside is called an intelligent being; and the same is a soul. The Sánkhya may reply, that, in his nomenclature, that is called a soul, which is unendowed with apprehension and other qualities. My answer is, that such a soul cannot, in any wise, be proved to have existence,† or to be such a one as I have, or as he has. For it

---

* The Sánkhyas repudiate virtue and vice, withal, as attributes of the soul, and style them qualities of the internal organ. Vijnána Bhikshu, as appears from an extract previously adduced, denounces the Vedántins as Bauddhas, for their doctrine, that everything is unreal, virtue and vice included. See the citation from the *Sánkhya-pravachana-bháshya*, at the foot of p. 71. But are not the Sánkhyas obnoxious to a similar reproach, for denying, that virtue and vice belong to the soul?

It may assist the reader, if he is told, that, in order fully to take in the present chapter, he should give a well-weighed consideration to the conspectus of the Sánkhya system contained in Chapter 2, and to the passages appended in the foot-notes.

† Singular it is, that the evidence brought forward, by the adherents of the Sánkhya, in proof of the existence of the soul, concludes it intelligent, not insentient, as they would fain have it to be. Witness these words:

प्रकृतिमहदादिकं परार्थं खेतरस्य भोगापवर्गफलकं संहतत्वात् श्-य्यासनादिवदित्यनुमानेन प्रकृतेः परोऽसंहत एव पुरुषः सिध्यति

is beyond doubt, that we both apprehend, and will, and energize, and become happy and miserable; that is, we have the qualities apprehension, will, activity, &c. Nor can our consciousness of these things be illusive :* for there is said to be illusion, where there is a notion, but not a corresponding object; as where, nacre being mistaken for silver, there is the notion of silver, but not silver as the object of that notion. But the like of this cannot have place as concerns our consciousness of apprehension, will &c.; for here a notion and its object are one. Apprehension, will, and the rest are objects; the consciousness of them is the notion: and, in my opinion, they are identical. To be sure, when the light reveals a

---

Sánkhya-pravachana-bháshya, pp. 53, 54. "Nature, the great *principle*, and the rest, are 'for another,' *i. e.*, they have for their end the experience *of happiness and misery* and the liberation of what is other than themselves; insamuch as *they are* composite : like a bed, a seat, &c. By this argument, soul, as distinct from nature, and incomplex, is made out *to exist*."

One that experiences and has need of liberation cannot, it is manifest, be insentient. In what manner the Sánkhyas go about to show, that the soul is an experiencer, and requires to be freed, and that it is, at the same time, void of sentience, will be seen in the progress of this chapter.

* अहं कर्ता सुखीत्यादिप्रत्ययास्तु अहं गौर इत्यादिभ्रमप्रतान्त:पातित्वेनाप्रामाण्याशङ्काक्रन्दिता नोक्तानुमानस्य बाधकाः । प्रत्युत

प्रकृत्यैव च कर्माणि क्रियमाणानि सर्वशः ।
यः पश्यति तथाऽऽत्मानमकर्तारं स पश्यति ॥

इत्यादिस्मृत्युपोद्बलितेनोक्तानुमानेनैव बाध्यन्ते ॥ *Pátanjala-bháshya-várttika*, MS., *fol.* 7, *verso*. "As for the consciousnesses 'I am a doer,' 'I am happy,' &c., since, being comprehended among hundreds of misconceptions, such as 'I am fair,' and the like, they are involved in the suspicion of unreliableness, they do not contravene the argument adduced *to prove the soul devoid of activity, happiness, &c.* On the contrary, the forementioned argument, corroborated by this and other *smṛitis*, 'He who beholds all works as done by nature alone, and likewise the soul as no doer, beholds *aright*,' disproves *those consciousnesses, or evinces them to be erroneous*."

jar, the light is the manifester, and the jar is manifested; but the light, when we see it, is itself alike manifester and manifested. So, when will arises in me, itself manifests itself; for I express, that I have a will of something. From this it is plain, that simultaneously* I both will, and am conscious, or have a notion, of willing; whereas, if those acts, however speculatively two, were two in reality, they could not arise in the soul at the same time. Accordingly, since my own conscious-

---

* Further proof, not only of the simultaneousness, but of the identity, of apprehension and the consciousness of it, of will and the consciousness of it, &c., is found in the fact, that it seems impossible, considering their nature, that unperceived apprehension, will, happiness, or the like, can have existence.

To those who think otherwise, that is to say, that will and the consciousness of it, for instance, are consecutive and distinct, the author would propound these two questions. Do they hold the notion, that will first arises, and, soon afterwards, the consciousness of it; and that the two for some time co-exist? Or do they hold the notion, that an act of the will is followed by the consciousness of it?

If the first, the Pandit replies, that—as is expressed in the text—he cannot conceive how two qualities can either arise or remain in the soul together: and herein his opinion is, to some extent, supported by the doctrine of the Naiyáyikas; who contend, that the specific qualities of the soul are antagonistic to the length of mutually displacing each other. The maxim on the subject is आत्मविशेषगुणानां ख्योत्तरगुणनाशत्वात् । In order, however, that one such quality may displace another, their theory is, that the displacing quality must remain with the quality displaced during the last moment of the subsistence of the latter. See the note at the foot of p. 93. This view the Pandit rejects as an absurdity.

To the second position indicated above, the author makes answer, that it is not consciousness which is there implied, but remembrance. On this ground, additionally to the one just mentioned, he considers as faulty the Naiyáyika idea, which supposes, that the consciousness of will co-exists for one moment with will, and then subsists without it. What is here called consciousness,—*anubhava*, as it is esteemed by the Nyáya,—is not so, its object having departed: it is memory.

At all events, if it be insisted, that will and the consciousness of will, &c., are distinct, still it is certain, that they are inseparable; and that they are so is sufficient to show the Sánkhyas, that the definition of mistake, given above, is inapplicable to such cases of consciousness.

ness, and my opponent's, of our acts of apprehension, will, and other qualities, are not distinct from their objects, viz., those acts of apprehension, will, &c., our consciousness cannot subsist sequestered from their objects; and, therefore, to characterize it as illusive would be erroneous; and, this being the case, my soul, or my opponent's, is not such a thing as he describes to be destitute of apprehension, will, and the rest. If the Sánkhya bestows its labour in order to the emancipation of such a soul, its labour is superfluous; and, besides, it devolves upon every one of us all to strive to save himself. But my opponent does not acknowledge this; he asserting, that the soul described in the Sánkhya is, in verity, such as his and mine, and yet contending, that it has no apprehension, will, or other qualities. I reply, that this is totally at variance with all that is rational.

I have distinctly shown, that my consciousness of my apprehension, will, happiness, misery, and so on, cannot be illusory. The Sánkhya, who, shutting the eyes of his common sense, declares, that it is illusory, should take notice of this also, that, if it be proved so, neither can the fact of apprehension, will, happiness, misery, &c., be proved; since, but for consciousness, there is no means of establishing their existence. Should it be replied, that the consciousness of will, &c. is said to be an illusion only in this respect, that its objects, as will, &c., though having existence as qualities of one subject, seem to appertain to a different subject, that is to say, being qualities of the internal organ, they seem to belong to the soul; I rejoin thus. The Sánkhya says, that the consciousness "I" is an affection of the internal organ alone, and that will, happiness, and so forth, are also affections thereof. It is clear, accordingly, that they appear in their proper subject: and how, then, can the consciousness of them be illusion even in the respect in which he declares it to be so? As I am aware, the mystery of the Sánkhya's fantastic economy consists in this. He holds, that the consciousness "I" is, in fact, an affection of the internal organ, but that it cognizes the soul, as being its proper object; though, by reason of misapprehension, intellect also is cognized,* as identical with the soul. Hence, the consciousness "I will," "I am happy," or the like, taking the soul for its object, attributes to it the alien qualities will, happiness, &c. This consciousness, accordingly, is illusory. Further than this limit error could not extravagate. Can it be, that the consciousness "I" can refer to another than that which entertains it? It is certain, that, when one who has a consciousness of "I" uses the word "I," he means his own self; for there cannot be any other word more unmistakably denoting one's self. If "I" denotes self, tell me whether any one but its subject can be that self. It appears to me, that a consciousness such as the Sánkhya assumes has its parallel in a lamp whose light proceeds from another lamp, or in the shadow of a man cast by his neighbour. For the object of the consciousness "I" is self; and that in which there is this consciousness is its self: but, in that which is different from itself, there is not this consciousness; and that in which there is not this consciousness is not the object of such consciousness.

But perhaps the Sánkhya will say, that I, their opponent, who hold, with the Naiyáyikas, that the notion "I" is a quality of the soul, must grant, that it is not unusual for the soul to identify things other than itself with itself; inasmuch as all men who lack right apprehension erroneously consider the body, &c., which are distinct from the soul, to be themselves; for, if they did not so consider, they would not

---

* ज्ञकानामहमिति प्रत्यये चाऽवश्यं बुद्धिरपि भासते अनादिमिथ्याज्ञानवासनाख्यदोषस्य प्रतिबन्धे मानाभावात्। *Pátanjala-bhàshya-várttika,* MS., *fol.* 87, *recto.* "And, in the consciousness 'I' of ordinary people, *who lack right apprehension,* intellect also, *i. e., besides soul,* is, of necessity, cognized; for there is no ground *for the supposition,* that the defect of the impression of unbeginning misapprehension is, *in the case of this consciousness,* debarred, *or becomes inoperative.*"

speak of themselves as being dark, or fair, as is conceded by the Naiyáyikas also: and thus it is decided, that the consciousness "I" may take cognizance of an alien object. I reply, that, in my opinion, men do not generally take their bodies, &c. to be their souls; and the fact, that they say "I am fair," or "I am dark," does not prove that they so take them. This shall be shown, when I come to consider the Nyáya and Vais'eshika systems. Even if I granted, that some men thus misconceive, still such a mistake would not be one of perception, but one of inference. If it be said, that it is from using his eyes, that a man calls himself dark, or fair, and that, therefore, his notion is a perception; I have to reply, that, on looking at his body, he indeed sees it to be dark or fair: yet the notion "This dark body, or fair, is myself" is not a perception, or immediate cognition. For the immediate cognition "I" cannot have for its object either the body, or its darkness or fairness. Know, therefore, that men apprehend only their proper selves in the immediate cognition "I;" and that, as, by means of their eyes, and other organs of sense, they cognize a jar, or cloth, precisely so do they cognize their bodies. When they perceive, that, from changes in the body, cognitions of happiness, misery, &c. arise in the soul, they infer, and wrongly, that the body is the soul. Thus, then, it is certain, that their error is not of immediate cognition, but inferential. They reason, that, since the soul receives happiness and misery through the medium of the body, the body is self. The consciousness "I" is an immediate cognition; but it cannot have the body for its object. Again, the body or the like is cognized by means of the eyes, or other organs of sense; but those organs cannot have the soul for their object. Hence, the confounding together of soul and body is the work of inference, not the work of perception. I was correct, therefore, in saying, that the immediate cognition "I" can have no other object than self. And, just as it cannot have an object different from itself, so the qualities will, happiness, misery, and the rest, of one cannot appear, in immediate cognition, as located in another. For I have already said, that will and other like qualities are their own manifesters. They must appear where they reside: and how can they appear elsewhere? Moreover, since the consciousness "I" can have only itself for object, how can the will, happiness, &c. which seem to belong to another, be the objects of such a consciousness as "I will," &c.?

But the Sánkhyas, though they deny cognition and other qualities to the soul, perceive, that, if it neither cognizes, nor wills, nor is miserable or happy, it cannot be called bound. Why, then, their philosophy, and all their toil to liberate the soul? This objection they anticipate; and, to rebut it, while they refuse to regard cognition, &c. as qualities of the soul, they maintain, that, in some sort, it experiences cognition, will, and so on. To arrive at this conclusion, they speculate as follows. Cognition, &c., which they call affections of the internal organ, are reflected in the soul; and these reflexions* of cognition and so forth are supposed to be experiences of cognition, &c.: a distinction being taken between the two classes. In this way the soul becomes an experiencer of cognition, will, happiness, and misery. The experience of cognition being itself a cognition, the soul may be said to cognize. But the experiences of will, happiness, and misery cannot, suitably with the Sánkhya system, be denominated will, happiness, and misery. Hence, it is not allowed, that the soul wills, and is happy and miserable, but only that it is the experiencer of will, happiness, and misery; though, occasionally, the reflexions of happiness and misery are found spoken of as happiness and misery, instead of experiences of them. Those experiences are, however,

---

* The European reader must be constantly on his guard against supposing, that, by reflexions, the Sánkhyas mean, figuratively, impressions made in the essence of the soul. What the Sánkhyas do mean will be seen from the present chapter, and from the second, with the notes attached to the latter.

pronounced to be unreal; for an experience of this sort, while the reflexion of an affection of the internal organ, is likewise an evolution from that organ, precisely as its affections are, and extrinsic to the soul. When it is termed unreal, it is not meant, that it has no real existence, but that it does not inhere in the soul, and that it is incapable of producing any change in its essence. It is like the reflexion, in crystal, of a red rose: where, only from misapprehension, would it be thought, that the colour reflected belongs to the crystal. Now, in our view, the soul cannot be an experiencer in consequence of the reflexions spoken of. For, when a man has an experience, a change really takes place in his soul. This would be the case, the Sánkhyas admit, if cognition, will, happiness, and misery could be regarded as qualities of the soul; as they are regarded by the Naiyáyikas, whose dogma on this point, as making the soul changeable, the Sánkhyas arraign as unsound. On the Sánkhya ground, then, that the reflexions in question work no change in the soul, and are alien to it, the soul cannot, by reason of them, become an experiencer. Nevertheless, the Sánkhyas, strange to tell, for all that they say these reflexions are extrinsic to the soul, declare, that, owing to them, the soul becomes an experiencer of cognition, will, &c. In this there is a plain contradiction in terms; for it amounts to an assertion, coupled with a denial, that the soul has experience. The following remarks will enable us to understand how the Sánkhyas came to entangle themselves in such an incongruity.

Most imperfect and erroneous, generally, are the notions of the so-called Hindu philosophers about things metaphysical and physical. Whatever two things these schemers see to be in relation, they must straightway ascertain the species of that relation. For instance, after laying down the proposition, that, wherever there is smoke there is fire, the first step to be taken, towards completing the proposition, is, they say, to ascertain the relation that subsists between the smoke and the place of its appearance. So, likewise, the relation of the fire to the site it occupies must be ascertained. And it is only by these relations, that the smoke is a token, and the fire that which is betokened.* The two relations here instanced are of the same sort, known as *sanyoga*. Again, it is deemed necessary to determine the relation between a quality and that to which it belongs, and between a whole and its component elements, &c. &c. The evil that has sprung from thus theorizing is, that the pandits came to look upon relations, *sanyoga*, *samaváya*,† &c., as real objective entities, as having existence apart from the objects they connect, and were led to sunder things further than it is reasonable to sunder them. Thus, according to the Naiyáyikas, substance may sometimes be so far independent of qualities as to want them altogether. The qualities of what they reckon as originated substances are not produced, they affirm, until after the production of those substances themselves. Take a

---

* Such relations are called, respectively, *hetutávachchhedaka* and *sádhyatávachchhedaka ;* or "the determinator of tokenness," "and "the determinator of betokenedness."

† *Sanyoga*, one of the four and twenty qualities of the Nyáya, is contact, the mutual touching of two substances. Only, as mentioned in the text, it is an entity, and has existence irrespectively of the substances to which it belongs. Moreover, it is destroyed by *vibhága* "separation"; which also is a quality. But, as a cause must exist prior to its effect, separation, before performing its destructive office, is fabled to coexist with contact for a single moment.

Samaváya, like *sanyoga*, is, in the first place, an entity. It is the relation between substance and quality, between a whole and its parts, &c. &c. It is eternal; so that, though the things which it stands between perish, itself remains. Numerically, it is one; and thus it is the same *samaváya* that connects a jar and its colour in India, and another jar and its colour in Europe; and that connected Adam's soul with its qualities, and that connects the reader's with its own. As the reason for maintaining its unity, the Naiyáyikas simply refer to the *lex parcimoniæ*, and leave common sense altogether out of the question. It is useless to try to translate *samaváya*. Colebrooke substitutes "aggregation, or intimate and constant relation;" Dr. J. R. Ballantyne, "intimate union," "inherence," "coinherence," "coinhesion."

jar, for example. During the first moment of its production, it is devoid, in their view, of all qualities whatsoever, as colour, smell, taste, and tangibility. In the second moment it becomes endowed with them. Again, the Naiyáyikas contend, that a whole is a different thing from the mere sum of its parts. By the joining together of the parts a new entity is generated in the whole which results:* as has been remarked, it has, for a single moment, no qualities,† whereas its parts have; and it

---

* It was a favourite pleasantry of a late most celebrated Naiyáyika pandit at Benares, that, in rigid accordance with his system, on receiving back from a goldsmith ornaments wrought from metal furnished to him, it would be quite just to demand double weight; that of the original gold, and, again, as much in ornaments.

For it is not held, that, on the production of a whole, the parts concurring to it are annihilated.

It is because of their notion regarding the novelty of wholes, that the Naiyáyikas are designated as *asatkáryavádins*, in contradistinction from the Sánkhyas and Vedántins, who are termed *satkáryavádins*; the former holding, that an effect is non-existent before its production, and the latter, that an effect has existence, in its material cause, antecedently to its manifestation, or eduction, *abhivyakti*. Hence, the Sánkhyas do not hold, that a property and its substrate, *dharma* and *dharmin*, are altogether alien to each other. In one sense, it is true, they are taken as different; but, in another sense, they are reputed one. The reader will have observed, repeatedly, in foregoing notes, the expression *dharma-dharmyabhedát*, "because of the non-difference of a property and that which is propertied."

In this case, the Sánkhyas and the Vedántins approve themselves nearer to rationality than the Naiyáyikas: but the case is rare of its kind.

† The reason assigned is this. Every effect must have three causes, the *samaváyi*, *asamaváyi*, and *nimitta*. A jar, when produced, is considered to be a new entity; and the same view is taken of its qualities Of the jar its parts are the *samaváyi* cause; the contact of those parts, its *asamaváyi*; and the potter and his implements, its *nimitta*. Of the qualities of the jar, itself is the *samaváyi*; and the qualities of the parts of the jar, are the *asamaváyi* of those qualities. Their *nimitta* is as before. As every cause must precede its effect, the jar, a cause of its own qualities, must exist previously to the production of its qualities.

A very recent authority, of most respectable weight, speaks thus of the three Naiyáyika causes: "It is commonly understood, that the Nyáya philosophy acknowledges three sorts of causes, substantial or inherent, non-substan-

resides in its parts by the relation styled *samaváya*. It is because a whole is predicated as residing thus in its parts, that the Naiyáyikas, in respect of the enunciation, that smoke betokens fire, set about, first of all, to ascertain by what relation it does so. For, as smoke is said to reside in a place by the relation of *sanyoga*, so it is said to reside in its parts by the relation of *samaváya*. Therefore, by simply asserting, that, wherever there is smoke there is fire, one is apt to mislead; since smoke, besides residing in a given place, resides, by the relation of *samaváya*, in its own parts, where fire is not.

We have now learnt how the Naiyáyikas, by transmuting relations into entities, and interposing these entities between things correlated, dissever what in nature we find most closely allied. Accordingly, these philosophers, though they profess to believe cognition, &c. to be qualities of the soul, are seen—when we come to understand how they speak of qualities and substance—to make them extrinsic to it. When, therefore, cognition &c. are said, in their character of qualities, to belong to the soul by the relation of *samaváya*, we recognize a position inadequate to that of their residing in the soul by inherence;* and yet the Nyáya, on the

---

tial or exterior, and a third which might, perhaps, be conveniently styled the *operative* cause." Professor Banerjea's *Dialogues on the Hindu Philosophy*, p. 127.

* Let it not be supposed, that, because the Naiyáyikas repute substance the *samaváyi* cause of its qualities,—as was said in the last note,—they look upon qualities as being intrinsic to substance. For, in the twenty-four qualities, they include differentness, contact, separation, remoteness, &c , as real entities. Of these also the substance in which they reside is the *samaváyi* cause; and they cannot, with any propriety, be said to be intrinsic to such substance.

Obviously enough it was the old, and all but universally diffused, ex-nihilian maxim, which suggested to the Naiyáyikas, that every effect must have a *samaváyi* cause; a cause which, by legitimate deduction from that maxim, ought to mean one from which an effect is evolved, or developed. From this notion the Naiyáyikas have, however, strayed afar; and what they intend by their *samaváyi* cause is equally unintelligible and unaccountable. This

point immediately under discussion, is much nearer to the truth than the Sánkhya and the Vedánta.

And now we are prepared for easy apprehension of a transition to a much graver error. If the soul, ask the Sánkhyas, may become a cognizer &c., from possessing cognition &c. by the relation of *samaváya*, why may it not become so from possessing cognition and so forth by any other relation? That the soul becomes thus possessed by the relation of *samaváya*, they refuse to admit; since the admission would imply a change in the soul's nature. Still, studious to make out the soul a cognizer &c., or else an experiencer of cognition &c., they proceed in this wise. The reflexions of cognition, will, happiness, misery, &c. are experiences of them, severally. These reflexions, or experiences, rest upon the soul. To the Sánkhyas an alternative is here, they think, presented. They allow themselves to suppose, that the soul cognizes, wills, &c., in the affections of the internal organ, cognition, will, &c., which are connected with the soul by the relation of reflexion; or to suppose, if they choose, that the soul is an experiencer of cognition &c., in those reflexions, the experiences of cognition &c., which rest on the soul by the relation of *sanyoga*. In order to the soul's cognizing &c., what does it matter, the Sánkhya asks of the Naiyáyika, if cognition and the rest do not reside in the soul by the relation of *samaváya;* seeing that the soul has them by some other relation; and there being no ground for restriction to the relation of *samaváya*. The Naiyáyika, thus controverted by the Sánkhya, cannot, in my opinion, return, with his imperfect views, any answer founded in reason.

Precisely the error of the Sánkhyas which has just been detailed is that of a distinguished Pandit of Benares, to whom

---

is evident from their contending, that an effect is altogether a new entity, as compared with its *samaváyi* cause; and from this, that they maintain substance to be such a cause of its own qualities; these being extraneous to it, and of a different category.

I applied for solution of divers of my doubts. One of my questions was as follows: Since, if the Sánkhyas believe that misery resides in the soul as a reflexion only, which reflexion is held to be an evolution from the internal organ, the soul cannot really be miserable, why all the toil of the Sánkhya system to liberate the soul? The reply was, in part, as follows:* "And, if thou intendest *to imply*, that, *according to the Sánkhya*, the soul cannot be miserable through the unreal relation of reflexion, * * * thou shouldst be asked, in return, 'Though *thou holdest, as in the Nyáya*, that the suffering of misery, which is an experience, is a quality, *still*, how, either by that quality, or by *samaváya*, can the soul be miserable?'"† In passing, the Pandit assumes, inadvertently, that I here go the whole way with the Naiyáyikas. I take his purport to be this. If, with a view to prove the soul miserable, a relation between it and misery, an affection of the internal organ, is demanded, the relation of reflexion is available; and, should it be objected, that the soul cannot become miserable by such a relation, it may be enquired, how it can become so even by the relation of *samaváya*. Then he goes on as follows: "And what superiority, save *thy* long conversancy *with it*, dost thou see in the Naiyáyika system, that it alone pleases thee? And what inferiority, waiving that

---

* First, he detected an inaccuracy in the expression "if the Sánkhyas believe, that misery resides in the soul as a reflexion only;" for, in strict Sánkhya phraseology, the reflexion of misery is not misery, but is its experience. Ever and anon, however, the Sánkhyas express themselves as the author expressed himself. See the first passage from the *Sánkhya-pravachana-bháshya*, given at the foot of p. 60.

† यदि च प्रतिबिम्बरूपावास्तवसम्बन्धेनाऽऽत्मनो दुःखित्वं न सम्भवतीति तवाऽऽशयस्तर्हि * * * भवानेवं प्रतिष्टव्यः । स दुःखभोगः साक्षात्काररूपः साक्षात्कारश्च गुणविशेष इति तेन वा समवायेन वाऽऽत्मा कथं दुःखी स्यात् ।

it is novel *to thee,* dost thou see in the Sánkhya system, that thou findest the acceptation of it difficult?" *

Another question proposed by me was this: If misery belongs to the internal organ, how can its removal profit the soul? The Pandit replies: "The fact, that misery resides in another *than the soul* does not prevent its cessation from being a good to the soul. For misery, which is held, by those who abhor the relation of reflexion, *to reside* in the soul by *samaváya,* resides, by some other relation, in what is not soul."† In the Nyáya, cognition and other qualities, though residing in the soul by the relation of *samaváya,* are spoken of as residing in time by temporal relation, in space, by spatial relation, &c. &c. What the learned Pandit means is, then, this. If it be argued, that, because the Sánkhyas believe misery to reside in another than the soul, that is to say, in the internal organ, its removal cannot benefit the soul, neither can its removal benefit the soul even according to the Naiyáyikas; inasmuch as, in their view, misery resides, by various relations, in other things besides the soul. As we are aware, agreeably to the Sánkhya, misery &c. are qualities of the internal organ. If they are so, what has their continuance, or their elimination, to do with the soul? But of this weighty objection the Pandit makes small account. The reason is, that, to his mind, *samaváya,* here a relation of the first importance, is quite on a parity with what are here inferior relations, such as the temporal and the spatial. This will

---

* कं च विशेषं नैयायिकमते पूर्वपरिचयव्यतिरिक्तं पश्यसि येन तदेव भवते रोचते कं चाऽभिनवत्वादन्यमपकर्षं सांख्यमते पश्यसि येन तस्य ग्रहण आयस्मान् क्लिष्यति ।

† दुःखनिष्ठत्वे पुरुषार्थत्वे हि दुःखस्याऽन्यगतत्वं न बाधकं प्रतिबिम्बसम्बन्धविद्वेषिभिः समवायेनाऽऽत्मनि स्थितस्याऽपि दुःखस्य केनचित् सम्बन्धेनाऽनात्मनि सत्त्वात् ।

serve as a sample of the degree to which the common sense of the pandits has become distempered. And I shall now address myself to show what that relation is between the experience of cognition, will, happiness, misery, &c., and that which is in truth the experiencer of them.

First, however, I must bestow a few words on the great error, committed by the Sánkhyas, of distinguishing between happiness and the like, and their experiences. Who is conscious of any such distinction? From experience of happiness deduct experience: can one then form any idea what happiness is by itself? Not at all. Consequently, all the qualities of the soul, to-wit, cognition, will, activity, happiness, and so on, ought to be regarded as so many different sorts of experience; as was previously exemplified, in the case of will. Or, should there be some very nice distinction between happiness, or the like, and the experience of it, the two, at all events, are inseparable. It follows, that there is no foundation for the theory of separating cognition &c. from their experiences, on which the doctrine depends, that the internal organ is the subject of happiness and so forth, and that the soul is their experiencer.

And now I purpose to make out, that the soul cannot, by any chimerical reflexions of cognition, will, &c., erroneously regarded as experiences of cognition and the rest, become an experiencer thereof. It is self-evident, that the experiences of cognition, will, happiness, misery, &c. are qualities of their experiencer: for a quality is that which cannot exist abstracted from its substrate. For example, the existence of colour, or of taste, or of length, or of breadth, under such abstraction, is impossible. And it is the same as concerns the experience of cognition, or the like, considered severally from its experience. Indeed, experience, thus circumstanced, is brought into the category of the son of a barren woman and the horn of a hare. From this it is clear, that the experiences of cognition, will, &c. are qualities; and, being such, they are connected with their substrates by the relation through which every other quality belongs to that which possesses it.

In the terminology of the Naiyáyikas, the relation between quality and substance is that of *samaváya*. But this *samaváya*, as they describe it, seems to me not only hypothetical, but irrational; and so I decline to designate by it the relation between quality and substance. To this relation I assign no name whatever. When, in our argumentations, we have reached the boundary of the certain and of the intelligible, there is nothing left for us but to be silent. As for the relation of quality and substance, reason teaches us, that it is widely different from *sanyoga* and such other relations. It is a relation through which quality penetrates and permeates the very essence of substance, and participates in it. Just so does experience with reference to an experiencer.

A reflexion, though, in respect of space, it is very near the soul,—in fact, within it, like everything else; for, in the Sánkhya, the soul is all-pervading,—is far remote from its essence. In the Sánkhya scheme, it is an evolution from the internal organ, and must reside in the soul by the relation of *sanyoga*, and not otherwise. Now, how can the soul, by virtue of it, be an experiencer? For, if it has not experience in its proper essence, it has none at all. Analogically, let it be, that a sage sits ever so close to a fool, or embraces him, if you will: can the fool, in consequence, be pronounced wise?

The European physicists, who have explored acoustics, optics, and other similar departments of science, declare, that, when a man sees an object, the following process is transacted. First, the object is imprinted upon the retina, behind which is a sensory nerve connecting it with the brain. The nerve and the brain are, thus, successively affected. Then, owing to some relation between the brain and the soul, that is to say, between matter and what is not matter, the object seen is cognized. That relation is incomprehensible: and yet of so much we are certain; that neither does the object's being reflected into the eye, nor does the effect produced in the sensory nerve, through the reflexion, nor does the action upon the brain, through the sensory nerve, constitute the soul's cognition. For, though the relation between the brain and the soul is most intimate, still the brain is distinct from the soul, and extrinsic to it. The soul's cognizing consists in this, that itself, that is to say, by its essence, apprehends an object through the eye and the other media enumerated.

The conclusion is, that, if the Sánkhya's reflexions of the affections cognition, will, activity, happiness, and misery are distinct from the soul's proper essence, they are not the soul's experiences of cognition, will, &c.; since, though, as to space, they are exceedingly proximate to the soul, yet, viewed essentially, they are as distant as the east from the west. Inasmuch, therefore, as the soul can neither cognize, nor will, nor energize, nor be happy or miserable, nor be an experiencer of cognition, &c. &c., why should the Sánkhyas strive so hard to liberate it?

In another way, moreover, the Sánkhyas deceive themselves and others. They say, that happiness and the like are not really in the soul, but that, from non-discrimination, the soul thinks itself miserable and bound: this is its wretchedness, emancipation from which is desirable. In this statement there are two great errors. One is this. The non-discrimination spoken of is itself an affection of the internal organ. As such, it has no intrinsic relation to the soul; only that of a reflexion: and how, then, can the soul be prejudiced by it? The other error is this. Even if the soul, from non-discrimination, did think itself miserable and bound,—which the Sánkhyas will not grant,—still, it could take no harm merely from thus thinking, so long as it did not, in reality, incur misery by reason of non-discrimination. If, then, the Sánkhyas conceded, that it thus incurs misery, it would be really miserable. And, if they deny—and they do deny—that it does, it follows, that it stands in no need of being emancipated.

Therefore, that position only, which is laid down in the sixty-second stanza of the *Sánkhya-káriká*, can be justified on Sánkhya principles; namely, that it is not the soul, but nature, that is hampered and that is disengaged.

I have already shown, that the Sánkhyas go to all the trouble they take to prove the soul devoid of apprehension, desire, &c., in order that the soul may be proved susceptible of emancipation.* They allege, that, if apprehension, desire, happiness, misery, and the rest be acknowledged to be qualities of the soul, they must be a part of its proper nature: and the nature of anything is inalienable. Only by making out the soul to be unendowed with apprehension and the like, they say, does its emancipation become possible. For, in the view of all the pandits, there is no emancipation apart from insentience. That riddance from pain is indispensable, we all hold alike. Now, let it be granted, for a moment, that these notions are correct; that is to say, that emancipation cannot take place without the abolition of apprehension, and that misery, like cognition, &c., if a quality of the soul, must continue forever. Still, it is improper, out of fear for the soul, to describe a thing as being other than it is, and to give aid to such a deceit by sophistry. I mean, that it is wrong to insist, that apprehension, desire, and so on, which are really qualities of the soul, are not so. Man, we know, is mortal. But, if, from dread of death, I, a man, affirm, that I am not a man, shall I, on that account, escape death? If, therefore, the Sánkhyas are convinced, that whatever has apprehension, desire, &c. for qualities is doomed to the fearful evil of never parting with them, it is the counsel of wisdom, seeing that they are left without resource, to abide their lot in patience, and not to belie reality.

---

* It cannot but seem extraordinary blindness, in the Sánkhyas, not to perceive, that the very efforts which they put forth to show, that the soul is capable of being emancipated, go to prove that it has no need of being emancipated.

The truth is, however, that the pandits' notion is baseless, that emancipation consists in definitive alienation of apprehension, &c. And the assertion of the Sánkhyas is erroneous, that, whatever has misery for a quality can never be discharged of it. When the cause of misery is removed, the misery likewise takes its departure; and Almighty God will deliver from it whomsoever He blesses with His grace. I shall treat of these points when I discuss the Nyáya.

CHAPTER. 6.

Brief Consideration of one Topic of the Mímánsá, with a few Remarks on the Intellectual Peculiarities of the Pandits, and on their Style of Reasoning.

Greatly do the Mímánsakas err, in not acknowledging God;[*] and, again, while they do not acknowledge Him, in believing in virtue and vice, and in laying upon the heads of men the burthen of rites and ceremonies; and, lastly, in maintaining, that the Veda has existed from eternity. My refutation, in the third chapter of this section, of the first two of these errors, as held by the Sánkhyas, will equally well apply to the Mímánsakas. But there is this difference of view between the two schools, as regards the Veda. The Sánkhyas hold, that, at the beginning of every renovation of the universe, it issues anew from the mouth of Brahmá, but without his composing it; whereas, according to the Mímánsakas, it has always existed: and the same arguments that are good against the former notion are just as cogent when applied to the latter. However, as for this latter view, that is to say, that the Veda was made by no one, but of itself has been in existence from all duration, one may indeed wonder at such an irrational theory.

---

[*] To name one Mímánsaka,—Párthasárathi Misra, in the first chapter of the S'ástra-dípiká, labours at length to overset the arguments adducible to prove the existence of Deity.

If asked for their proofs of this, the Mímánsakas can only reply, that no name of the writer of the Veda has come down to us.* But what sort of a proof is this? Many is the book whose author's name nobody knows : but do we infer, therefore, that such a book never had a beginning in time? And how, pray, differs an ancient book from an ancient house? And who ever concluded, that an old house had been built from the beginning of all things, on the ground, that its builder's name has been lost in oblivion? There is, in short, only one topic connected with the Mímánsá, on which I purpose to remark. It is as follows.

To find, that the Mímánsá esteems the Veda to be infallibly authoritative, and, nevertheless, decides, that the gods named in it are all imaginary,† and that the relations concerning them there are mere fables; and to find, that, though Indra is denied to exist, yet to make offerings in his name is sufficient to ensure great reward; cannot but strike one with astonishment. Wherever, allege the Mímánsakas, the gods and their exploits are spoken of in the Veda, it is not intended to recount actual facts: the end in view being to magnify the benefit of ritual acts, and so to allure men to engage in them. But how can any one who has the slightest discrimination say, after reading the Veda, that the persons who originally addressed its hymns to Indra and others, did not themselves believe these to be real divinities? And who can imagine a man's doing worship to an unreal god, and singing praises to a nonentity, and imploring nobody, in the expectation of receiving therefor eminent recompense?

---

* यदि वेदानां कर्ता कश्चिदभविष्यत् ततोऽस्मन्मध्येऽपरम्परया बुद्धादिवदस्मरिष्यत । Párthasárathi Mis'ra, in the first chapter of the S'ástra-dípiká. "Had there been any author of the Veda, surely remembrance of him would have been preserved by successive students *of the Veda ;* as has been the case in respect of Buddha and others."

Párthasárathi goes on to urge, that, if the Vedas had had an author, it is impossible he could ever have been forgotten.

† See the extract from the *Bhátta-dípiká,* cited at p. 67.

On this subject the Mímánsakas seem to reason thus. All our strivings are for the attainment of reward; this reward being dependent upon works; and information about works being obtainable from the preceptive enunciations of the Veda. If we accept these three things, why need we accept more? If we hold the precepts of the Veda to be true, what harm is there in our looking upon the rest of the Veda as a romance? And, if reward comes of works, these suffice; and what is the use of the gods and the rest? Again, if works give rise to various fruits, then, as a seed possesses an innate power of originating a sprout, so, by maintaining, that works possess an innate energy, we are enabled to account for the production of the world; and what necessity, in that case, is there of a God? To refute such strange notions may be spared: the very statement of them is refutation. Still, I shall reply to them in the third chapter of the second section, where I speak of the error into which the pandits fall on the subject of virtue and vice.

Thus I have examined, in the present and three preceding chapters, the main doctrines of the Sánkhya—the Yoga included—and of the Mímánsá. Any man whose common sense is unsophisticated, on inspecting these doctrines as set forth and defended in the Sánkhya and Mímánsá, must perceive, that the pandits are most faulty in their manner of argumentation. As compared with those systems, the Nyáya and the Vais'eshika are greatly eligible. And yet their adherents also, ancient and modern, betray the intellectual defects common to all the pandits; as will before long be evinced.

Even as concerns things that are self-evident, these scholars go deplorably amiss. When a person reaches this state, it is most difficult to bring truth home to him. If a man, for instance, gets to doubt whether he has twenty fingers and toes, who can resolve his misgiving for him? You count them, one by one, to him; but, nevertheless, he cannot satisfy himself that they make up a score. After this, there is no hope of removing his uncertainty. Something similar to this state of mind is that of the pandits; as one cannot but see, on looking into the Sánkhya and Mímánsá. To dispel their difficulties is, consequently, no easy task; and yet I have ventured to undertake it. But, such are the peculiarities of my countrymen,—as I know from old experience,—that they will not understand my answers; and the real reason is, that they do not wish to understand them. Where there are persons who cannot be reached by rational arguments, we can only commend them to God; for to Him is possible what to man is impossible.

In this, again, the pandits manifest their wrong habits of mind, that, when they set about considering a subject, they do not, first of all, soberly ask themselves what the facts are, bearing on it, which they and others are acquainted with. Such is the spell over their minds, and, from prepossession towards what they wish to believe, such is the partiality of their contemplation, that they adopt maxims which are baseless, as if they had no imperfection, and accept defective illustrations in place of proofs, and reason on the strength of them: nor do they reflect whether their arguments are cogent or futile, or whether they may not be met by counter-arguments. And so they go on, rearing one thing upon another, utterly regardless of the preposterousness of their conclusions.

One more defect of their intellectual constitution is this, that they fail to enquire what things are within the range of human reason, and what are beyond it. With the short cord of human wit they vainly essay to measure the profundities of God's fathomless perfections, and to determine their limits. He who will act thus cannot but stumble, and at last fall disastrously.

People who follow the dictates of common sense steer clear, for the most part, of such errors. Common sense is that sense which is shared by the generality of mankind. By its aid, even the illiterate and rustics are able, in their daily occasions and transactions, to judge between the true and the false, and between the useful and the harmful. When any one, abandoning it, sets about adducing grand arguments in support of his favourite notions, he is very apt to get lost in a wilderness of nonsense, and to think, that the ground is above his head and the sky beneath his feet. But, to obey the admonitions of common sense is not the way of the pandits; and so we see how such wonderful dogmas as they profess came to be suggested to them.

Their style of reasoning may be illustrated by the following story. Once on a time, two men, travelling in company, laid a wager as to who would first reach the end of the next day's journey. One of them, getting up early the following morning, saw that the other was still asleep. With great complacency, he thereupon dressed, tied up his kit, and set off. In his haste, however, unawares to himself, he put on the other's turban instead of his own. Hurrying forward, on reaching the end of the day's journey, he found his companion had not got the start of him, and was not even within sight. And then he sat down, opened his bundle, took out his mirror, and began to inspect himself. Seeing that he had on the other's turban, he flung down the mirror, exclaiming: "Alas! well-a-day! I have taken all this trouble to get here first; and, after all, my friend has outstripped me." On this, a bystander, who had heard his lament, began to reason with him. "What do you mean?" said he. "Here you are, arrived and waiting; and how can you say, that your friend has, after all, outstripped you? Can you be so bewildered as to believe, that your sense of self has been transferred to another?" But still he turned a deaf ear. He had resolved on taking it for an invariable rule, that his friend's turban could be on no one's head but his friend's; and, accordingly, he must infer, that he himself had become the other, and that he had all along been labouring under illusion, in thinking it was himself who had started first on the day's journey, and prosecuted it, and completed it.

SECTION II.

CHAPTER 1.

Briefly prefatory, with an Examination of the Nyáya and Vais'eshika Doctrines touching God.

I shall now consider the Nyáya and the Vais'eshika. But, as I have before noted, there are many doctrines common to almost all the Systems. When I take up such points, in discussing the Nyáya and Vais'eshika, what I shall offer will, therefore, be applicable to the Systems generally.

At the outset I remarked, that the authors of nearly all the Systems announce, as the great end of their compositions, the attainment of final beatitude. At their respective beginnings, the Nyáya and the Vais'eshika Aphorisms make distinct statements to this effect. And so far forth they are worthy of commendation; it being most fitting to all men, and it being of all things most necessary, that they should strive, with their entire might, to find out the means of salvation. Yet I cannot concur with the partizans of the Systems, in regarding right apprehension as the chief cause of emancipation; my own belief being, that this effect springs from the spontaneous grace of God. I acknowledge, indeed, that right apprehension is instrumental to salvation; but it is not that right apprehension, consisting in discriminating between soul and what is not soul, which the authors of the Systems teach to be the sole means thereto. That sort of right apprehension, taken by itself, I hold to be of no benefit; a position which I shall substantiate by and bye. The sort of right apprehension which I maintain to be beneficial is this: rightly to apprehend God, and oneself, and one's wretchedness, and the way of escape from it, and what man ought to do, and what he ought to forbear. I do not mean, however, that to acquire, in its entirety, a right apprehension of these things is absolutely necessary; for this is impossible to man. I mean, that he ought to make this acquisition in so far as it is indispensable to his good. Requisite right apprehension, as concerns God, should be such as to move man to honour, to love, to worship, and to fear Him; such as to purify man's nature, and to lead him to love virtue and to abhor vice. And, further, a man's right apprehension, pertaining to himself, should be so much as to enable him to appreciate his place in the order of the universe; to think of himself as he appears in the sight of God; and to understand his relation to God, and his relations to his fellow-creatures, in order that he may be qualified to act according to those relations. And, again, a man's right apprehension should be sufficient to qualify him to realize his own wretchedness, so that he may take thought how to escape from it; and sufficient for him to acquaint himself with the means calculated to bring about such escape, so that he may avail himself of those means. But of these things there is no correct account in the Nyáya, or in the other Systems. Far from it, they inculcate numerous errors concerning them.

Most inappropriate is the account given, in the Nyáya and Vais'eshika, of the divine attributes, such as God's greatness, power, wisdom, holiness, and justice.

The soul, atoms, the mind, and many other things, no less than God, they hold to have existed from eternity. Like God, they have been, of themselves, from all duration, and were created by no one. How far does this view fall short of God's greatness, absoluteness, and sovereignty! According to the Naiyáyika, souls and atoms are innumerable; and, if they have always had spontaneous existence, it is manifest, that their existing is not in subordination to the will of God. As they had not their origin from God's will, so neither could they be by Him brought to nought. Even if God had willed otherwise, no change could have been operated as to their existence: nor will He be able to operate any such change. How, then, can absoluteness and sovereignty be predicated of God, as regards them? Him we call absolute and sovereign, on whose will, or permission, everything depends; and without entire subjection to whose will, nothing can be or happen. If the existence of souls, atoms, &c. be not subject to the will of God, His sovereignty does not extend to their existence. On this principle, God cannot be proved to be God: for God is He who is over all.

To this view the pandits would bring forward this objection: "If you deny unbeginning existence to atoms, what cause of the origin of the world can you produce? For every effect must have a material cause; as a jar clay. But for the clay, of what will the potter make his jar? In this way God formed the world out of atoms; and how could He have made it without atoms?" In reply, I would ask the pandits, whether they consider the power of God to be of like kind to that of the potter. If the powers of the two be similar, then God required limbs and appliances; just as the potter, in fabricating a jar, is obliged to use his hands, feet, and sundry other implements. And, if it be conceded, that God, unlike the potter, had no need of limbs and appliances, but could have made the world by His mere will, where is the difficulty in acknowledging, that He could have created it without a material cause? By His inscrutable power He was able to originate the entire world, material cause and material effect together. If it be objected, that this is inconceivable, I would ask, whether it be not equally inconceivable, that God could have framed the world out of atoms, by His will alone, and without recourse to bodily members. Do we see, anywhere among men, a workman of such skill, as that, by a simple operation of mind, he can call effects into being? My opponent may perhaps say, that the human soul answers these conditions; for, by its mere will, it sets the hands and feet in motion: and he may add, that, in like sort, at the beginning of the world, God, by His will, imparted motion to the terrene and other atoms. Let the parallelism of the illustration be granted; yet the main difficulty, that of inconceivability, is still where it was. We know, to be sure, that the soul, by its mere will, moves the hands and feet. But who can comprehend how this comes to pass? The will is invisible and intangible: resembling neither a cord, with which a thing may be brought near; nor a staff, with which a thing may be raised or thrown down. How can it have any influence on the hands and feet, which are insentient matter? And how can it raise or depress them? The whole is inconceivable. If, then, the works of God outreach our conception, how can we assign limits to His power, which is inscrutable? But the soul's communicating motion to the hands and feet cannot properly be drawn into analogy: for the hands and feet are of the body which belongs to the soul; but terrene and other atoms are not of the body of God, He being bodiless. The difficulty of operating, by the mere will, upon what is not of one's body remains, therefore, precisely where we found it. Nor can you call terrene and other atoms the body of God;* for you cannot maintain, that the qualities and nature of body are possessed by them. Thus, the body influences the soul; but you cannot affirm, that God is affected by terrene atoms, &c., in the same manner. Since there are, thus, numerous characteristics of body which do not appertain to the terrene and other atoms,

---

* According to the author of the *Dinakarí*, the following opinion was held by the adherents of A'chárya, by which title Udayana A'chárya, most probably, is intended: वस्तु ∗ ∗ ∗ ईश्वरस्य नित्यं शरीरं तथाऽपि नेश्वर-स्याऽतिरिक्तशरीरसिद्धिः परमाणूनामेव तच्छरीरत्वोपगमात् ।

"Let it be *granted*, that I'swara possesses an eternal body: still it is not established, that I'swara has a distinct, *or proper*, body; for it is held, *by us*, that the atoms themselves are his body."

if you give the name of God's body to these atoms, still our bodies cannot be adduced as analogous to them. My meaning, in sum, is, that, whereas the tenet, that God created all things by His infinite and inscrutable power, is not open to exception, the opinion, which, in arguing the independent and unbeginning existence of the material world, undeniably abridges God of His supreme absoluteness and plenary sovereignty, is imbued with error.

There are two particular objections, say the pandits, to the view, that souls had their origin from God. The first is, that it involves, as against God, the imputation of unequal dealing and cruelty. The second is, that, if we hold souls to be generated, we must hold them to be destructible. I shall return to these points in a short time.

The Nyáya and Vais'eshika dogma, which is also that of the Yoga and Vedánta, that whatever God does,—as in framing the world, for instance,—He does solely for the purpose of awarding to souls the fruit of their works,—He doing nothing of His own free will,—is, likewise, exceptionable. On what ground is God believed to be thus fettered ? To know, to will, and to do are natural faculties of an intelligent being ; and, if God is an intelligent Being, it is congruous to maintain, that, by virtue of His free will, He can act whenever it may seem good to Him so to do.

To this the pandits would reply, that, if God, without reference to the works of souls, of His mere will fashioned the universe, the blemish would be imputable to Him, that there was some want, to satisfy which He engaged in creation :* but,

---

* Nearly all the Hindu philosophers, the Bauddhas included, have taught the eternity of the soul and the tenet of metempsychosis. Had occasion been presented to them of assailing the position, that God created the world irrelatively to the works of souls, we may judge, from the ensuing passage, how, in all likelihood, they would have made answer : प्रेच्यावत्र ष्टेः खार्थकार-त्वाभ्यां व्याप्तत्वात् । ते च जगत्सर्गाद् व्यावर्तमाने प्रेच्यावत्र्व-

if it be held, that He did so in accordance with the works of souls, the blemish of His having a want will not attach to Him; and it follows, that He made the world for the sole purpose of awarding to every one the consequences due to his deeds. My answer is, that neither do I maintain, that God made the world to fulfil any want implying that He lacked aught, to obtain which He engaged in creation: but I do maintain, that, by reason of one of the perfections of His nature, goodness, He was pleased to make manifest, through the medium of creation, His supremely loveworthy and wondrous attributes. God made the world, says my opponent, in order to requite the good and evil deeds of souls. But why should He requite?* The very objection intimated

चित्पूर्वकत्वमपि व्यावर्त्तयतः । न ह्यवाप्तसकलेप्सितस्य भगवतो जगत् सृजतः किमप्यभिलषितं भवति । नाऽपि कारुण्यादस्य सर्गे प्रवृत्तिः । प्राक् सर्गाज् जीवानामिन्द्रियशरीरविषयानुत्पत्तौ दुःखाभावेन कस्य प्रहाणेच्छा कारुण्यम् । *Tattwa-kaumudí*, p. 52.

"The action of the prudent, *or sane*, is *ever* accompanied by *wish of* self-profit, or else by compassion. And these, being impertinent as concerns the creation of the world, refute the notion, that it, *such creation*, was due to the act of a prudent person: for there can be no *unfulfilled* desire of a Lord whose every wish is already satisfied, that he should be creator of the world. Nor could his creative agency be *exerted* from compassion. Inasmuch as, prior to creation,—since the senses, bodies, and objects were *as yet* unproduced,—there was no misery of souls, for dispelling what *misery was there scope* for compassionate desire ?"

Váchaspati Miśra, while engaged in upholding the atheistic doctrines of the Sánkhya, writes as above, in opposition to those who maintain the belief of a Creator.

The last two words of the Sanskrit are of very doubtful correctness; but no manuscript is at hand, by which to mend them, if wrong.

* We have seen above, at p. 38, that, in the view of the theistic Hindus, to save the Deity from the imputation of unequal dealing and cruelty, it is thought necessary to refer the unequal portions of souls in this world to the diverse works of those souls in bygone states of existence. To Váchaspati Miśra, in his character of advocate on behalf of the Sánkhya, this seems unsatisfactory. We find him saying : अपि च कर्मणा प्रेरित ईश्वरः सु-

against me, and which I set aside, here arises, to-wit, that there was some want of God's to be supplied by such requital. If it be replied, that, in virtue of the equity* of His nature, He awards to each the fruit of his works, I rejoin, that it is in virtue of an excellence of His nature, namely His goodness, that He made manifest His supremely loveworthy attributes by creating souls and by making them to rejoice in the contemplation of His perfections. Any one has discrimination enough to perceive, that, from mere vanity, to go about exhibiting one's importance, under the impulse of a longing to hear it proclaimed by the world, is one thing; and that it is quite another thing, to make manifest the excellence of anything, because such manifestation is fitting and laudable. When a foolish man, actuated by vanity, goes here and there to display his importance, everybody laughs at him. But, if a learned European were to bring some very extraordinary machine to this country, and invite people to his house, and show them the wonders of the machine free of charge, no one would deride him, but, on the contrary, all would thank and praise him for his gratuitous kindness and trouble. Just so, the manifesta-

खिन् एव जन्तून् सृजेन् न विचित्रान् । कर्मवैचित्र्याद् वैचि-
त्र्यमिति चेत् कृतमस्य प्रेच्यावतः कर्माधिष्ठानेन तदनधिष्ठानमा-
विदेवाश्चेतनस्यापि कर्मणः प्रवृत्त्यनुपपत्तेरार्थशरीरेन्द्रियविष-
यानुपत्तौ दुःखानुत्पत्तेरपि सुकरत्वात् । *Tattwa-kaumudi*, pp. 52, 53.
"More than this, I'swara, *if* moved, by compassion, to create, would create creatures in happiness, not of diverse conditions. If *to this* it be replied, that the diverseness *of the condition of souls* is owing to the diverseness of *their* works, it is a pity, *I reply*, that he, *Iswara*, prudent, should superintend works; since, but for his very superintendence, works, being unintelligent, could not proceed to act; and, consequently, as their effects, *viz.*, the body, the senses, and sense-objects, would not be produced, the non-production of misery would be a matter of facility."

* Indeed, the reply here put into the mouth of the Hindu gives him credit for clearer notions touching God's equity than he could really come by from study of his so-called sacred books.

tion of anything that is excellent is no fault, but itself an excellence. God, therefore, because of the very excellence of His nature, makes known, through creation, and otherwise, His loveworthy and wondrous attributes. That such attributes, calculated to awaken affection and joy, should forever remain hidden, would seem most unmeet.

Let us now consider God's attributes of justice and holiness, as viewed in the Nyáya and Vais'eshika. As for His justice, if we scan these systems superficially, it may seem, that the doctrine of His bestowing requital according to works involves it. And, when the followers of those systems declare, that even the most trifling pain endured in this world must be taken to have had sin for its cause, and that, therefore, a former state of existence must be admitted, or else God's equity suffers the imputation of imperfectness, it looks as if they believed, in all its fulness, in justice as an attribute of Deity. On looking more closely, however, we find, that here too they are quite in the dark, as also touching God's holiness.

As I have before remarked, the Systems receive the Vedas, the Smṛitis, the Purāṇas, &c. as authorities. The former, therefore, share with the latter any faults ascribable to them on the score of portraying amiss the justice, holiness, and other attributes of God. Let it not be supposed, that I am going out of my way to fasten faults on the Systems. Secrets, which else lurk unperceived, necessarily stand forth in any thoroughgoing examination such as that with which I am occupied.

No man is ignorant, that God is just and holy; and we need not be surprized to find Him so called in religions of human origin. But man, unaided, cannot attain to a correct knowledge of the holiness and other attributes of the Deity. His inability betrays itself, when he ventures into details on the subject, or, incidentally, when he is treating of matters cognate to it. Hence, the express declarations regarding God's holiness and other attributes, which we find in a book on any religion, are not a sufficient warrant, in the examination of that religion. Further and fuller exploration is indispensable. We should consider all that there is in the book, and also what is there omitted, and likewise all that has legitimate connexion with its subject-matter; and then we are in a position to pass judgment on it. From the fact, with reference to the Systematists, that they admit as authorities the Vedas, the Puráṇas, &c., it comes out, that, if the Nyáya and Vais'eshika do not, in express words, militate very greatly against the justice and holiness of God, it is not because the writers on those schemes entertained fit and correct notions of the divine attributes, but simply because they did not dilate on those topics. Had they done so, they would have exhibited errors of every description.

Again, if we search out what the Systematists teach concerning those things which man is to do, and those things which he is to forbear, and other points allied with religion, we may learn what views they hold of God's justice, and holiness, and other attributes. For, so strict is the connexion between morality and theology, that any faults which are found in views about the former imply, of necessity, faults in the views held about the latter. Of morality grossly wrong ideas occur in the Vedas, the Puráṇas, and the rest; and, where these err, the Systems participate their errors.

I shall, moreover, show, in the sequel, that the doctrines of the Systems, taken by themselves, touching virtue and vice, are signally faulty; and, such being the case, from this ground also it results, that they mistake as regards holiness and others of the divine attributes.

According to the tenets of the Nyáya and Vais'eshika, God can in no wise possess the attribute of mercy. It being one of the dogmas of these systems, that no effect can take place irrelatively to the works of souls, whatever a soul receives must be accounted a consequence of its works; and, if it succeeds in attaining to salvation, it earns salvation. It is evident, that there is an exercise of mercy, when God bestows what has not been merited. The existence of such mercy is at variance, however, with the dogmas of the Nyáya, of the Vais'eshika, and of all the other Systems.

Moreover, since the Nyáya and Vais'eshika deny, that God made the world of His free will, but affirm, that He did so to requite souls, they altogether do away with the goodness which He evinced in creation. When we behold God's world, on every side we perceive evidences of His wonderful goodness and bounty. In the first place, man, before he was created, was nothing; but, in vouchsafing to him existence, and life, and the faculty of knowledge, how has God constituted him capable of happiness! Though, now in our fallen state, it is ours to suffer much misery, still all our suffering, nay, death itself, is the fruit of our sin; and we alone are to blame for it. Had man never sinned, his happiness, and especially that which, by reason of his rectitude of mind and purity of original nature, he would have enjoyed from knowing God, from devotion and love to Him, and from communion with Him, would have surpassed description. When we behold the sun, the source of so much gladness and benefit, or the moon and the sidereal world, it seems, indeed, as though the goodness of the compassionate Author of our being were holding converse with us in a bodily form. The very trees, which comfort and refresh us, and yield us their luscious fruitage, and the charming mountains and rivers which embellish the earth, almost call upon us, with united voices, to give praise for the love and bountifulness of our merciful Father. But who could adequately depict the countless sources of happiness which God has created? And each and all of them are manifested to us as tokens of His goodness, when we come to believe, that He fashioned the universe of His own free will, and from the bountifulness of His nature. But the Naiyáyikas and Vais'eshikas, having established it as a maxim, that all things are indebted for their origin to the works of souls, have overspread these glories with the blackness of gloom. And they have transformed God into a hard-natured huckster, who secures his pay from his customers, and sells his wares by rigid tale, weight, and measure. So much for the description of the Supreme Being which we meet with in the two most reasonable of the Hindu Systems.

CHAPTER 2.

Examination of the Nyáya and Vais'eshika Tenets relative to the Soul; namely, that it had no Beginning, that it is All-pervading, and that it takes Birth again and again.

Numerous are the faults of the Nyáya and Vais'eshika, even in their account of the soul. Souls they hold to have existed from eternity, and to be, each, diffused throughout all space. I have already pointed out, that, if unoriginated existence be ascribed to any but God, His deity is impugned. I now purpose to consider the grounds on which souls are maintained, by the Nyáya and Vais'eshika, to have existed always, and to be diffused everywhere. If we do not so believe, say the advocates of those systems, the soul must be perishable. As for existence from all duration, it is argued, that whatever had a beginning will have an end; as a jar, cloth, &c.; and, therefore, if a soul once began to be, it will some time cease to be.* But I would ask, what foundation there is for the maxim, that all which has had a beginning shall have an end. Should it be replied, that the history of a jar, or the like, supplies foundation for it, I rejoin, that what may be predicated of jars and such-like material things is not on that account predicable of the soul; so great is their disparity. Moreover, the origin, continuance, and termination of any-

---

* What the Hindus esteem to be the most unanswerable argument of the soul's eternity will be considered at p. 124.

SEC. II., CHAP. 2.   119

thing depend solely upon the will of God. If it pleased God, could He not, by His infinite might, preserve a jar for ever and ever? By evidence* which I do not here adduce, it is established, that human souls are immortal; and so it is evident, that it is the will of God, that they should be so. And can anything thwart His power to do as He wills to do? Can the aforesaid maxim of my opponents obstruct His infinite power? It is a great mistake, in them, to take up a maxim gratuitously, and then to wish to fetter with it the whole world, nay, God himself, whether it be appropriate or inappropriate.

As a proof of the maxim of the pandits, that whatever had a beginning must have an end, it is alleged, that every originated substance is necessarily made up of parts,† and that the parts of anything thus constituted may come asunder, and so the thing some time perish. To this I have to say, as before, that all such suppositions are applicable to material things alone; and that the origination, continuance, and end of all things depend solely upon the will of God.

That the soul is all-pervading must also be believed, say the pandits, if we would consider it to be indestructible.‡ Ac-

---

* It is not opportune, at this place, to indicate more distinctly than in this manner, the only certain warrant for believing in the soul's immortality, namely, the Holy Scripture.

† Dharmarája Díkshita, speaking of the internal organ, holds this language: न तावदन्तःकरणं निरवयवं सादिद्रव्यत्वेन सावयवत्वात् । *Vedánta-paribháshá*, p. 3. "The internal organ is not without parts: being an originated substance, it is made up of parts."

‡ यदि च घटादिवत् पुमान् मूर्तः परिच्छिन्नः स्वीक्रियते तदा सावयवत्वविनाशित्वादिना घटादिसमानधर्मापत्तावपसिद्धान्तः स्यादित्यर्थं । *Sánkhya-pravachana-bháshya*, p. 35. "And if it were acknowledged, that the soul is 'limited', or finite,—like a jar and such other *things*,—since, as is the case with these, it must possess the properties of having parts and of being destructible, the result would be a tenet contradictory *to that of our system.*"

Annam Bhaṭṭa says, speaking of ether: विभुत्वादेवास्मवन् नित्यत्वम् ।

cording to them, dimension is of three descriptions; atomic, intermediate, and infinite. Atomic dimension is the last degree of minuteness. Intermediate dimension is that of a jar, of cloth, or of any originated substance whatsoever. However great it may be, it has limits. Infinite dimension, the third kind, is unlimited. It is this species of dimension which, the pandits teach, belongs to God, to souls, to ether,* to time, and to space; and whatever has this dimension is all-pervading. Further, according to them, things of atomic or of infinite dimension are indestructible, but those of intermediate dimension cannot be indestructible.† A soul, then, to be in-

---

Tarka-dípiká, MS., *fol. 7, verso.* "As being, like the soul, all-pervading it is, like it, eternal."

* A characterization of *ákás'a* will serve to show how inadequatively it is represented by "ether." In dimension, it is, as has been said, infinite; it is not made up of parts; and colour, taste, smell, and tangibility do not appertain to it. So far forth it corresponds exactly to time, space, I'swara, and soul. Its speciality, as compared therewith, consists in its being the material cause of sound. Except for its being so, we might take it to be one with vacuity.

In passing, this is, doubtless, the fifth element referred to in the following words of Megasthenes, as cited by Strabo: Πρὸς δὲ τοῖς τέτταρσι στοιχείοις πέμπτη τίς ἐστι φύσις, ἐξ ἧς ὁ οὐρανὸς καὶ τὰ ἄστρα. Schwanbeck's *Megasthenis Indica*, p. 138.

† Vijnána Bhikshu says of the soul: मध्यमपरिमाणत्वे सावयवत्वा- पत्त्या विनाशित्वम् ‌। *Sánkhya-pravachana-bháshya,* p. 35. "If it were of intermediate dimension, it must be constituted of parts, and, therefore, would be destructible."

The following also refers to the soul: न मध्यमपरिमाणः । तथा सत्य- नित्यत्वप्रसङ्गेन कृतनाशाकृताभ्यागमप्रसङ्गात् । *Tarka-dípiká*, MS., *fol. 8, verso.* "It is not of intermediate dimension. If it were so, from being uneternal, *and hence perishable*, there would follow the destruction of what is done, and the accession of what is not done."

What is meant is this. The works of the soul are assumed to be inalienable and inevitable. On the theory, then, of the soul's perishableness, its works would miss of their effect, which, by the hypothesis, cannot thus fail. Further, newly created souls would reap fruit which they had not sown.

destructible, must needs be, in size, either atomic or infinite. If it be the first, then its qualities, as apprehension, will, &c., cannot be subject to immediate cognition; for there is another maxim, that the qualities of an atom—as, for instance, the colour or taste of earth in its atomic character,—are incapable of being so cognized.* It is, however, a fact of universal consciousness, that the qualities of the soul are cognized immediately; and hence the pandits are compelled, on their principles, to regard the soul as of infinite dimension. The reply which I gave at the end of the last paragraph is equally applicable in this place.

Another relevant objection that would offer itself to the pandits, is this. "If the soul be not all-pervading, but bounded by the body, it must vary in dimension as the body varies: and the same soul may, in one state of existence, inform an ant; in another, a human being; and, in a third, an elephant. Assuming the soul to be bounded by the body, it must be very minute in an ant; and, when it passes into a man, or into an elephant, how can it discharge its functions?†

---

* मनसोऽणुत्वात् प्रत्यक्षे च महत्त्वम् हेतुत्वात् मनसि ज्ञानसुखादिसत्त्वे तद्व्यक्तानुपपत्तेरित्यर्थः । *Siddhánta-muktávali*: *Bibliotheca Indica*, Vol. IX., pp. 38, 39. "Since the mind is atomic *in dimension*, and since grossness is essential in order to perception, if cognition, happiness, &c. had their seat in the mind, they would not be perceived, *or immediately cognized.*"

A further objection, and one more ordinarily urged, against the hypothetical notion, that the soul is of atomic bulk, will be found in the words of the Sánkhya and Vaiśeshika writers adduced in the second note forward.

† S'ankara A'chárya, in the passage about to be cited, is writing against the Bauddhas, who, as he asserts, maintain, that the soul is commensurate with the body. शरीराणां चानवस्थितपरिमाणत्वान् मनुष्यजीवो मनुष्यशरीरपरिमाणो भूत्वा पुनः केनचित् कर्मविपाकेन हस्तिजन्म प्राप्नुवन् न कृत्स्नं हस्तिशरीरं व्याप्नुयात् पुत्तिकाजन्म च प्राप्नुवन् न कृत्स्नः पुत्तिकाशरीरे सम्मीयेत । *S'áriraka-sútra-bháshya*; the MS.

And how can it take cognizance of the sense of feeling throughout such a bulk? For it cannot dilate so as to fill it.* We must conclude, consequently, that the soul increases and diminishes with the increase and diminution of the body. And since, thus, from repeatedly increasing and diminishing, it undergoes alteration of constituent parts, it follows, that it must repeatedly be generated and destroyed: for to undergo such alteration is, according to the Naiyáyikas, to be generated after having been destroyed."

Now, for my part, I repudiate the notion of metempsychosis; and so I might hold myself dispensed here from returning answer to the pandits. Nevertheless, I reply to them; since the objection just detailed will recur. A human being has, in infancy, a body of small size as compared with what that body becomes subsequently. They will say, then, that, on my view of the soul's being bounded by the body, it must be, that the small soul of the infant becomes a large soul in the full-grown man: for the small soul of a small body could not take cognizance of the sense of feeling, for instance, from head to foot of a body greatly augmented in magnitude.† To

---

not at hand for reference. "Since bodies are various in dimension, if a human soul,—coextensive, *according to the Bauddhas*, with the human body,— were, by a special maturation of works, to be born an elephant, it would fall short of filling the whole of an elephantine body; and, if born a bee, an apian body would be inadequate to contain it."

* Vijnána Bhikshu and Annam Bhatta argue after the manner of the text, in opposition to the view, that the soul is atomic.

अगुत्वे च देहव्यापिज्ञानादनुपपत्तिः । *Sánkhya-pravachana-bháshya*, p. 35. "And if *the soul* were atomic, there would be no accounting for cognition, &c., which extend all over the body."

सच न परमाणुः शरीरव्यापिसुखानुपलब्धिप्रसङ्गात् । *Tarka-dipiká*, MS., fol. 8, verso. "And it, *the soul*, is not an atom, *as to size*; else it would result, that pleasure would not be perceived throughout the body."

† Such an objection is brought by S'ankara A'chárya, in continuation of his words quoted in the note before the last: समान एघ एकस्मिन्नपि जन्मनि कौमारयौवनस्थाविरेषु दोषः । "The same objection ap-

this I say, that, though one holds the soul to be bounded by the body, still it does not follow of course, as an article of belief, that, in proportion as the body changes in size, so does the soul. When a child begins to grow, the apprehension and other faculties of his soul increase in strength; but it is not necessary to say, that his soul itself augments. And, when I allege, that the soul is bounded by the body, my meaning is not, that its dimension tallies exactly with that of the body. I simply intend, that the soul does not reside beyond the body. As for its nature, that is most hard to understand; and no one, in fact, can give a full description of it. That the soul takes cognizance of the sense of touch in all the parts of a body, small or great, is nothing difficult to it: for, in its operations, it subsidizes all the sense-organs; and its power of apprehension is more or less in proportion to the vigour of those organs. Thus, a man whose sight is impaired sees ill; and, when it is improved, he sees better. In like manner, tact is apprehended through the nerves; and these increase with the body; and, through them, there is apprehension of tact throughout the parts of the body, whether it be small or great.

The truth is, that the nature of the soul transcends our knowledge, and does not lend itself to description. All that we know of the soul is, that it is something which possesses apprehension, will, and other qualities. More than this we cannot affirm concerning it; as, for instance, that, like earth, water, and other material substances, it has dimension and such-like qualities. Much, therefore, that is predicable of a jar, of cloth, and of other material substances, is not to be predicated of the soul. Such, however, is the disposition of the pandits, that they refuse to consider what things are within the reach of our understanding, and what things lie beyond. They would fain take the visible and the invisible, God and souls included, and measure them, and turn them round and

plies even to *the case of* a state of existence taken by itself, in its *several stages of* childhood, middle age, and senescence.'

over, and pry into them, and at last get their complete quiddities inside their fist. To their minds, if one is to know anything, one should know everything: otherwise, it is better to know nothing. And so they wander on in the wilderness of vain inquiry. I would remind them, that, be the essence of the soul of what sort soever, its origin, duration, and end are in subordination to the will of God; and, therefore, if God thinks good that the soul shall exist for ever, it can in no wise incur destruction.

But the weightiest reason, in the estimation of the pandits, for arguing, that the soul has existed from all eternity, is as follows. First, they argue, that the doctrine of metempsychosis must be accepted. " Otherwise, the imputation of partiality and cruelty must attach to God. Partiality consists in not looking upon all alike; in treating some with more favour, and others with less; in giving some a high rank, and others a lower. Cruelty is uncompassionateness; the giving pain where no fault has been committed. Now, we see, that, in this world, some enjoy a high rank and great power, and others are wretched, and afflicted with poverty: and what is the reason, that God has ordered it thus? Again, almost all men suffer misery and misfortune; and what is the cause of this? It is not enough to say, it is the sins that have been done in the current state of existence; for it is matter of experience, that many a grievous offender has great power and pleasure, and that many a man whose conduct is observably meritorious is oppressed with poverty and pain. And what can you say with respect to infants and beasts? Consciously, they have never committed sin; and yet they suffer greatly. Hence, we maintain the doctrine of the transmigration of the soul, and so remove all these difficulties. We can, therefore, say, when we see a bad man to be powerful and in comfort, that he must have been eminently virtuous in a former state of existence, and is now reaping the reward of his virtue. Similarly, when we see a good man suffer more than ordinary affliction, we are able to affirm, that, in a former state of existence he was eminently sinful, and is now receiving retribution for his sin. And, in like manner, infants and beasts undergo punishment for the offences of which, in a prior birth, they were guilty. A single former state of being will not suffice, however; as the good and evil experienced therein must likewise be accounted for by the works of a birth that preceded. Moreover, the getting a body is also a consequence of works;* and, therefore, as often as a soul is invested in a body, antecedent works must be postulated in connexion with it. We hold, therefore, that the vicissitude of works and births, the alternate production of each from the other, has been going on from time without beginning."

I reply, that, neither by this reasoning can the soul be proved never to have originated. Even if I admitted the truth of what you have alleged touching the present felicity of some bad men, &c. &c., and metempsychosis as an explanation thereof, still I should not feel myself under any compulsion to argue, that souls have always existed, and that birth and death have had place from a foregone eternity. The difficulties above mentioned would all be repelled, if it were maintained, that, in the beginning, souls were created by God; originally in a state of happiness, but condemned, by reason of sin, to repeated embodiment. But to say, as you do, that works must be taken to have been done prior to the body,—for that the having a body is the consequence of works,—is in the last degree unreasonable. Your maxim, that every effect must have for its cause the

---

* स हि धर्मादिनिमित्तप्रभवः । *Tattwa-kaumudí*, p. 43. "For this *obtaining a body* is due to merit and the like, as causes.'

पूर्वकृतस्य यागदानहिंसादेः फलस्य धर्माधर्मरूपस्यानुबन्धात् सहकारिभावात् तस्य शरीरस्योत्पत्तिः । *Nyáya-sútra-vritti*, p. 160. " 'The production' of 'that', *i. e.*, of the body, is 'owing to the aid', or co-operation, of merit and demerit, 'the fruit of foredone' sacrifices, donations, harm, &c."

works of souls, I have previously exploded: for effects follow from the free will of God. But the pandits say, that the body is intrinsically an abode or site of misery,* and hence is itself a misery. Out of the twenty and one miseries enumerated by the Naiyáyikas, this is one. If, then, God invests a soul with a body, irrespectively of works, He does injustice. My reply is, that the body is not, intrinsically, an abode of misery. On the contrary, not a little happiness is derived by means of it; and, as for the pain caused by the body, owing to illness, &c., it is in the power of God to remove it. If He so willed, He might preserve us constantly at ease, though in the body. How crude here also is the reasoning of the pandits! Those who follow the Nyáya and Vais'eshika, hold, that God exists. Still, when they argue upon other points than His existence, they seem to forget, that He exists, and, as it were, refer all things to a law of chance. For the ground of their doctrine, that misery inevitably accompanies the body, is, that they everywhere see such to be the fact; and hence they infer, that it is its nature to be so accompanied, and that God could not make it to be otherwise. In like manner do they err in their maxim, that nothing which has had a beginning can be indestructible. Thus to think will be made out to be proper, when we are convinced, that the course of nature is fortuitous, and subject to some blind law. If, however, God is Governor of the course of nature, all things spring from His will. Some things are perishable, because He wills them to be so; and, for the same reason, other things are imperishable. In like manner, we men suffer misery, because

---

* न च सशरीरस्य सतः प्रियाप्रियसंस्पर्शो वारयितुं शक्यः ।

S'ankara A'chárya on the *Brahma-sútra*: *Bibliotheca* Indica, No. 89, p. 115. "And the contact, with one who is embodied, of good and evil cannot be prevented."

The शरीरस्य of the printed edition has been changed, on manuscript authority, as above.

it has been decreed fit, in His unfathomable and incomprehensible counsel, that thus it should be. If He thought good, it would not be at all difficult for Him to cause, that, though clothed with bodies, we should constantly remain happy. Indeed, it is manifest, from the true Word of God, that, when man was in a state of sinlessness, he was entirely exempt from misery. Neither did sickness, nor sorrow, nor death befal him: nay, the body was, to him, a door to many felicities. Only since he became a sinner has he been subject to the countless griefs of the soul and of the body. Earth, water, air, and all other external objects, were, in the beginning, sources, to him, of happiness only, and afterwards became sources of misery. The doctrine, therefore, of the pandits, that to abide in the body is intrinsically misery, is in every wise erroneous.

The refutation which I have detailed, of the notion of an unoriginated succession of works and births of souls, has proceeded on grounds maintained by my opponents. For, as regards myself, I reject the doctrine of metempsychosis; and I account as inadequate all the reasons that they bring forward in support of it.* With respect to the first defect which, according to them, has place, if metempsychosis be rejected, namely, partiality in God, I reply thus. If you simply mean, that He has not bestowed upon all men equality of rank and happiness, your objection has no weight with me: since I hold, that it

---

* This argument against the metempsychosis, however drawn out, will not seem to be gratuitously diffuse, if one but takes these three facts into consideration: first, that the doctrine here impeached is all but ineradicably rooted in the mind of very pandit; secondly, that, in the estimation of the pandits, any religious economy which does not acknowledge it is almost self-evidently false in its very first principles; and thirdly, and by way of consequence, that the rejection of it by Christianity is, to them, a well-nigh insuperable obstacle to their acceptance of the Gospel. The writer, in here combating a favourite and fundamental dogma, has, with his best thought and diligence, selected and marshalled his reasons in such a manner as is, he apprehends, best calculated to impress the minds of his erring countrymen, and to win them towards the truth.

was to show forth His all-sufficient attributes, that God framed the world; and that He creates souls irrespectively of works; and that He makes them diverse, as exhibiting the manifoldness of His creation. For instance, there are souls of one kind, in the form of angels, who surpass man, by far, in rank, majesty, wisdom, power, and other particulars. Inferior to them is man; and, again, below him are other creatures, such as beasts. These varieties we know of: but who shall say how many more different grades there may not be in God's vast universe? Again, there are distinct orders of angels; and of mankind also the ranks are numerous. All alike are the creation of God's free will; and, if He has given a high place to one, and a humble place to another, has any one a claim on Him? If we, who were once nothing, have, on receiving existence, been given anything whatever, it is from God's mere mercy. And can this mercy become injustice, from His giving another more than He gives me? If any one gives a poor man ten rupees, the man thinks himself greatly indebted to the giver. But, if the donor gives a hundred rupees to another poor man, does his favour towards the first turn to no favour? Does he prove himself unjust? I am aware, that, our nature having become corrupted by sin, almost any man, if he sees that others are favoured beyond himself, takes it ill, and is jealous and unhappy. But this unhappiness arises from the fact, that his nature is corrupt; and there is no right ground for it. There is no injustice, then, in giving less to one, and more to another. If, indeed, all had a claim to receive equally, there would be injustice. No one, however, has any claim upon God.

But now you may say, that, though there is no injustice in bestowing mean rank or small power on one, and high rank or great power on another, yet is there not injustice in causing pain gratuitously? And how many great sinners are happy, and how many good men are miserable! As for infants and beasts, too, who have never sinned, do not they suffer much affliction? Pray, how are these things to be accounted for? I reply. Without doubt, the fruit of sin is misery; and, as all men are sinners, it is meet, that, being so, they should be miserable. There are some men whom we call good; but, in the sight of God, they are all guilty: for God and man behold things under very different aspects. From sin, the discernment of man has become blunted; and the heinousness of sin is not altogether clear to him. Some men are called good, simply because they are better than most others. And yet there is not, in all the world, even one man whose heart and nature are undefiled by sin. Those, therefore, whom we call good are, before a most holy God, guilty, and deserving of punishment.

Moreover, mark, that this world is not man's place of judgment. Full judgment will not be till after death; and not till then will each receive exact and complete requital for his deeds. The present world, like a school, is a place where man is disciplined; and the happiness or misery which we here experience is not always by way of requital, or, when so, proportioned to our actions. In most cases, God sends happiness and misery to men, as being calculated for their good; but, to us, it is impossible to decide what is for any one's good, or the reverse. For none of us can know another's heart and nature, and his history, past, present, and future, and the eventual result of his happiness or misery. Should we, then, pronounce all misery in this world to be evil, we should err greatly. We ought, rather, to consider misery to be sent to us, in this world, by God, in mercy, for our warning, that we may turn to Him, and so escape future punishment. Therefore, to entertain doubt as to God's justice, because of the distresses of this world, is most rash. If a man who has been blindly walking in the path of sin, has his heart opened by some great calamity, and takes warning, repents, and turns to God, must he not look upon that calamity as a great blessing from God; and will he not praise God for it all his life long?

And do not suppose, that men of proper life and of amiable disposition have no need of the discipline which is furnished by misery. They too commit many an error, and have many a defect. And often it so occurs, that he who is a chosen servant of God is especially visited with affliction, not for punishment, but to the end, that he may be tried, like gold, in the crucible of misery, and thereby be purified. What folly, then, to let the idea of evil be suggested, whenever one hears the name of misery, and, with one's feeble intellect, to decide as to its hidden causes!

It is often wondered, why, if there was no former state of existence, some persons are born blind, and others are born lame. God has made many men thus, while he has made many of whole body. And it is asked, whether there be not partiality in this. But what are we, to attempt to find out the secret counsel of God! Can we learn the heart, and nature, and all the external and internal condition of another? Who shall say what good may not accrue to the immortal souls of the lame and blind, from their few days of misery? It is very true, that, though God, in His great mercy, sends us various remedial miseries for the eternal benefit of our souls, still, so infatuated are we with sin, that most of us refuse to take warning from our misery, and to repent of our sins, and to turn to God. The fault is our own, however. As for God's dealing, it is mercy. Is it not written even in one of the books of the Hindus, " From him whom I would favour, by little and little do I take away the riches"?*

It remains for me to speak of the misery of infants and beasts. And here, entering upon a strict logical argument, I would ask the Hindu: Is it certain, that the suffering of souls can have no just cause but their offences? When a man commits a great state-crime, the king has him executed,

---

* यस्याऽहमनुगृह्णामि हरिष्ये तद्धनं शनैः ।

This half-couplet is from the *Bhágavata-purána*, X., 88, 8.

and confiscates his property. As a consequence, and even though they may have taken no part in the crime, his children and household are involved in extreme distress. But does any one, for this, call the king unjust? Or take this case. The king's subjects are in every way loyal, and their sovereign is perfectly satisfied with them. But an enemy comes to attack him. He orders his people to give him their aid; and thousands of them suffer greatly, or are slain, and that, although they have not offended against their lord, but, on the contrary, have always obeyed him. Now tell me, whether the king did any injustice in sending them to war. Take a third illustration. A king entrusted his son to a pandit, to be instructed. The pandit was very learned and expert; and the prince, on his part, was of a good disposition, laborious, and heedful of his teacher's directions. The teacher initiated him in every branch of learning. When the prince became a thorough scholar, the pandit took him to the king, whom he addressed as follows: "Sire, I have taught your son all things but one. That one thing is most necessary, in my opinion; but I cannot teach it to him, till I have your promise of pardon." "Why do you speak thus?" replied the king. "In securing your services, I count myself most fortunate; and I made over my son to you; and I am sure, that whatever you propose to do must be for his good." "Very well," said the pandit: "let a horse be saddled." When the horse was brought, the pandit mounted, and called out to the prince. The prince drew near; upon which the pandit laid his whip over him smartly, and spurred on his horse, telling the prince to run along with him. The king, seeing this, was at his wits' ends, hastened after the pandit, and begged him to tell what it all meant. The pandit reined in his horse, and thus made answer: "Pardon me, Sire, for what I have done. I wish only good to your son; and, in my opinion, it was most necessary to teach him the one thing I have now taught him. For he is a prince; and he was altogether ignorant of the pain of being beaten and of violent exertion. He knew it only by name, as he had never tasted it. On coming to the throne, how could he have realized the sufferings of others; and, if any one offended, how, when awarding punishment to him, could the thought have presented itself to his mind, of leaning to tenderness and to mercy? These attributes are, however, necessary to a good king; and what I have done was done with a view that he might not be without them." Now, observe, that the prince had done no wrong in his relations with the pandit; and yet no one would charge the pandit with doing injustice in occasioning him pain. And, if a foolish man, ignorant of the pandit's motive, on seeing this strange scene from a distance, had said to himself, that either the prince must have been guilty of some grave fault, or else the pandit was most unjust, what rashness and want of consideration would such an inference have manifested! But do not understand me to mean, that the actions of the king and of the teacher, in these illustrations, afford exact parallels to the ways of God; or that the subjects, whose misery was caused by their king, and the situation of the prince, are altogether like the condition of infants and beasts; or that the fruit of the misery of them all is of the same character. I pray you not thus to misapprehend me: for it often happens, in controversy, that, from not seizing the drift of one's opponent, one takes words that fall from him, otherwise than as he intended them, and then blames him for opinions which he does not entertain. Do not deal by me in this way. Understand, that my design, in adducing these illustrations, is simply to refute the notion of its being an established fact, that, when misery befals any one, it must be referred to his offences against the author of his suffering, and admits of no other explanation. I have only wished to show the baselessness of this your maxim. The inference of a former state of existence, in the case of children, from observing, that they experience suffering, can have no ground but that maxim; and, if the maxim is shown to be false, the inference built upon it is so likewise. As for the illustrations of the king and pandit, perhaps you will allege, that they do not go to disprove your maxim, that suffering presupposes sin: inasmuch as, according to your system, the persons who, though they had not offended against the king and the pandit, suffered pain from them, received therein the retribution of sins done in a former birth; and so their offences are made out to have been the cause of their pain, and your maxim stands intact. I have to reply, that you have not exactly taken in the intent of my illustrations. If the persons in question had sinned in a former birth, they must have been offenders in the sight of God. What I meant was, that they had not offended against the king and the pandit; and yet the king and the pandit, though bringing suffering on them, cannot be called unjust. If there could be no proper reason, other than offences against the causers of suffering, for causing suffering to others, the king and the pandit were certainly unjust. When any one, without due cause, brings about the death of another, even then, suitably to your view, he who dies reaps, in his death, the fruit of the sins of a foregone birth: and is the person who took his life, on that account guiltless? In conclusion, my illustrations certainly prove, that there may be an adequate cause, other than offences against him who inflicts suffering, to which suffering may be referred; and, by consequence, your maxim is baseless.

As concerns the fearful punishment which every evil-doer must suffer in the world to come, that maxim is, indeed, correct; but there is no satisfactory and convincing proof of it with reference to the frivolous distresses we suffer in this transitory life. Be assured, also, that the sufferings of infants and beasts, though to the onlooker they seem terrible, are very trivial in comparison with those of a person of full consciousness: for we know, with certainty, that, the less the consciousness, the less the pain. In fact, very likely a father and mother, when they see their infant in pain, suffer more than the infant itself. As for its pain, though we may see no fruit coming from it now, still you may be sure, that God sent it for some most good and salutary end; such an end, that, when it becomes known to us, we shall confess, that the misery from the pain is of no account whatever, as weighed against the consequent benefit.

Again, we learn, from the true Word of God, that the chief and primary cause of the entrance of pain into this world was sin; and that all misery has immediate or mediate connexion with man's bad deeds, or with his evil nature, which is the seed of ill-doing. Nevertheless, I affirm, that, so deep and so far transcending understanding are the ways of Almighty God, and in such a manner does He, in His inscrutable wisdom, educe various results from every single thing He does, that, assuredly, we cannot say, when a soul receives pain in this world, that such pain can have no just cause but in the sin that soul has committed. Many and many a just cause may it have, of which our feeble understanding can know nothing. How hasty is it, therefore, for us, when we contemplate the sufferings of beasts, or of children, or of any other creature, to make up our minds, forthwith, that they had a former birth, and that they were then guilty of sin. To establish such strange doctrines, satisfactory and convincing evidence is necessary. It is manifest, that metempsychosis is most improbable. Hindus, because they have constantly heard of it from their childhood, look upon it as not improbable. Still, in reality, it is exceedingly improbable; and it does not deserve instant credit, that we have been in existence, times innumerable, and from duration without beginning, as gods, men, elephants, horses, dogs, cats, monkeys, mice, scorpions, and centipedes. What scenes we must have passed through, of which we have not, now, even the faintest remembrance! If it be replied, that, as we who are grown up have forgot many circumstances of our childhood and adolescence, so we have forgot the circumstances of our former births, I would ask, whether, in those so many births, we were always like children. Moreover, though we forget many things that passed in our adolescence, there are thousands of other things, belonging to that stage of life, which remain in our memories all our lives long. Should it be replied, that, not altogether inconceivably, at the time of each new birth, we must forget the transactions of the former birth, I assent. But there are many things that are not altogether impossible, which, yet, we are unable at once to believe. Is it wholly impossible, that wings should sprout out of an elephant, and that he should soar up into the clouds? At the same time, if any one should come and tell us, that he had seen such a thing, we should scarcely credit him off hand. Only on his producing the most indubitable evidence of the truth of what he was asserting, should we believe him; not otherwise. For, in proportion as a thing is extraordinary, we require strong proof of it. And, inasmuch as metempsychosis is in the highest degree improbable, and is supported by no satisfactory and convincing evidence, I cannot accept it; your maxim, that suffering presupposes sin, and cannot else be accounted for, being altogether impotent. In my foregoing illustrations I have shown, that suffering may have other just causes. Consider, too, that the king and the pandit, in those illustrations, are infinitely surpassed, by the Deity, in amplitude and profundity of counsel. Where there is one reason to justify an act of a king, who can say how many there may not be to justify any one act of God? Can you, indeed, find out the whole mind of God, and say, with assurance, in respect of any particular, that such or such is the cause of it, and that it can have no other cause? Countless are the things in this world, of which we cannot in the least discover the purpose: and will you therefore conclude, that they exist without a purpose? Who can tell the bounds of God's wide and complicated universe? And, as for the innumerable things which constitute it, who can point out the hidden cause of each, or its result, or its countless relations to other things? God, keeping in view all this, created the whole, and controls it. Of this whole we see but a very small portion of a part; and yet, when anything in it seems otherwise than suits us, we begin to raise objections to it. But God, who beholds all, and who knows how everything in it relates to everything else, and the result of each thing, and what consequences will finally flow from all things taken collectively, knows, that whatever He has made is in every wise good, and is assigned to its proper place.

When a cultivator casts his precious seed into the dust, and presses it down, if a foolish man were to ask him why he was destroying it, would he not smile, and tell him to wait a little, and he would see, that the seed had not been destroyed, but would turn to great profit? Be advised, that, in like manner, God has made this world for some most excellent end. At present, we are unable to perceive what it is; and some things seem to us to be reversed, and others to be useless, and even wrong. The laws by which God governs the world, and His reasons for them, are so deep, that not only we, but even the angels, stand confounded before them. The foundations of His counsel have been laid time that had no beginning; and its pinnacle, so to speak, pierces the remotest futurity. Know, however, of a surety, that all things will conspire to a final result, such as shall make manifest His supereminent glory and His supremely love-worthy attributes.

But the pandits do not take these things into their consideration. All the actions and plans of God they treat as if they were those of a man. They cannot realize, that the counsels and the ways of God are far beyond our understanding,—so far beyond it, that, search as we may, we can never find them out. Nor can they believe, that there are, in God's world, things past computation, of which we know not the causes, and of which there are, nevertheless, numerous and just causes, known to God. And hence they would settle everything by their own poor judgment; and hence they arbitrarily postulate maxims and dogmas. In this lies the root of all their errors. Be persuaded, I entreat you, to quit this most faulty method. If you learn the right method, you shall never go astray. When you have to reason on any matter pertaining to God, first of all consider what things are within the scope of our understanding; and reason on them alone. As for what transcends our understanding, to be silent regarding it is a token of wisdom. Who knows but God has kept back from us the causes of many things in His creation, expressly with a view to teach us humility, and to discipline our faith in Him? Indeed, a chief mark of piety is this: that, though many things relating to God seem to us not only to have no obvious causes, but even—such is our short sight—to be improper, we should yet bow our heads, and confess, with unwavering faith, that they are all most excellent and right. In so doing, our humility and the firmness of our faith are put to the test. When a given thing is referred to God, we must first ascertain, whether it be correctly so referred: if correctly, of course our humble belief in it is justified. Such belief is not, however, binding upon us with regard to what is written of God in your Vedas and Puráṇas; for it is not proved, that what is there said of God belongs to Him. On the contrary, thousands of proofs render it most indubitable, that those books were the invention of men. Whatever things we see before us in God's creation—the sufferings of children, for instance,—are from God, without doubt; and these, as I have said, we are to believe, with humility, to be most excellent and right.

The Naiyáyika dogma of the existence of the soul from eternity appears, further, as a great error, in that it detracts from the real relation in which the soul stands to God, and from the consequent duties which it owes to God. If I believe, that God created both my soul and body, and that my continuance in life, and whatever I have, are from Him, I must regard Him as having complete authority over me; and it is seen to be my duty to love and to honour Him with all my soul and strength, and to remain entirely His. But, if a man believes that his soul is self-existent, and that whatever he receives from God is the fruit of his own works, he must consider God's authority over his soul to be very partial; and, as a result, the duty of his soul to love and to honour God must likewise be partial.

CHAPTER 3.

Examination of the Cause, laid down in the Nyáya, Vais'eshika, and the other Systems, of the Wretchedness of the Soul, that is, its Bondage, and the Means of escaping therefrom; a Succinct Description of the True Nature of Virtue and Vice; and a Criticism of the Views of the Systematists touching Virtue and Vice, their Consequences, &c.

Now, other things with which we ought to acquaint ourselves are, the wretchedness of the soul, the cause of this wretchedness, and the means of getting rid of it. On these topics there are very many errors in what we find in the Nyáya, Vais'eshika, and others among the Systems. All the Systematists concede, that all men are wretched; their wretchedness consisting in metempsychosis and the resultant suffering. It is not this, in my belief, that constitutes man's wretchedness: and yet his real wretchedness is far more terrible than any of that nature. But this point I will not pursue. Let me ask the Systematists, what is the cause of human wretchedness. They allege, that it is misapprehension, —the identifying oneself with one's body and so forth. And, if I wish to know what harm, in their opinion, comes of this, they tell me, that the identifying the body with the soul originates desire and aversion, from which spring good and evil works, whence arise merit and demerit, to reap the fruits of which follow repeated births, Elysium, Hell, happiness, and misery: and that such is human wretchedness. All this wretchedness they think the soul can escape from, and then be liberated, on its coming to know itself to be diverse from the body, &c. A full account of this has been given in the second chapter of the first section. All the dogmas of the Systematists on this topic contain grave errors; and I shall consider those dogmas, one by one, in the present chapter. The matter before us, I implore the reader to remember, is most concerning. It is to the salvation of our priceless souls that it relates; and it should be pondered with freedom from partiality, and with patience and fixedness of attention.

There must be very few who regard the body and soul as altogether one. In general, men know and believe, that the soul, which is intelligent, and the body, which is unintelligent, are of different substances. All men, however, you declare, in saying "I am dark," or "I am fair," evidence, that they labour under misapprehension. I reply, that such locutions do not betoken misapprehension. For, though the soul and the body are different as to substance, yet God has established so close a connexion between them, that, as it were, the two make up one, and we call both together man. When, therefore, a man says "I," he does not mean his soul only; nor does he mean his body only; but the two. He may predicate of himself things which pertain solely to the body, as when he says "I am dark, or fair;" and so of things which belong only to the soul, as when he says "I am conscious, or ignorant:" but this does not prove him unaware, that his soul is distinct from his body. It is true, that a man sometimes seems to identify his wealth, or the like, with himself, and, when he loses his property, says, "I am lost."* But does any one really believe, that a man who so expresses himself actually regards his property as one with his soul?† And

---

* The sense of the original has here been preserved at the cost of compromising idiom.

† It is singular, that the pandits adduce locutions similar to those in the

again, since, of the body and soul, the soul is chief and the more excellent, a man sometimes speaks as though he were soul only, as when he says "my body," or "I shall leave the body." Baseless, therefore, is the opinion of those who maintain, on the ground of such phrases as "I am black," and "I am fair," that men labour under great misapprehension,—a misapprehension which gives rise to all their wretchedness.

Again ; though some men may be so ignorant as to identify the soul and body, still, they are not enabled, by being taught their separateness, to escape from good and bad works. The pandits, however, may argue,* that a conviction of their separateness is necessarily operative of such escape. "For, when a man knows, that his soul is separate from his body, he must also believe, that the soul will not perish with the body, but will continue to exist after death, and will receive the requital of its good or evil works. And, when he reflects, that, in order to receive such requital, he must fall into Hell, or go to Elysium ; and that even the happiness of Elysium is alloyed by various kinds of misery ; and that, after all, when his desert is exhausted, the very happiness which was enjoyed becomes a source of misery ; and that successive births and deaths must follow, and various sorts of happiness and misery be experienced ; how great is the wretchedness ! And, when, from heed to the numerous admonitions of the scriptures, the vanity of all the happiness of this world and of the next becomes

---

text, to prove the direct opposite. When, they allege, a man whose son is prosperous says "I am prosperous," it is proved, that the man, through ignorance, regards himself as strictly and in fact identical with his son. See the *Vedánta-sára*, p. 14 ; and the extract from S'ankara A'chárya at pp. 13, 14.

* This argument has not been met with ; nor does the author suppose, that a pandit would be likely to employ it. It has been brought forward, and answered, to meet possible contingencies. The Hindu theory is, that the intuition of the soul's separateness from the body and so forth, has the effect of extirpating desire and aversion, and so of conducing to emancipation. See pp. 25 seqq.

clear to him, he will assuredly grow averse from both virtue and vice, and will estrange himself equally from good works and from evil." I reply, that the expectation of his doing so is vain. As I have said already, the generality of men know, that the soul is distinct from the body. Interrogate even a very ignorant man, and he will tell you, that he looks to receiving, after death, the fruit of his deeds. But does this prospect keep him from good and evil works? Perhaps you will say, that the ignorant are, indeed, informed about this matter, but do not seriously reflect upon it; and hence they do not rid themselves of desire and aversion. If, nevertheless, they received instruction, and meditated on the subject, why would they not so rid themselves? To this I have to say, that it becomes evident, if we thoroughly study the condition of human nature, that no labour such as you have spoken of is enough to root out desire and aversion altogether. And here I must observe, that, to count both good works and evil works a cause of bondage is, to my mind, wholly wrong. A little further on I shall expose the error of the pandits on this point. As for evil works, they are really a cause of bondage. Most necessary is it to avoid them; and even the consideration of the future punishment which they entail ought to induce men to avoid them. But, alas! so corrupt is the nature of man, that, let him reflect however much, yet he cannot, on that account, abandon bad works entirely. Your solicitude to shun good works is quite superfluous; for, so corrupt is the nature of man, that, let his works be ever so good, still there cleaves to them much of evil and imperfection; and he is incapable of a single good work wrought with purity of body, speech, and heart. For good works a man may receive praise from his fellow-men; but, in the sight of God, who knows everything without and within, these very works are tainted with evil. Know, then, that miserable man of himself forbears good works: there is no need of pointing out the way to avoid them. But to escape from evil works is impossible by any human device. Suppose that one avoids practical theft, murder, adultery, contention, injustice, and so forth: yet is this the avoidance of all evil works? Not at all. The whole duty of man consists in two things: to love God with all his heart, soul, and strength; and to love his fellow-men as he loves himself. To do contrariwise, or to do less, is sin. He who does his whole duty must never offend in either of the two things I have specified. And who can thus never offend? Most men are unaware of their secret faults, which lie hidden from them; and, on the ground of certain visible good works, they hug themselves on their goodness. But, if a man habitually explores, with the lamp of discrimination, that gloomy crypt, the dark dungeon of his heart, and looks into all the corners, and weighs all his thoughts, words, and deeds, he perceives, all too plainly, that he is a vile, fallen, weak, and helpless sinner. Countless are the instances of secret pride, hypocrisy, deceit, selfishness, and other blemishes, not to be described, that he will discover in himself; and the conviction will be forced upon him, that he does not love God as he ought. Such is the state of man. And be assured, that no man will be saved by right apprehension, or by works, but only by the free grace of God, the means of obtaining which are indicated in the real Word of God.

Again, you yourselves acknowledge, that even he who has attained to fulness of right apprehension,—whom you call saved-in-life,—goes on, so long as he is in the body, doing good and bad works: for you hold, that the accumulated works of the rightly apprehensive man are destroyed, and that his current works are inoperative. By this it is proved, that he does works which, but for his right apprehension, would have produced merit and demerit,—that is to say, good works and bad. How, then, is it established, that misapprehension is the cause of all works? And what turns out to be the difference between a man of right apprehension and one of wrong apprehension? You may allege, that there is this great difference, that the good and evil works of the misapprehensive man serve to fetter him, and that the rightly apprehensive man cannot be fettered by his works. The fallacy of this I shall lay bare in due course.

Another, and a greater, error on this point, into which the Systematists fall, is, in saying that virtue itself enthrals the soul. Vice does so, to be sure; but how can virtue? The fact is, that the Systematists do not understand aright the nature of virtue and that of vice; and on this account they go astray so variously. This being the case, I shall first briefly set forth the true nature of virtue and that of vice, and then treat of the errors just adverted to.

God created man a moral creature; capable of knowing God, and his own relations to God and the world; and capable of honouring and of loving God, his Creator and Lord, and of discharging his duties towards his fellow-creatures. And this capacity also he possesses, of knowing, that to do these things is right, and that to do the reverse is wrong. By a moral creature I mean one who answers this description. And now understand, that, man being a moral creature, certain things, in respect of his rank and nature, are, of themselves, binding on him; such as devotion, justice, truth, compassion, and the like: while other things are, of themselves, wrong for him; such as atheism, injury to others, uncompassion, falsehood, and so forth. The former are virtue, and the latter are vice. Now, God, in His essential character, is good and just. Consequently, any action proper for man is, in itself, pleasing to Him; and any that is improper is displeasing to Him: and, inasmuch as He is just by nature, He must show favour to the virtuous, and award punishment to the wicked.

Three points are to be kept in view. First: God has not established, without cause and at hap-hazard, the distinction between virtue and vice; but He has fixed that to be virtue, which is binding on men with respect to their nature and rank, and that to be vice, which is wrong for them. Hence, in no circumstances is it right for man to commit sin; and in no circumstances is it wrong, or unnecessary, for him to do what is right. Secondly: God's favour to the virtuous, and His punishment of the wicked, are not because He receives aught of benefit from our virtue, or aught of injury from our sin. His requital of us is solely because of the justice of His nature. For it is of the essence of justice to reward the virtuous for their rectitude, and to inflict pain on the vicious for their wickedness. If God did not do thus, He would not be just; and imperfection would attach to His superlatively excellent and perfect nature. Thirdly: It is not the case, that the good and bad consequences which follow virtue and vice spring spontaneously from works. God has appointed those consequences.

Such are vice and virtue, and their consequences. But the understanding of man, when it became blind to the justice, holiness, and other attributes of God, got confused as to virtue and vice, and took to inventing a variety of perverse doctrines about them. Such has been, not exceptionally, the history of the Systematists. Of the grounds of the laws of virtue and vice, on which I have touched, they know nothing. Otherwise, they would not speak of both virtue and vice as causes of bondage; nor would they pronounce, that he who wishes for emancipation should be alike free from the one and from the other.

The reason why the Systematists hold virtue to be a cause of bondage is this. Good works, they say, hinder the soul of emancipation: for emancipation consists in the soul's independence of the body, mind, apprehension, will, &c.; but good works, in order to reap the fruits appertaining to them, compel the soul, until this end is accomplished, to wear the form of a god, or of a man, or such-like. Moreover, happiness, the fruit of good works, is beneath the ambition of a wise man; it being implicated, in two ways, with misery. In the first place, it is fugacious: since whatever has a beginning must have an end; and the fruit of virtue, like other things that have not always existed, must pass away. When a man obtains happiness, he is happy; but, when the happiness comes to a period, there supervenes misery: and so happiness itself amounts to misery. In the second place, there is inequality in the fruit of virtue; that is to say, he whose virtue is inconsiderable is meagrely rewarded, while he whose virtue is more abundant receives a larger recompense. The former must repine at seeing the latter; and thus his very happiness makes him wretched. In this way all happiness whatsoever partakes of the character of misery; and hence, to be freed from both, and to become insensible, is the most transcendent aspiration of humanity.

But how erroneous is all this! God, I have shown, has appointed those things to be good works, which, in respect of the nature of man, are incumbent on him, and, for forbearing to do which, man, in the eye of justice, deserves punishment. Can, then, the fruit of those works which are incumbent on man, ever be evil? In your opinion, since the wish for the fruit of good works, happiness, misbeseems a man of prudence, that fruit is an evil. Again, since you maintain, that the true well-being of the soul consists in its parting with apprehension and will, and in becoming insensible, you ought rather to consider this state to be the fruit of virtue. Herein you have exactly inverted things. What! has God enacted the law of virtue and vice after the manner of a net, with no reason but to entangle souls in it, like so many birds, and to divert Himself withal? Has He fixed at random, that some works are bad, and that others are good, so that souls may sometimes be entrapped in one snare, and sometimes in the other? But, if God, simply because of His just and excellent nature, has established those works to be virtuous, which, in respect of the nature of the soul, are incumbent on it, will not He— a sea of mercy and goodness, and Who, as the Father of all, desires the welfare of all, nay, Who devises a way and a means for the welfare of even such as do what is amiss,—give to such as do what is right, that which will constitute their true well-being? Instead of well-being, will He, indeed, decree to such a soul a recompense to its harm? The fact is, however, that the attainment of a state of insensibility is not true emancipation; and they who, by God's mercy, arrive at true emancipation, will suffer no injury in their faculties, as those of apprehension and will. This I shall show further on.

Again, you mistake in arguing, that the fruit of virtue, happiness, is perishable. I have already made out your maxim to be utterly baseless,—that all products must, as such, come to an end. Further, if perishable happiness is of the nature of misery, it cannot be the fruit of virtue; for, since that which it is obligatory on man to do is virtue, will God requite with misery him who does what is obligatory? You think, too, that virtue is a thing which is to be done for only a limited time, after which, it being discontinued, the reward follows. Hence your fear, that the reward also will, after a time, be discontinued. As I have said, however, virtue is a thing which it is perpetually incumbent on man to do, whether he be in this world, or in another. As long as he has being, so long should he go on practising virtue. While he continues in virtue, its beneficent requital will ever remain with him; but, when he falls away from virtue, its reward terminates. But the misery which then ensues is not the consequence of virtue, but of vice; for even desistance from virtue is vice. Who, one may here ask, is equal to such unintermitted virtue? Grant, that endless happiness is the reward of such virtue as you speak of: still, what shall we profit by hoping for it? It is true, I reply, that we men have all become so corrupt in our nature, that we are incapable of practising virtue; and, therefore, if we hope to compass the loftiest aim of man on the strength of our virtue, we shall be benefited nothing. But God, in compassion for us sinners, has revealed His Word, and has thereby marked out a way, by following which, all our sins will be pardoned, and that reward, by His mercy, will be bestowed upon us, which would have attached to virtue, had virtue been practicable to us. Then will our fallen nature be purged and purified; the ability to practise virtue will be vouchsafed to us; and we shall abide near to God, and dwell in the realms of glory, and enjoy everlasting beatitude.

The second objection which you oppose to the fruit of virtue is, that it implies inequality; some being rewarded more, and others, less: and this also is a ground of misery. My answer is, that this inequality is no real ground of misery. The misery which proceeds from envy has its real root in man's corrupt nature. Envy is a blemish in human nature. It is not found in a pure nature; it is found in a fallen nature. Of him whose nature is fallen the virtue is not really virtue; and, accordingly, he cannot obtain the fruit of virtue. How evident is it, from this, that the Systematists were not acquainted with the true character of virtue and that of vice! Little did they know of the nature which virtue requires. How can he whose nature is corrupt do works that are right? Outwardly, he may imitate them; but still he retains his corrupt nature, which renders genuine virtue impossible to him. Works only externally good are not the whole of virtue. That, in the sight of God, is virtue, which comes from a pure heart. I will exemplify what I mean. It is proper for a man to show friendship to a friend. But, if a simulator, merely from sense of shame, is outwardly courteous to his friends, but inwardly bears them malice, can he, in the sight of God, be a doer of proper works? Know, then, that they alone whose nature is pure are capable of virtue, and that only such as they will receive the reward of virtue. Others, they may see, are, for greater virtue than their own, rewarded more largely: but they will not, on that account, feel envy. On the contrary, it belongs to a pure nature to take pleasure in the increase of the happiness of others. And thus, that which is a source of misery to an evil nature is, to a pure nature, rather a source of joy.

From their ignorance of the true character of virtue, and that of vice, the pandits err, again, in maintaining, that, on the acquisition of right apprehension, all previous sins are effaced, and that current works become inoperative, or, in other words, that nothing piacular inheres in the bad actions which the rightly apprehensive man is constantly committing. This is altogether untenable. For what connexion is there between the conviction, that I am not my body, and the effacement of sin? To sin is to do that which, in all circumstances and conditions, is improper for man; and hence, by so doing, man becomes, before God, guilty and deserving of punishment. Is all this set aside by my knowing that I am not body? Moreover, if accumulated and current works are obliterated, why not fructescent works as well? The issue of the whole matter is, that it is vain to hope for salvation on the score of knowing the body to be not identical with the soul; for this knowledge cannot avail to save a man from evil works, or from their penalty.

From this it is clear, that the Hindu, in his ignorance of the nature of virtue and that of vice, supposes their laws to be baseless and fortuitous. He seems to have little notion of the moral goodness or badness of works, and to regard them as producing their effects physically, or mechanically. It plainly appears, from what the pandits have written on this subject, that, in their opinion, pretty much as food possesses an inherent property of appeasing hunger, and as poison possesses an inherent property of causing death, so some works have an innate virtue to ensure celestial happiness, while others have the efficacy of consigning to Hell. Whatever produces happiness is virtue; and whatever produces misery is vice. A foolish man, therefore, who desires the happiness of Elysium, &c., will aim to practise virtue. But he who, weary alike of the happiness and of the misery of an existence of vicissitude, gives up both, and yearns after emancipation, will assuredly free himself from such a plague. He cannot, however, rid himself of it readily. For, if, so long as he is in a state of misapprehension, in order to escape from the bondage of virtue, he resolves to give up good works, in so doing he transgresses. Hence he must acquire right apprehension, which is the only panacea against virtue.

Similarly, with regard to vice, the pandits think, that, as some substances, poison, for instance, possess an innate virtue of injuring, which, yet, under certain conditions, is neutralized, so, though bad works have an intrinsic property of entailing evil,—as the torments of Hell,—yet, in the case of the rightly apprehensive man, that property is rendered inefficacious. It is his right knowledge which serves to counteract it. And, therefore, the sin of such a man does not affect him.*

But, more especially, the fact of the pandits' maintaining, that good and bad works produce their effects, happiness and misery, in a physical manner, becomes plainly manifest from their invention of requitative efficacy as an objective entity. Their reason for believing in what they style requitative efficacy† is this. "Good works," they say, "are the cause of elysian happiness, and bad works are the cause of infernal dolor. And how can this be so? For, if a man does a good act to-day, he does not, therefore, at once go to Elysium,

---

* If the Hindus had a correct conception of the moral goodness and badness of actions, they would not be found to argue, that Krishṇa and other members of the pantheon were not defiled by their deeds of wickedness, simply on the ground that those gods were endowed with great power, and were secured from the evil consequences of what they did. On moral grounds, the very commission of such wickedness is defilement.

† In Sanskrit, *apûrva*.

but after the lapse of perhaps a long period, when he dies. How, then,—a cause being that which immediately precedes an effect,—is that good work the cause of his going to Elysium?" Involved in this grave embarrassment, the pandits, with a view to liberate themselves from it, allege, that there is produced, in the soul, by good or by bad works, the quality denominated requitative efficacy; and it is this which consigns the soul to Elysium, or to Hell. It is, then, through the medium of requitative efficacy that good and bad works lead, respectively, to Elysium and to Hell. This requitative efficacy is what they mean by merit or demerit. But what, I would ask, is the necessity of this embarrassment? Good and bad works are not immediately originative of desirable and undesirable consequences, but mediately. And how are they so mediately? As I have said before, God, who is just, in consideration of the virtue and vice of men, Himself appoints corresponding reward for them. Since, therefore, this reward depends on the will of God, when it seems proper to Him, He bestows it,—at once, it may be, or bye and bye. And so there is no need of the invention of requitative efficacy. One man serves another, and is daily entitled to wages; and yet his master pays him at a time which he himself determines; monthly, or half-yearly, or annually. But, possibly, some one may say,* that, as the hireling, from serving his master, becomes entitled daily to his wages, just so man, from doing good works, or evil, becomes an heir of Elysium, or of Hell; and his having such a heritage is, for him, requitative efficacy. If, I reply, the pandits had said only thus much, there would have been no harm. But they lay down requitative efficacy as being a real and distinct entity. For example, the Naiyáyikas and the Vais'eshikas reckon it among the qualities of the soul,—apprehension, will, happiness, misery, and the rest:

---

* Not that any pandit would hold such language; but a foreigner might, if bent on rationalizing Hinduism.

and I affirm, that such a thing cannot be proved to exist. Furthermore, I would say to the pandits, that, if you believe in requitative efficacy as a distinct thing generated by good and evil works, you ought to believe it to be generated by service, in the instance of one man who works for another; for the same objection presents itself in both cases alike. In fact, you ought to believe in a similar efficacy in countless other instances besides that of service; and then, instead of twenty-four qualities, you would have qualities innumerable.

The error which I have here charged on the pandits, though it is not perfectly manifest in the Naiyáyika and some other Systems, is yet very clear in the Sánkhya and Mímánsá; these not believing in God, and yet affirming, that good and bad works, through requitative efficacy, lead to Elysium and to Hell. In their opinion, from casting an offering into the fire, with utterance of the formula "To Indra; may it speed," requitative efficacy is engendered, the which, of its own motion, fructifies in elysian bliss and so forth. What need, then, of God? How strange is all this!

On the point at present in discussion, the Sánkhyas and Mímánsakas labour under miserable misconception; and the rest of the Systematists, also, are more or less in the wrong. For, at the beginning of this book, where I have spoken of the doctrines held in common by the Systems, it will have been seen, that, though the Systematists dissent among themselves on some few matters, yet, on almost every capital question they are alike as to method of consideration and as to reach and bias of intellect. They have all of them tenements of the same sort of foundation, and fabric, and model, however different in outer aspect. One of them may carry a certain error to greater extremes than the rest; but in these as well inheres that error, in embryo.

CHAPTER 4.

Examination of the Views concerning the State of Emancipation, professed, in common, by the Naiyáyikas and by the Vais'eshikas.

I have thus given an account of the Naiyáyika and Vais'eshika theories as regards God, the soul, the soul's wretchedness, the cause of that wretchedness, the way of escape from it, and virtue and vice. The treatment of a single topic more will bring this second section to an end. And that topic is, the miserable condition to which the Naiyáyikas and Vais'eshikas give the name of emancipation; their views on this article growing out of their lamentable conceptions touching God, &c. Is to lose the faculties of apprehension, will, and all manifestations of sensibility, and to become like a stone, the loftiest aim of the soul? In what, I would ask, does this state differ from annihilation? In reply to two objections of the pandits, the one real, and the other presumed:—that, if the fruition of happiness be allowed to belong to the state of emancipation, and, if that happiness varies in degree to different recipients, some among the emancipated must be envious of others less favoured than themselves; and that, if cognition, will, and other such faculties survive in emancipation, the emancipated might admit evil desires, and hence incur danger of falling into sin; I maintain, that they who know not the power of God, and the greatness of His grace, may have such fears. But we, for our parts, who possess the true Word of God, learn, from it, that such as accept the terms of salvation which God has offered, and become participators in His grace, will be translated, after death, to the abodes of bliss, and that God will so purify their nature, that they shall never more be affected with evil desires, envy, enmity, pride, and such like. To them will be given, in Heaven, celestial and indefectible bodies; and they will retain all the mental characteristics of conscious beings, and will be for ever blest with the beatific vision, and with the highest joy, ineffable and divine, in being near to Him, and in paying Him adoration, and,—their nature being made pure,—with serenity of soul, and with peace;—their happiness always increasing, and subject to no intermission. And tell me, pray, which state deserves rather to be called the highest aim of man; this, or one of total unconsciousness? This latter is, indeed, not the highest aim of man, but, contrariwise, the lowest of degradations. You say, that souls have existed from all duration, and have, in the meantime, passed through births and deaths unnumbered, suffering incessantly the miseries of an existence of vicissitude. Now and then one has grown wise, and has aspired to escape from its wretchedness, and, to this end, has practised, during several births, austerities, contemplation, and similar observances. And what reward has it received at last, except the becoming insensible, like a stone,—a state equivalent to annihilation? Of nothing, then, is the destiny so cruel as is that of the soul. So long as, dating from past eternity, it remains conscious, it is subject to wretchedness; and it can hope for no exemption from this wretchedness, other than annihilation. If we were atheists, not believing in God, and if our deliverance from misery depended on our own efforts, to look for emancipation such as yours might be fitting. But, as we believe in a God, inscrutable in power, replete with all goodness, most bountiful, all-merciful, and the Giver of every felicity; and as we hope for emancipation at His hands; it seems to us reasonable to expect an emancipation better than the miserable state to which you give that name. Two ways of attaining the chief aim of the soul are found in the true Word of God; by human actions, and by the grace of the Lord. According to the first, on a man's doing that which it is binding on him to do, the reward of his works is bestowed upon him by God. A soul that should always thus do would be rewarded with constant happiness; and to enjoy such happiness is the highest aim of man. But, again, it is written, in the Word of God, that it surpasses our strength to follow this way; for we have all become corrupt, through sin, and our works are unworthy of God's acceptance. Our well-being is, therefore, wholly dependent upon the grace of God. By our works we can merit only Hell; but, since God is merciful, He desires to save us by His free grace. In order that we may secure this grace, He has contrived a wondrous plan, giving proof of His illimitable and ineffable compassionateness, and altogether in harmony with His justice and holiness. And, since He has opened, on our behalf, the treasury of His boundless mercies, will He make our highest happiness to consist in being conformed to the condition of a stone? Endless happiness, whether compassed by works, or by God's grace, alone deserves to receive the name of the highest aim of man. Why, then, will you have it to consist in unconsciousness? The truth is, that this matter cannot be understood save with the help of the illumination derivable from God's own Word; and he who rests solely on his own intelligence, in reasoning about it, may well end in some such doctrine as that of the Systematists; namely, that to be emancipated is to become unconscious. The speculators just mentioned proceed somewhat as though they thought they were to be saved by a scheme and by labour of their own: and whence can they, unfortunates, hope to obtain everlasting happiness? Hence it is, that, in their estimation, they will secure everything that is to be secured, if only, bereft of all consciousness, they get quit of the distress which infests an existence of vicissitude. But know, ye Hindus, that to achieve even thus much is impossible for you. God made the soul cognitive; and who shall make it incognitive? The nature with which God endowed the soul cannot be annulled by reflecting, that "I am not mind, I am not body." Be assured, that our souls will forever continue conscious. Two things are, however, placed before us, between which to make our election. God, in His Word, points out the way of salvation. If we accept it, we shall make our consciousness the instrument of eternal joy. If, on the other hand, we reject it, we shall make our consciousness the instrument of eternal affliction and torment. As, therefore, you seek for well-being, accept the genuine Word of God.

My motive in exposing the faults of the Systems has not at all been, to convict their authors of error, for the purpose of holding them up to ridicule. My aim has been, to show, that whoever—whether they, or I, or any one else—undertakes to argue, in reliance on unaided reason, about divine and spiritual things, must constantly fall into error; the mind of man being impotent to understand them rightly. When you are convinced, that they are correctly described in the Christian religion, you will know, that this is the true religion of God. Accordingly, it is my wish, that you should study the Christian Scriptures, and with candour. To this study fixed attention, docility, and patient thought are indispensable; for, when a man has, during a long space of time, entertained any particular set of opinions, he is slow to perceive their faults, and to recognize the excellence of what conflicts with them. But, if you conduct this investigation with humble prayer to God, you shall attain to a knowledge of the truth.

SECTION III.

CHAPTER I.

Description of the Three Sorts of Existence held in the Vedánta: the Key to a Right Understanding of that Scheme of Philosophy.

HAVING briefly considered five out of the six great Hindu Systems, I shall, in this section, examine the Vedánta. And to engage in such an examination in the present day is especially important. The Hindus, it is true, refer all the Systems to Rishis; but, in our time, these systems, the Vedánta apart, have no followers, except perhaps here and there an individual. As for the Vedánta, it is held by a large majority of all Hindus.

The Vedántins argue three sorts of existence; and one must thoroughly comprehend and ponder them, in order to take in the meaning of their scheme. These they designate as true, practical, and apparent.* That which verily exists is called true, and its existence, true existence;† and this ex-

---

* त्रिविधं सत्त्वं पारमार्थिकं व्यावहारिकं प्रातिभासिकं चेति। तच पारमार्थिकं सत्त्वं ब्रह्मणः व्यावहारिकं सत्त्वमाकाशादेः प्रातिभासिकं सत्त्वं शुक्तिरजतादेः। *Vedánta-paribháshá*, p. 18. "Existence is of three sorts, true *(páramárthika)*, practical *(vyávahárika)*, and apparent *(prátibhásika)*. True existence is *that* of Brahma; practical, *that* of ether, &c.; apparent, *that* of nacrine silver and the like."

† Dr. J. R. Ballantyne takes *páramárthika* to denote "being, in its highest sense." *Christianity contrasted*, &c., p. 38.

That *páramárthika*, popularly, is everywhere used to signify "true," one may learn without any very laborious search. The adverb *paramárthatah* means "in truth," "indeed," &c. &c.

istence, according to the Vedánta, is predicable of Brahma exclusively. The second species of existence has the name of practical. The things to which it belongs do not veritably exist: only the misapprehensive, or ignorant, mistake them for existent, and by means of them transact practical life; whence the epithet. And it must be kept in mind, that, as the things just spoken of are thought to be not veritably existent, but to be imagined by ignorance, precisely so is it with the use made of them. For instance, a man in a dream drinks water, or mounts a horse: the water and the horse are visionary; and so are the drinking and the mounting. If the use to which one puts a thing is veritable, the thing also must be veritable; for, to have veritable dealings with that which is false is impossible. Can a man in his waking senses bathe in a river that he saw in his sleep? The things which, agreeably to the phraseology of the Vedántins, are practical, are the very things which all men, themselves excepted, call true: and such are I's'wara, or the maker of the world, souls, and all the world besides.* Their existence these philosophers hold to be the

---

The fact, that the Vedántins, in contradistinguishing practical and apparent existence from the first species, style them *mithyá*, or false, is a further proof, that the sense here attached to *páramárthika* is alone correct. Though the word is technical with the Vedántins, they have done no violence to its ordinary meaning.

Vijnána Bhikshu, on an occasion where he employs *páramárthikatwa*,—the abstract substantive of *páramárthika*,—in the sense of "unchangeableness and eternalness," clearly intimates, that his acceptation of the term, as a follower of the Sánkhya, is different from that of the Vedántins. See the *Sánkhya-pravachana-bháshya*, p. 25.

The torture to which Vijnána habitually—and especially in the *Sánkhya-sára*—subjects the whole compass of the Vedánta nomenclature, reminds one forcibly of the sanctimonious vocabulary of free-handlers and secularists among our contemporaries in Christian countries.

* यद्यद्वितीयं खलोऽसंसारि ब्रह्म वेदान्तप्रमाणकं तर्हि कथमव-स्थानयविशिष्टा जीवा भोक्तारोऽनुभूयन्ते भोजयिता चेश्वरः श्रूयते भोज्यं च विषयजातं पृथगुपलभ्यते । तदेतद्दैते त्रिविध्येत्याह्नु.

result of ignorance; and such existence is termed, by them, practical. The third species of existence, denominated apparent,

ब्रह्मैव जीवा जगदीश्वरेति सर्वं काल्पनिकं सम्भवतीत्यभि-
प्रेत्याऽऽह । A'nanda Giri, commenting on S'ankara A'chárya's *Mándú-kya-bháshya: Bibliotheca Indica*, Vol. VIII., pp. 326, 327. "If Brahma, secondless, and essentially unconnected with the world, be established by the Vedánta, how is it, that there are souls, subject to three conditions, *those of waking, dreaming, and insensible sleep*, and employers *of objects*; and *how is it, that* an I'swara, effecting the experience *of souls*, is revealed by scripture; and *how is it, that* the aggregate of objects subserving experience is found *as a thing* apart *from these?* If monism were true, all these would present themselves as incompatible. With reference to such an objection, it is set forth as follows, with intent to declare, that souls, the world, and I'swara can all *reasonably* be admitted as things of imagination *surmised* in Brahma."

A little further on, A'nanda Giri says : अतो ब्रह्मैवावस्थानयं
तदन्तो जीवा मायावि ब्रह्म च ब्रह्माणि परिशुद्धे परिकल्पितं सर्वमि-
त्याह । "Therefore it is enunciated, that the three conditions, and the souls subject thereto, and the illusive Brahma, *i. e.*, I'swara, are all imagined in the pure Brahma."

The reason why the Vedántins use such an expression as "silver imagined in nacre," is, of course, that the nacre is the substrate of the imaginary silver. Strictly analogous, in their view, to the nacre and silver of this illustration are Brahma and the world, &c., where they speak of the world, souls, and I'swara, as imagined, by the ignorant, in Brahma. It is to be understood, that Brahma is not the subject of the imagination, but its object.

A most eminent authority in Vedánta matters, Sarvajnátma Muni, thus instructs the learner:

तव गाढमूढतमसा रचितं जगदीशजीववपुषा सकलम् ।
प्रतिभाति तावदृढं दृढवत् समुदेति यावदवबोधरविः ॥
इति । *Sankshepa-s'áríraka*, from a MS. not at hand for reference. "All that is devised, *or fancied*, in the form of the world, of I'śa, and of souls, by the ignorance forcibly possessing thee, appears—albeit unsubstantial, *viz., barren of true existence,*—substantial, until the sun of right apprehension rises."

This couplet has been interpreted in accordance with the gloss of Madhusúdana Saraswatí, who takes *gádham* as an adverb.

I'śa, or I'swara,—the maker of the world,—and souls, since the Vedántins consider them as, no less than the world itself, ignorance-imagined and false, come under the category of things practical.

resembles the practical, in that it is false, but, by mistake, seems to be veritable. It differs, however, from the practical in three respects. First, the ignorant, that is to say, ordinary men, do not constantly, but only now and then, mistake for veritable the apparent objects to which it appertains; as nacrine silver, and the matters of a dream. Nor, secondly, is there any practical dealing with these things. Let a man who mistakes nacre for silver offer it for sale: he will not get for it the price of silver; for it will be recognized, by others, as another substance. Thirdly: it is because of ignorance, that the practical seems to be veritable; but it is by reason, additionally to ignorance, of distance and other causes, called defects, enumerated by the Naiyáyikas, &c., that the apparent seems veritable.* Such are the Vedántin's three sorts of existence, the true, the practical, and the apparent.

To obtain a just view of the Vedánta doctrine, or even to appreciate its fallacy, it is all-important to master its theory of three existences. It must be understood, that it is not because existent things are—in any way to us intelligible—of

---

* घटाद्यध्यासेऽविद्यैव दोषत्वेनापि हेतुः शुक्तिरूप्याध्यासे तु काचादयो दोषाः ।   *Vedánta-paribháshá*, p. 12. "Nescience, the cause of mistaking *Brahma* for a jar, or other *practical object*, is *to be considered as* a defect also. When, however, nacre is mistaken for silver, an ocular affection, or similar defect, *is the cause of the misapprehension.*"

It is not to be understood, that, in the case of nacrine silver, nescience is excluded as a cause. The defects specified are causes additional thereto. This appears from the two pages of the *Vedánta-paribháshá* preceding that here quoted from.

The term *dosha*, "defect" is a technicality generalizing certain causes of misapprehension.

दोषोऽप्रमाया जनकः प्रमायास्तु गुणो भवेत् ।
पित्तदूरत्वादिरूपो दोषो नानाविधः स्मृतः ॥
इति । *Bhásha-parichchheda*, 130th couplet.
"A defect is a cause of wrong notion; a virtue, of right notion. Defects are pronounced to be multifarious, as bile, *giving rise to jaundice*, distance, &c."

various kinds, that the Vedántins contend for a difference in their existence. In other words, they do not predicate a difference between the existences of things, because one is eternal and another is uneternal, or because one is self-existent and another exists dependently.* It is a difference in the very nature of existing, not in its mode, that they insist upon. Their view on this subject will now be exhibited.

To the Vedántins the establishment of monism, or non-duality, is most essential. They wish to make out the soul to be Brahma, and the world to be false; whence it would follow, that Brahma solely is true, and that nought but him exists, or ever existed, or at any time will exist. From the couplet of the *S'iva-gítá* which I shall quote in the sixth chapter, and from numberless other passages of Vedánta works, it is manifest, that, in their view, the world is false, and imagined by ignorance. Not that they only figuratively call it false,—as we sometimes call things of an evanescent and perishable character; but they mean, that it is indeed so, like nacrine silver.* As

---

* According to the Vedánta, souls, as souls, and also ignorance and I'swara, are beginningless and self-existent. Still, we find ascribed to them a different existence from that of Brahma. It is called false.

For the unoriginatedness of souls, &c., see the last quotation in p. 35. The source of the couplet there given has not been ascertained. Its statements are, however, called in question by no Vedántin. Among the various treatises which cite it is, besides the *Siddhánta-ratnamálá*, the *Krishnálankára* of Achyutakrishna Ananda Tírtha, a commentary on Appayya Díkshita's *Siddhánta-leśa*. Moreover, it is at the tongue's end of almost every student of the Vedánta.

Achyutakrishna reads, as the second quarter of the distich: तथा जीवे-श्वयोर्भिदा, "likewise, the distinction between the soul and I'śa." This lection is by much to be preferred.

Máyá, illusion, *avidyá*, nescience, and *ajnána*, ignorance,—when these two denote collectivity,—are synonymes. Nescience and ignorance, when referred to souls in several, are only fractional portions of illusion. See the *Vedánta-sára*, pp. 4, &c.

* ब्रह्मभिन्नं सर्वं मिथ्या ब्रह्मभिन्नत्वात् । यदेवं तदेव यथा शुक्तिरूप्यम् । *Vedánta-paribháshá*, p. 17. "All other than Brahma

such silver is nothing, and wholly from ignorance seems to be something, just so, they say, is the world nothing; it being imagined by ignorance, that is, it seeming, simply by reason of ignorance, to exist. To maintain otherwise would be to surrender non-duality.

Further, it is surprizing to find, that the ignorance which imagines the world is laid down as being itself ignorance-imagined, and hence false.* They refuse to grant, that even this is true; and consistently: else, non-duality would be

---

is false, because other than Brahma. Whatever is thus *different* is thus *false;* for instance, nacrine silver."

Those of the Systematists who are not Vedántins apprehend the doctrine under comment in the manner in which it is apprehended in the text.

न केवलमद्वयस्यैवाऽद्वैतवादिनो हेया अपि तु जगदसत्यता-
ग्राहकप्रमाणाभावेनाऽपीत्यत आह ।

जगत्सत्यत्वमदुष्टकारणजन्यत्वाद् बाधकाभावात् ।

निद्रादिदोषदुष्टान्तःकरणादिजन्यत्वेन स्वप्नविषयशुक्तीतिमा-
दीनामसत्यत्वं लोके दृष्टं तच् च मह़दादिप्रपञ्चे नाऽस्ति तत्का-
रणस्य प्रकृतेर्हिरण्यगर्भबुद्धेश्चाऽदुष्टत्वात् । *Sánkhya-pravachana-bhá-shya,* p. 225. "Not only on the ground of the aforesaid argument are the monists to be shunned, but, further, because there is no proof to establish the untrueness of the world. To this effect it is set forth, *in the aphorism:* 'The world is true, since its origination is from a cause that has no defect, and since there is nothing to make out *the world to be* false.' The objects of a dream, the *imagined* yellowness of a *white* conch-shell, &c., are found, among men to be untrue, by reason that they owe their origin to the internal organ, &c., infected by the defects of sleep, &c. This *untrueness* does not belong to the universe, *made up of* the great *principle* and the rest; for the causes of that *universe,* nature and the intellect of Hiraṇyagarbha, *the creator,* are free from all defect."

The aphorism cited in this extract is VI., 52.

Vijnána, in continuation, will have it, that the Vedántins wrest from their legitimate drift the passages of the Veda which they adduce to establish, that the world is false. For, he says, if those passages mean as is pretended, the result is suicidal; the Veda being itself of the world.

* See the eighth chapter of this section.

Y

impeached by the presentation of another entity than Brahma,—ignorance. Thus it is, that they would establish Brahma alone to be true, and all besides to be illusory. When, therefore, they give the epithet of true to the existence of Brahma, and that of practical to the existence of the world, we are to understand, that, in their system, that existence which is indeed real is called true, and the epithet of practical is given to false existence, or existence which in fact is not, but, owing to mistake, seems to have place.

In only applying names to real things, and to unreal, there is no fault. The extraordinary error of the Vedántins is of quite another character. I have already said, that they would prove both the world and ignorance to be ignorance-imagined and altogether false. But, earnestly as they desire to have them so, their inner consciousness refuses to rate them as altogether nothing: for the mind of man will not give willing entrance to an absurdity. The world, the Vedántins allege, is veritably nothing, but, because of ignorance, appears to exist; after the manner of nacrine silver. Now, can the mind assent to the notion, that even that ignorance is nothing whatever? Never: and he who tries to reconcile with it his own views generally, and the common experience of mankind, will encounter obstacles at every step. Moreover, to call such ignorance nothing, is, evidently, most venturesome. Nor do the Vedántins feel, that the world is nought. Let it be believed, that, when they denominate ignorance and the world false, they cannot help feeling, that they are not so far false as to be nothing at all: they must possess some sort or other of existence.

On gathering, from this, that the Vedántins allow to the world a certain sort of existence, one might suppose, that they must give up non-duality: for, however they may designate the world's existence, if they concede, that the world really exists, their Brahma does not remain without a second; and the consequence is duality. This brings us to the knot of their error. They argue, as was said before, for distinct kinds of existence,—not various modes of existence. The world, according to them, really exists; but its existence differs from that of Brahma. They call this existence a false existence; and their so calling it brings them into error: and this error blinds them to their inconsistency. The world's existence is, they allege, false existence; if true, of course the issue would be duality. Analogously, though a madman, alone in a room, thinks himself one of a crowd, his so fancying does not invalidate his being there by himself. Mark, how the Vedántins herein err. Their assertion, that the untrue existence of the world is of no prejudice to monism, would be correct, if they understood such existence to be non-existence; as is the existence of the aforesaid madman's crowd. Since that existence is allowed, by them, to be in fact, they do not mend the matter by calling it untrue. As for themselves, they think otherwise. They urge, that we have two* kinds of existence, the true and the untrue. As that thing which possesses the former kind exists, so does that which possesses the latter; for it has existence: but the thing is untrue, because its existence is of that stamp. And so the doctrine of non-duality is saved uninjured. Observe, that the Vedántins believe in two classes of objects, true and untrue, and both of them really existent; only an object of the first class is really real,† and an object of the second class is unreally real.‡

---

* For convenience, the third kind of existence is here kept out of sight.

† It is not claimed, that the expression "really real," and especially that of "unreally real," does not savour strongly of the absurd. But it is things altogether absurd that are here taken account of.

Among unreally real things are included, with the practical, things apparent, soon to be spoken of. Added to these, and the true, there is a fourth class, to comprehend positive unrealities. Examples of objects of this class are, the son of a barren woman, a hare's horn, sky-blossoms, &c. &c. Their technical ephithet is *tuchchha*.

‡ The notion of practical existence, entertained by the Vedántins, is,

Furthermore, the aspect of these classes of objects varies according to the point of view from which they are beheld.

---

summarily, a combination of two contradictory ideas, that of existence, and that of non-existence. This assertion may be made good simply by showing, that, while they endeavour to prove the world, and all other practical things, no less than all that are apparent, to be nothing whatever, they believe, that the same things are something. The first of these antagonistic positions has been illustrated, and will be illustrated further; and, as for the second, it is evident, on inspecting the books of the Vedántins, that they receive as realities the world and whatever else they call practical. Moreover, as has been seen, they comprehend their I'swara, maker of the world, among practical and false objects, and yet believe, that he really exists. On perusing the eighth chapter, the reader will, further, be satisfied, that, though they would prove the ignorance which imagines the world to be nothing at all, yet they cannot but allow, that it has a certain real existence.

That the view here taken is correct, confirmation is furnished by the words of two very celebrated Hindu philosophers, Párthasárathi Misra and Vijnána Bhikshu, writers on the Mímánsá and on the Sánkhya, respectively.

Párthasárathi, refuting the Vedánta, urges, that, inasmuch as the universe is certified, by perception, to be true, it cannot be made out false. If, he says, it is held, on the word of the Veda, to be false, the Veda itself, as being included in the universe, must be false; and, consequently its proof is invalid.

Then he introduces a Vedántin, and refutes him, as follows: नासत्त्वं प्रपञ्चस्य ब्रूमः प्रत्यचादिप्रमाणतः सिद्धत्वात् । नाऽपि परमार्थतः सत्त्वमात्मज्ञानेन बाध्यमानत्वात् । तस्मात् सदसद्भ्यामनिर्वाच्योऽयं प्रपञ्च इति । तदिदमसारम् । सतोऽन्यत्वमेवासत्त्वम् । तद् यदि प्रपञ्चः सन् न भवति व्यक्तमसन्नेवायम् । असत्त्वाभावे वा सत्त्वापत्तिः । सदसत्त्वयोरेकतरनिषेधस्येतरविधिनान्तरीयकत्वात् । न च विधादयरहितं विधान्तरं सम्भवति । अथाऽपि यन् न कदाचित् प्रतीयते तदसद् यथा घटविषाणं यत् प्रतीतं न कदाचिद् बाध्यते तत् सत् यथाऽऽत्मतत्त्वं प्रपञ्चस्तु प्रतीयमानत्वाद् बाध्यमानत्वाच्च भावाभावाभ्यामनिर्वाच्य इति मतम् । तदनुपपन्नं लोकविरोधात् । यदि प्रतीतं बाध्यते मृगतोयरज्जुसर्पादि तदसदेवेति हि लौकिकी प्रसिद्धिः । न हि घटविषाणादीनां मृगतोयादीनां च कश्चिद्भेदो लोके । सोऽयं प्रपञ्चो बाध्यते वेदसन्नेवेति नाऽनिर्वाच्यत्वम् ।

Conceive true existence and practical existence as two stations, with a station intermediate. A person located at practical

S'ástra-dípiká, MS., fol. 57, *verso.* "'We do not say, that the universe is unreal; since it is established, by perception and other proofs, *to exist.* Nor *do we say, that* it has true existence; it being falsified by right apprehension of spirit. The universe cannot, therefore, be described either as true, or as unreal.' All this is hollow. To be other than true is to be unreal. If, then, the universe be not true, manifestly it is nothing but unreal. On the other hand, if not unreal, it follows, that it is true. For the denial of either *of these,* trueness and unreality, implies the affirmation of the other: and no alternative besides these is possible. 'That which never presents itself—as the horn of a hare,—is held for unreal; and that which presents itself, and is never falsified,—as the true nature of spirit,—is held for true; and, as for the universe, since it presents itself, and *yet* is falsified *by right apprehension,* it is not to be described as true, or, yet, as unreal.' The view thus *propounded,* as being at war with ordinary consciousness, is impossible of establishment. For that which presents itself, and is falsified,—as the mirage, or a snake *surmised* in a rope,—is positively unreal; as, to be sure, all the world is persuaded: there being no difference, in *the estimation of* mankind generally, between such a thing as the horn of a hare and such a thing as the mirage. Hence, if the universe be falsified *by right apprehension,* it is simply unreal, and so is not incapable of being described *as true, or as unreal.*"

Observe whence this argument sets out. Párthasárathi begins by arguing, that the Vedántins cannot uphold the falseness of the universe on the faith of the Veda; for that the Veda is part and parcel of their false universe Now, since the Vedántins fall back on the Veda as the foundation of their belief, it cannot be supposed, that they look upon it as altogether nothing. The end of the argument adduced above, by the Vedántin, is to reconcile these two positions: that the universe, the Veda inclusive, is indeed false, and that, nevertheless it is existent. Herein we have the combination of two irreconcilable ideas, spoken of at the beginning of this note. So understands Párthasárathi; and he proceeds, to deal with the idea on the basis of common sense.

The subjoined words of the same writer, which follow shortly after the passage just extracted, support what is asserted in the text. The Vedántin is asked, whether he takes nescience to import misapprehension, or something else, causative thereof. In neither case can it appertain to Brahma:

ब्रह्मातिरिकेण भ्रान्तिज्ञानं तत्कारणं वाऽभ्युपगतामद्वैतहानिः ।

"In respect of those who accept erroneous apprehension, or a cause of it, *as an entity* additional to Brahma, *for them* non-duality perishes."

It will be made plain, in the eighth chapter, that the Vedántins cannot

existence does not style its objects unreally real: for, to his eyes, there is only one sort of existence; and all that presents itself to him he must deem simply real. In circumstances similar to his are, according to the Vedánta, all who are known as misapprehensive, or ignorant. Again, a person located at true existence would not designate its one object, Brahma, as

repute their ignorance to be quite a non-entity; and yet, to save the dogma of monism, and other doctrines, they essay to prove, at the same time, that ignorance is false, or a non-entity. If, in assigning to ignorance false existence, an existence other than that of Brahma, they meant only, that it is subjective, transitory, or the like, and, on that account, different in kind from their eternal Brahma; and if they meant, by the tenet of non-duality nothing more than this, that, Brahma apart, there is nought of an ever-enduring character; there would be no want of reasonableness in the conception. This style of non-duality would take no harm from ignorance; and there would have been no opening for the polemics of Párthasárathi. The truth is, that they do not understand the falseness of ignorance, and that of the world, in this way; but, to preserve monism, they would make out both ignorance and the world to be positive non-entities. This, their aim, to establish ignorance as a non-entity, is ignored, by Párthasárathi, as an absurdity beneath his notice.

विरुद्धोभयरूपा चेत् । ननु विरुद्धं यदुभयं सदसच् च सद्-
सद्विलक्षणं वा तद्रूपैवाऽविद्या वक्तव्याऽतो न तया पारमार्थिकाद्वै-
तभङ्ग इति चेदित्यर्थः । * * * * न तादृक् पदार्थप्रतीतेः ।

Sánkhya-pravachana-bháshya p. 25. "'If it be held, that nescience is essentially of two contradictories.' But, 'should' it be alleged, that nescience ought to be pronounced 'essentially of two contradictories,' entity and nonentity, or else to be different from both; and thus there would be no invalidation, thereby, i. e., by nescience, of non-duality, the only true (páramárthika) state. Such is the sense.* * 'Not so; for such a thing is unknown.'"

This passage takes in the twenty-third and twenty-fourth aphorisms of the Sánkhya-pravachana, Book I. The first is put into the mouth of a Vedántin; and the second curtly replies to it.

Vijnána Bhikshu asserts, that the portion of the Sánkhya-pravachana here quoted from is directed, primarily, against the Bauddhas, but that it tells with equal relevancy in confutation of the illusionists (máyávádin) and crypto-Bauddhas (prachhanna-bauddha). The Vedántins are denoted by both these titles. The latter is applied to them dyslogistically; and the application is far from infrequent.

really real : for, with him likewise, only one sort of existence would offer itself for inspection; and that, as above, as simply real. Such would be the standing point of the Vedántins' Brahma, except for his lacking the faculty of cognition, —as will be seen by and bye. A person located at the intermediate station, just now mentioned, is enabled to pass in review the objects of both the other stations; and he alone can speak of those objects as they veritably are. By him they all alike are seen to be real; the true object, as really real, and practical objects, as unreally real. This person is the Vedántin.

To their third kind of existence the Vedántins give the appellation of apparent. A perusal of what is now to be said of it will elucidate the statements just put forth, and will serve to induce confidence in them. It is objects of error, such as nacrine silver, and a snake imagined in a rope, that are meant by apparent objects. As was before remarked, it is not because of any rationally assignable difference in the nature of things, but because of a belief in difference as to their very existence, that the Vedántins ascribe to them different sorts of existence. By what I am about to show, this assertion will be evinced as true. No one can suspect, as regards what is styled apparent existence, that it is so styled on account of any rationally assignable difference, in the nature of the things of which it is affirmed, from that of things true and practical; those things that are called apparent being, we are all aware, nothing. If it be said, that, for this very reason, apparent things may be held to differ in nature from other things, and that, therefore, for convenience, the Vedántins give a name to the false existence of apparent things, I reply, that I do not accuse them on this ground, but on the ground, that they reckon such existence, and the things to which it is ascribed, as possessing a species of reality. Respecting apparent things the partisans of the Vedánta hold this language;* that, when

---

* ननु विसंवादिद्रष्टच्या भ्रान्तिज्ञानस्य विषयसिद्धावपि तस्य प्राति-

a man, on seeing nacre, takes it for silver, apparent silver is

भासिकतत्त्वालोत्यद्रजतादिविषयकत्वे न प्रमाणं देशान्तरीय-
रजतस्य क्वचिदेव तद्विषयत्वसम्भवादिति चेत् न । तस्यासन्निकृ-
ष्टतया प्रत्यक्षविषयत्वायोगात् । *Vedánta-paribháshá*, p. 10.

"Though, by the efforts, *however* belying, *of a misapprehensive person*, to *obtain possession of* an illusory object, *such an object* is established as existent, yet there is no proof, that it, *the misapprehension*, has reference to an apparent object, as silver, &c., produced at that time. For silver which is extant elsewhere may be taken as its object. If this be said, I demur: since that *silver elsewhere*, not being in contact *with an organ of sense*, cannot be an object of perception."

There is room to suspect, that the word विषय in the first line of this extract, is an interpolation.

The objector here rebutted is a Naiyáyika, who, as such, holds misapprehension to be what is technically called *anyathá-khyáti*. By this is meant, the apprehension of an object otherwise than as it is. Agreeably to the Naiyáyikas, when, for instance, a man mistakes nacre for silver, the object of his mistake must be confessed to exist, but elsewhere than in the place to which he erroneously refers it. That is to say, the very silver which he has seen in some other place is supposed, by him, to be then present before him. To copy the Naiyáyika expression, instead of perceiving nacreness, he transfers the silverness, which he has seen on some other occasion, to the nacre lying in his sight. This view the Vedántin rejects, on the following ground, implied in his answer. The misapprehension in question is, in the view of the pandits, one of perception; and, in all perception, the contact is essential of an organ of sense with the object perceived. Absent silver cannot, therefore, account for the mistake committed.

Misapprehension is, by others, explained under the designation of *asat-khyáti*, "the apprehension of what is not." This notion, on the ground of their argument given above, is also disallowed by the Vedántins.

An objection respecting things seen in dreams is thus adduced and answered:

ननु खप्नस्थले पूर्वानुभूतरथादेः सरणमात्रेणैव व्यवहारोपपत्तौ न
रथादिदृष्टिकल्पनं गौरवादिति चेन् न रथादेः कृतिमात्राभ्युप-
गमे रथं पश्यामि खप्ने रथमद्राक्षमित्यादनुभवविरोधापत्तेः ।

Vedánta-paribháshá, p 13. "Since, in the case of dreams, what *there* goes on may be accounted for by simple remembrance of a chariot, or the like, previously cognized, to imagine the production of those objects is not *admissible*, because cumbrous. Should this be urged, I except; for, to allow mere remembrance of a chariot, or the like, to be *here a sufficient cause* is contra-

really produced. If silver, I ask, is then really produced, vouced by the consciousness *of a man, in a dream,* that he sees a chariot, and *his consciousness, when afterwards awake,* that he saw a chariot in a dream."

How apparent silver is produced will be seen from what ensues: ननु रजतोत्पादकानां रजतावयवादीनामभावे शुक्तौ तवाऽपि कथं रजतमुत्पद्यते इति चेदुच्यते । न हि लोकसिद्धसामग्री प्रातिभासिकरजतोत्पादिका किन्तु विलक्षणैव । तथाहि काचादिदोषदूषितलोचनस्य पुरोवर्तिद्रव्यसंयोगादिदमाकारा चाकचक्याकारा च काचिदन्तःकरणवृत्तिर्भवदेति । तस्यां च वृत्तौ इदमवच्छिन्नचैतन्यं प्रतिबिम्बते तत्र पूर्वोत्तरीव्या वृत्तेर्निर्गमनेन इदमवच्छिन्नचैतन्यं वृत्त्यवच्छिन्नचैतन्यं प्रमाढचैतन्यं चाऽभिन्नं भवति । ततच प्रमाढचैतन्याभिन्नविषयचैतन्यनिष्ठा शुक्तित्वप्रकारिका अविद्या चाकचक्यादिसादृश्यसन्दर्शनसमुद्बोधितरजतसंस्कारसभ्रीचीना काचादिदोषसमवहिता रजतरूपार्थाकारेण रजतज्ञानाभासाकारेण च परिणमते । *Ibid.,* p. 10. "Since the originators of silver, its parts and other *causes,* do not exist in nacre, how, with thyself, is silver produced there? If so interrogated, I reply: It is not, that the constituents popularly recognized are the originators of apparent silver. These are different. Thus; when the contact takes place between, for instance, the eye, labouring under the defect of bilious humour, or the like, and a presented object, there arises an affection of the internal organ, in the form of that *object,* and likewise in the form of *its* glitter. In that affection intelligence, *i. e., Brahma,* appropriated to that *object,* is reflected. At that spot, *viz., where the object is located,* in the manner aforesaid, by reason of the egress *and advent there* of the affection, intelligence appropriated to that *object,* intelligence appropriated to that affection, and intelligence the subject of right notion, *these three,* become identical. Afterwards, nescience—residing in the object-appropriated intelligence, one with intelligence the subject of right notion; cognizing nacreness as the abstract nature *of the thing beheld;* aided by the impression of silver *before seen, an impression* resuscitated by the perception of similarity in the glitter, &c. *of the object present to that of silver previously seen;* associated with the *forementioned* defects, bile, &c.,—is evolved, in the form of the object, the *apparent* silver, and also in the form of a semblance of a cognition of *that* silver."

Just as, with the Sánkhyas, the whole world is evolved from nature, with the Vedántius, all practical things are evolutions from nescience, or igno-

how is there proved to be a misconception? In reply, I am

rance; and equally so are all apparent things, and the apprehension of them, styled, above, "the semblance of a cognition." In the evolution of apparent things there is, however, the association of defects, which have no place in the evolutions of things practical; as was mentioned in the text, at p. 158, and the related note. The statement which we have seen about the identification of three sorts of intelligence is designed to show, that the misapprehension of nacre for silver is an error of perception. This question is one of great difficulty; but some light will be thrown upon it in the fifth chapter. The idea of identification of three sorts of intelligence may be thus explicated. Intelligence, or Brahma, is, like ether, universally diffused; and, being so diffused, it is said to be appropriated to everything which it contains. Ether is laid down as being, in reality, one. Still, though the ether in a jar outside a house is said to be distinct from the ether within the house, yet, when the jar is brought into the house, identity is realized of the ether of the jar with that of the house. Similarly, when an affection of the internal organ and the object of that affection become collocal, the Brahma of the affection and that of the object coalesce into one. The doctrine of the impenetrability of matter is unknown to the pandits. In their view, the internal organ and its evolutions are strictly material; and yet an affection of that organ and a material object can take up the same space.

ननु शुक्तौ रजतस्य प्रतिभाससमये सत्ताभ्युपगमे नेदं रजतमिति चैकालिकनिषेधधज्ञानं न स्यात् किन्तु इदानीं न रजतमिति स्यात् * * * * इति चेन् न । न हि तत्र रजतत्वावच्छिन्नप्रतियोगिकाभावो निषेधविषयः किन्तु लौकिकत्वपारमार्थिकत्वावच्छिन्नप्रातिभासिकरजतप्रतियोगिकः । *Ibid.*, p. 14. "If it be admitted, that *apparent* silver exists, at the time of *its* appearance, in the nacre, the cognition, *to one not misapprehensive*, in the form of 'This is not silver,' of the non-existence, through tripartite time, *of silver*, would not have place; but *the cognition* would be in the form of '*This thing* is not now silver.' * * * * If this be affirmed, it is contested : for the object, here, of the cognition '*It is not silver*' is not the non-existence of silver as silver, but the non-existence of apparent silver, as true and practical."

Such is the sense of the Sanskrit. Some of its expressions, in a literal reproduction, would only perplex the reader, and entail a long comment.

It comes out from this, that, in the apprehension of the Vedántins, a thing may, contemporaneously, be both really existent and really non-existent. When, from misapprehension, a man takes nacre to be silver, apparent silver, is thought, is really produced, and exists for him. Another looker-on, not

told, that, if the silver were true, or practical, there would be under such a misapprehension, thinks, that there is no silver where the other fancies he sees it. His idea, it is asserted, is authentic; the non-existence of silver, apprehended by him, being supposed to have reference to apparent silver as true and practical.

Language similar to that about apparent objects, in the last extract, is found concerning practical objects also.

The falseness of these objects is defined as follows: **मिथ्यात्वं च खाश्र-यत्वेनाऽभिमतयावन्निष्ठात्यन्ताभावप्रतियोगित्वम् ।** *Ibid.,* p 18. "By a false *thing is meant* that whose absolute non-existence resides in the entirety of what is *erroneously* taken for its substrate."

This definition is thus applied to things practical. Take a jar, for instance. Its parts are deemed, by the Naiyáyikas and others, to be its material cause and substrate. See pages 94 and 95. But those parts are erroneously so taken, assert the Vedántins, by all but themselves; since a jar, a practical object, being false, has no substrate. In the parts of the jar, wrongly supposed to be its substrate, resides the absolute non-existence of the jar itself; and, therefore, the jar is false.

The same definition is applied to the jar's parts, the absolute non-existence of which resides in their own parts, the material cause and the substrate of the primary parts. Intermediate effects and causes being traversed, ignorance the material cause and substrate of everything save Brahma, is at length reached; all the effects on the way having been proved false, since the non-existence of each resides in its material cause. Ignorance then comes to be dealt with. Its non-existence resides in Brahma, the imagined substrate, or, as it is also termed, illusory-material cause, of ignorance, as of all else than Brahma. Everything, Brahma excepted, is, thus, concluded to be false.

To this conclusion an exception is suggested and replied to: **न च घटादेर्मिथ्यात्वे सन् घट इति प्रत्यक्षेण बाधः अधिष्ठानब्रह्मसत्तायास्तत्र विषयतया घटादेः सत्यत्वासिद्धेः ।** *Ibid.,* p. 18. "Let it not be thought, that *the notion of* the falseness of a jar, or the like, is contradicted by the perception of the jar as existent; for, since the object, in that *perception,* is the existence of Brahma, the substrate *of the jar, not the existence of the jar,* the verity of the jar, &c. is not established."

Another answer is subjoined. **घटः सन्निति प्रत्यक्षस्य यावद्व्यावहारिकसत्त्वविषयत्वेन प्रामाण्यम् । अस्मिन् पक्षे घटादेरेषाणि निषेधो न खरूपेण किन्तु पारमार्थिकत्वेनेति न विरोधः । अस्मिन् पक्षे मिथ्यात्वलक्षणे पारमार्थिकत्वावच्छिन्नप्रतियोगिकत्वमत्यन्ताभाववि-**

no room to speak of misconception; but, since it is neither, but apparent, misconception has place.* From this it is clear, that, when the Vedántins call the existence of an apparent thing,—a thing really produced,—apparent, it is not because the thing differs by nature from other things, but because its existence differs from the existence of other things. If the thing were different simply by nature, and not in respect of existence, how could the apprehension of it be reputed a misconception? The same reasoning will apply to practical things, no less than to apparent: for, as the apprehension, by one

मेषं द्रष्टव्यम् | *Ibid.*, p. 18. "The perception, that the jar exists, *can be made out to be* correct, inasmuch as it has practical existence for its object. Conformably to this position, the existence, in Brahma, of a jar as true is denied, not *that* of a jar as a jar. Thus there is no incongruity. According to this opinion, *viz., that in the perception of a jar as existent, practical existence is apprehended*, the qualification 'relative to a thing *considered* as true' is to be added to 'absolute non-existence,' in the definition of falseness, lately given."

By the definition of falseness, practical things have no existence; and yet these words assign to them a sort of existence. On referring, for comparison, to the passage from the fourteenth page of the *Vedánta-paribháshá*, at pp. 169, 170, the reader will perceive, that practical and apparent things differ in no respect, among themselves, in being both true and false.

To return to things apparent, the Vedántins do not, in all cases of misapprehension, contend for their production. | यञ्चाऽऽद्रोप्यमसन्निकृष्टं तदैव प्रातिभासिकवस्तुत्पत्तेरङ्गीकारात् | *Ibid.*, p. 14. "Only when a false thing imagined in one veritable is not in contact *with an organ of sense*, is an apparent thing acknowledged to be produced."

Where, however, the object is near, the Vedántins concur with the Naiyáyikas in admitting *anyathá-khyáti;* for, since the object is brought into contact with an organ of sense, the fact, that the misapprehension, is perceptional, is accounted for. To argue the production of an apparent object may, therefore, here be dispensed with.

* शुक्तिरूप्यादिभ्रमस्य संसारकालीनबाधविषयप्रातिभासिक- रजतादिविषयकत्वात् | *Vedánta-paribháshá,* p. 10. "Because misapprehension about naorine silver and the like has, for its object, apparent silver, &c., which are proved, by correct perception in the state of practical existence, to be false."

labouring under mistake, of nacrine silver, is considered, from the standing point of practical existence, to be misconception; in like manner, the apprehension of the world, and of the things therein, by those whom the Vedántins call ignorant, or even by the wise while detained in the body, from the standing point of true existence, is considered to be misconception.*

Finally, it should be understood, that, in fact, the aim of the Vedántins is, to make out the world, &c. to be veritable non-entities; for, this unestablished, even so is monism. It is the stubborn and irrefragable actuality of external things that compels them, as it were in their own despite, to enunciate a second kind of existence, one applicable to such things; and the character which they give to that existence compels them to add a third. Their inward impressions, however, touching their views, vary with varying occasions. Thus, when they turn their contemplation towards the world, it presents itself to them as having really an existence. Then, that no harm may come to their notion of monism, they apply to that existence the epithet of false, and so relieve their discomfort. Yet, when they pass to reflect on their secondless Brahma, and, in order to prove his secondlessness, and the world's falsity, assert, that the world is ignorance-imagined, it appears to their minds as if the world were really nothing whatsoever.

---

* Since, according to a tenet of the Vedánta, all things but Brahma are false, how can the cognition of them be regarded as right notion ? In reply to this interrogatory, it is said :

देहात्मप्रत्ययो यद्वत् प्रमाणत्वेन कल्पितः ।
लौकिकं तद्वदेवेदं प्रमाणं त्वाऽऽत्मनिश्चयात् ॥

इति ।   Cited in the *Vedánta-paribháshá*, p. 2. " As the notion, that the body is one's self, is imagined, *by the ignorant*, to be correct ; even so the practical *apprehension of worldly things is esteemed to be* correct, till *one attains to* right apprehension of soul."

The author of the *Vedánta-paribháshá* expressly states, that, in the fourth quarter of this couplet, there is a contraction of *á-átma-nis'chayát*. No one need doubt, that he is in the right. *Laukikam*, he likewise observes, points to practical apprehension of things of the world.

Their chief aim being as aforesaid, it must, consequently, be borne in mind,—and, throughout this work, it is taken as a postulate,—that, with the Vedántins, Brahma excepted, all is nihility. In a way, indeed, a real existence is allowed to what is other than Brahma: but, inasmuch as all this has no more substantiality than nacrine silver, however the Vedántins speak of it, how can we account it as, in any wise, existence? And, further, it has been made patent, that, according to the Vedántins themselves, only from the standing point of practical existence is reality ascribable to the world; which, from the standing point of true existence, is devoid of reality of every kind and degree.

The Vedánta recognizes, as existent, an I's'wara, maker of the world, all-wise, and all-powerful; and souls, also, and their ignorance, their doing good and evil, their requital in Elysium and in Hell, and their transmigration. And, again, all these are regarded as non-existent, and as absolutely so. Neither are they, nor have they been, nor are they to be. Brahma alone exists,—without qualities, and eternal. All besides—I's'wara, the world, and everything else,—has but a false existence, and owes its being to imagination by ignorance. In very truth, it is nothing. Such, in a few words, is the creed of the Vedántins.

CHAPTER 2.

Summary of the Vedánta System.

Though the Vedántins allege, that, from the standing point of the true state of existence, Brahma alone is real, and all else is unreal, still, from the standing point of the practical state of existence, I's'wara, souls, and the whole world, are real, that is to say, practically real, and distinct one from another.*

---

* And they have been distinct from all eternity. See the last Sanskrit extract in p. 35.

Their system, therefore, branches into two divisions; one of which has to do with the practical state of existence, and the other, with the true state of existence. Great part of the first is seen in one or other of all the remaining Systems. Here, as in the Nyáya and in the Yoga, we find an omniscient and omnipotent I's'wara, framer and ruler of the external world.* Pretty much as in the Sánkhya, and in the Yoga, we also here find statements of the order in which the world was developed. That which the Sánkhyas call nature, the Vedántins call illusion, or ignorance. As for the internal organ, its affections, and many other articles, the Sánkhya and the Vedánta coincide to a large extent. In several particulars, however, they join issue. He that would acquaint himself fully with those particulars must have recourse to special treatises on the Vedánta. It is neither my desire, nor is it my intention, to treat the subject exhaustively; an examination of its essential features being sufficient for my present purpose. Again, like the rest of the Systematists, the Vedántins receive the Veda, the Puráṇas, &c., as authoritative. They believe, likewise, in good and bad works, and that, to receive the favourable and unfa-

---

* तथा चेश्वरगीतास्वपि * * * * परमार्थावस्थायामीश्वरीमितखाभावः प्रदर्श्यते । व्यवहारावस्थायां तूक्तः श्रुतावपीश्वरादिव्यवहारः एव सर्वेश्वर एष भूताधिपतिरेष भूतपाल एष सेतुर्विधरण एषां लोकानामसम्भेदायेति । *S'ankara-A'chárya's Brahma-sútra-bháshya*, I., 2; MS. "And thus the absence, from the standing point of true existence, of a Ruler and ruled is likewise shown in the *I'swara-gítá*. * * * * But, from the standing point of practical existence, the Veda itself supports the notion of an I'swara, &c., *by the words* 'This *is* the lord of all; this, the sovereign of all beings; this, the protector of creatures; this, the preserving bridge against the disruption of the worlds.'"

By the *I'swara-gítá* the *Bhagavad-gítá* is here meant; the passage omitted,—two couplets, V., 14, 15,—being found there. In S'ankara's days the book now current under the title of *I'swara-gítá* could not have existed. Its minute development of the Vedánta marks it, undeniably, as a recent composition

vourable requital to which these give rise, souls must pass to Elysium and to Hell, and again and again take birth, and so forth. To animadvert on the errors of the Vedánta doctrines as confined to the practical state of existence, there is no need; as I have refuted them, by inclusion, in what I have written touching the Sánkhya and the Nyáya.

But entirely different from anything as yet encountered is the doctrine of the Vedántins touching the true state of existence, as they phrase it. And this doctrine is summarized in this half couplet: "Brahma is true; the world is false; the soul is Brahma himself, and nothing other."* As expanded and expounded by the advocates of the Vedánta, this quotation imports as follows. Brahma alone—a spirit; essentially existent, intelligence, and joy;† void of all qualities ‡ and of all

---

* ब्रह्म सत्यं जगन् मिथ्या जीवो ब्रह्मैव नापरः ।

Who wrote this half-couplet is not known, though it is familiar to every Vedántin. Selected here for its conciseness in expressing the substance of the Vedánta, it serves as text to all that follows this second chapter. Preceding it is the line:

श्लोकार्धेन प्रवक्ष्यामि यदुक्तं ग्रन्थकोटिभिः ॥

"In half a couplet I will declare that which is set forth in millions of volumes."

† In Sanskrit, *sat*, *chit*, and *ánanda*. All three words have numerous synonymes.

Chit, chaitanya, &c., "intelligence," when applied to Brahma, are, as will be seen, equally deceptive with the *bodha* of the soul, professed in the Sánkhya. Brahma, we shall discover, is utterly destitute of all intelligence to which the name can rationally be allowed.

‡ मन्मते ब्रह्मणो द्रव्यत्वासिद्धेः । गुणाश्रयत्वं समवायिकारणत्वं वा द्रव्यत्वमिति तेऽभिमतं न हि निर्गुणस्य ब्रह्मणो गुणाश्रयता नापि समवायिकारणता समवायासिद्धेः । *Vedánta-paribháshá*, p. 18.

"For, in my system, Brahma is not proved to be a substance. Thou holdest, that a substance is the substrate of qualities, or a *samaváyi* cause. But Brahma, being void of qualities, is not a substrate of qualities: nor is he a *samaváyi* cause; inasmuch as *samaváya* is not established *for an entity*."

See, for *samaváya* and *samaváyi*, pp. 93-95.

acts* in whom there is no consciousness such as is denoted by
" I," " thou," and " it ;"† who apprehends no person, or thing,
nor is apprehended of any ;‡ who is neither parviscient nor om-

---

* निष्कलं निष्क्रियं शान्तं निरवद्यं निरञ्जनम् ।

"*Brahma is* without parts, devoid of action, tranquil, irreproachable, emotionless."

This line is from the *S'wetás'watara Upanishad.* See the *Bibliotheca Indica,* Vol. VII., p. 370.

† In the annexed passage, isolated spirit, *i. e.,* spirit abstracted from all adjuncts originated by ignorance, such as the imagining the world, and so forth, is characterized:

असम्भवति सर्वस्मिन् दिङ्मूम्याकाशहृपिणि ।
प्रकाश्ये याटृशं रूपं प्रकाशस्याऽमलं भवेत् ॥
चिज्जगत् त्वमहं चेति दृश्येऽसत्तामुपागते ।
द्रष्टुः स्यात् केवलीभावस्त्वादृशो विमलात्मनः ॥

इति । *Yoga-vásishṭha,* p. 107 of the Calcutta edition of 1851.

" As would be the pure essence of light, if all *that is* illuminated *thereby*,— *as* space, the earth, and ether,—were non-existent; so becomes the isolation of the pure-essenced beholder, when the objects of apprehension—the three worlds, thou, and I,—*all* vanish into nothingness."

By "beholder" is meant knower, or apprehender. We have seen how the Sánkhyas attempt to justify their application of this term to their *purusha ;* and we shall soon see how the Vedántins endeavour to make good its applicability to Brahma. Both the *purusha* and Brahma are, really, unintelligent.

Vijnána Bhikshu, in citing this passage in the *Sánkhya-pravachana-bháshya,* p. 97, draws on a production notoriously ultra-monistic : but he has there to do with a point on which the Sánkhya and the Vedánta are quite agreed. On that occasion there was no room for misconstruction at his hands.

The *Yoga-vásishṭha,* though considered as the work of Válmíki, and as a supplement to his *Rámáyaṇa,* was doubtless composed subsequently to the full development of the system of S'ankara A'chárya.

‡ That Brahma apprehends no one and nought, will be proved in the fifth chapter. That he is apprehended by no one follows from the position, that all apprehension is an affection of the internal organ ; and Brahma, it is asserted, never comes within the cognizance of such affection. Even the affection in the form of "I am Brahma, essentially existent, intelligence, and joy," which immediately precedes emancipation, does not cognize Brahma, but only removes the ignorance that hides him. See the *Vedántasára,* pp. 21-23. Indeed, that which is then cognized is not the true Brahma,

niscient; neither parvipotent nor omnipotent*; who has neither beginning nor end; immutable and indefectible—is the true entity. All besides himself, the entire universe, is false, that is to say, is nothing whatsoever. Neither has it ever existed, nor does it now exist, nor will it exist at any time future.

but only his shadow, the nearest approximation to him that is apprehensible, on any terms, or at any time, by one destined to be liberated, or actually liberated. Hence, when the Vedántins affirm, that Brahma is inapprehensible and ineffable, their meaning is not like our own, when we use such language regarding God. We mean, that God cannot wholly, they, that Brahma cannot at all, be known or described. Nothing, it is said, that comes, or that can come, within the scope of apprehension, is in any wise Brahma.

* Both I'swara and the soul are held to be ignorance-imagined and false. See the note at p. 157. Of the same character are all their attributes; the omniscience, omnipotence, &c. of the former, and the parviscience, parvipotence, &c. of the latter. These attributes, cannot, therefore, appertain to Brahma.

"Parviscient" and "parvipotent" literally translate the technical expressions *alpajna* and *alpaśaktimat*.

प्रभुरेष सर्वविदेहं क्षपथोजगदेतदद्भुतवितानमिति ।
प्रतिपत्तयक्तिमिरघ्नमहृद्यो यदिच्छोद्भवन्ति न तदद्भुतकम् ॥

इति । From the *Sankshepa-śáriraka*, MS. "'He is the all-knowing lord; I am a pitiful *creature*; this *is* the world, wonderful in expansion. That such conceptions should arise in *the mind of* one whose *inner* eye is blinded by darkness, is no matter of amazement."

That Brahma does not possess omniscience, omnipotence, &c. will, further, be plain to any one who will read, in almost any body of Vedánta doctrine, the elucidation of the utterance "That art thou," *tat twam asi*, one of the twelve "great sentences."

The preceptor of the Vedánta, intending to instruct his pupil, that he is one with Brahma, is obliged, by reason that Brahma is inexpressible by language, to teach him, that he is one with I'swara, an object apprehensible, and the entity that is nearest to Brahma the inapprehensible; and a being lifted far above humanity, as not being liable to misapprehend. The pupil is to think of I'swara as shorn of all attributes, and of himself as wanting all his own. The residual part of I'swara, and that of himself,—Brahma in both cases,- he is to consider as unified. This also evinces, that the characteristics which severally contradistinguish I'swara and the soul do not belong to the essence of Brahma.

And the soul is one with Brahma. Such is the doctrine of the Vedánta regarding the true state of existence; and it is denominated non-dualistic, as rejecting the notion of any second true entity.

And here some one may ask, how it is, that, if the external world is nothing, it presents itself as existing; and why it is, that, if the soul be Brahma, it is not aware of the fact, and, more than this, endures various miseries. The answer which the Vedántins give to this is, that it is all due to the power of ignorance. This point I shall now enter upon with somewhat of detail.

The Vedántins assert, that the external world originates from ignorance; in other words, it is all actually Brahma, but, by reason of ignorance, appears to us as the world. Just so, a rope lying in certain circumstances may be mistaken, by a man, for a snake. He calls it a snake, it not being so, however, but a rope: and so one may speak of the snake and the rope as being one. And yet it is not meant, that the rope has actually undergone a change, or has turned into a snake: it is a snake merely in semblance. As the rope is to the snake, so is Brahma to the world. When, therefore, the Vedántins declare, that the world is Brahma, their meaning is not, that Brahma is actually transformed into the world, but that, in point of fact, the world is no entity; only Brahma presents himself as if the world. To use their technical phraseology, the world's existence is not its own, but Brahma's. Hence they designate Brahma as the illusory-material cause of the world. He is not really a material cause, as clay is of the jar which is made out of it, but a substrate, as the rope is to the snake, or as nacre is to silver, in the stock illustrations of the system under description. The existence, the apparent existence, of the snake and of the silver depends on the existence of the rope and the nacre; and yet these are not in reality transmuted, respectively, into a snake and into silver. Such is the explanation of the term illusory-material cause. As for illusion, or ignorance, in it we have the world's material cause,* and, from it, the world's name

---

* According to this, the world is the *vivarta*, or illusory effect, of Brahma, and the *pariṇáma*, or evolution, of illusion, *máyá*. These two expressions, as denoting acts, are thus explained: परिणामो नाम उपादानसमसत्ता-ककार्यापत्तिः । विवर्तौ नाम उपादानविषमसत्ताकंकार्यापत्तिः । *Vedánta-paribháshá*, p. 11. "Evolution is the production of an effect which has the same kind of existence as its material cause. Illusory generation is the production of an effect which has an existence different in kind from that of its material, *i. e., illusory-material*, cause."

It is stated, that some Vedántins formerly maintained Brahma to be the material cause of the world. But, from the time of S'ankara A'chárya, the dominant school of the Vedánta has held, that Brahma is the world's illusory-material cause.

न च विजातीययोरप्युपादानोपादेयभावे ब्रह्मैव जगदुपादानं स्यादिति वाच्यम् । प्रपञ्चभ्रमाधिष्ठानरूपम्य तस्येष्टत्वात् परिणामित्वरूपस्योपादानत्वस्य निरवयवब्रह्मण्यनुपपत्तेः । तथा च प्रपञ्चस्य परिणाम्युपादानं माया न ब्रह्मेति सिद्धान्तः । *Ibid.*, p. 31

"Let it not be said, that, if, of two heterogeneous things, one may be a material cause, and the other a material effect, then Brahma himself may be the material cause of the world. For this, *Brahma as a material cause* is admitted for such in the sense of *his* being the substrate in misapprehension, of the world, *i. e., the substrate of the world, the object misapprehended*: since that material causativity which consists in evolving is impossible in Brahma; he being without parts. Thus, then, the established doctrine is, that the evolutional material cause of the world is illusion, not Brahma."

S'ankara A'chárya often interprets literally those passages of the Upanishads, &c., which seem to speak of Brahma as the world's evolutional material cause; but he prefers to understand them as setting forth the view which, since his time has generally, if not universally, been adopted by Vedántins. S'ankara's opinion may be learned from what follows: ननु सोपादानत्वादिः प्रासादादीन् सृजतीति युक्तं निरुपादानत्वात्मा कथं लोकान् सृजति इति । नायं दोषः । सलिलस्थानीयेरूपेऽव्याकृते आत्मैकशब्दवाच्ये व्याकृतफेनस्थानीयस्य जगत उपादानभूते सम्भवः । तस्मादात्मभूतनामरूपोपादानः सन् सर्वज्ञो जगन् निर्मिमीते

and form. Agreeably to the Vedánta, of these five, existence, intelligence, joy, name, and form, the first three belong to Brahma, and the other two to illusion.* The existence, intel-

इति न विरुद्धम् । अथवा यथा विज्ञानवान् मायावी निष्पादान आत्मानमेवाऽऽत्मान्तरत्वेनाऽऽकाशे गच्छन्निव निर्मिमीते तथा सर्वज्ञो देवः सर्वशक्तिर्महामाय आत्मानमेवाऽऽत्मान्तरत्वेन जगद्रूपेण निर्मिमीत इति युक्ततरम् । *Commentary on the Aitareya-upanishad: Bibliotheca Indica*, Vol VII, pp. 175, 176. "'A carpenter, or similar *artificer*, possessed of material, constructs a house, or the like. This is *all* right, *or intelligible*. But how can the spirit, which is without material, create the worlds?' This is no *valid* objection. Like the foam, a thing developed, *existing potentially* in water, the universe can exist in its material cause, known as pure spirit, formless, and undeveloped. Therefore, it is not incongruous *to think*, that the omniscient, himself the material cause of names and forms, should create the universe. Otherwise, *and* preferably: as a dexterous juggler without material produces himself as it were another self travelling in the air, so the omniscient Deva, *or I'swara*, being omnipotent and great in illusion, creates himself as it were another self in the form of the universe."

Such is the construction put, by S'ankara and by all his discipular successors, on texts of the Hindu scriptures where Brahma is mentioned as a material cause. And to this construction the Vedántins are constrained, as they would render consistent either their own tenets or the Upanishads themselves. For the Upanishads again and again describe Brahma as being without parts, and as unchangeable; and this notion would be contravened by that of his being an evolutional material cause. Such being the case, in disputing with Vedántins now-a-days, one will gain nothing by indicating to them, that the prevailing doctrines of their school are out of harmony with those which obtained of yore. Their own doctrines, they will reply, do not conflict with those of their predecessors, but only unfold and supplement them. One may find, in the Upanishads, passages inculcating, that the world is an evolution from illusion, and many such things favourable to the position, that Brahma is the world's illusory-material cause only; and the pandits will urge, and perhaps justly, that, in arriving at their conclusions, they but use different texts for mutual explanation.

* अस्ति भाति प्रियं रूपं नाम चेत्यंशपञ्चकम् ।
आद्यं त्रयं ब्रह्मरूपं मायारूपं ततो द्वयम् ॥

ligence, and joy, which appear to be found in all things in the universe, are from Brahma, the illusory-material cause of the universe; as the existence of nacrine silver is from nacre, the illusory-material cause of the fancied silver. Name and form, appertaining to the universe and its contents, are from illusion, the world's material cause.*

The inconsistency and fatuity of the Vedánta, on the point under discussion, are most bewildering to the reader. In the first place he will enquire what is the nature of illusion, also called ignorance. If, he will say, it is that by reason of which the unreal world presents itself as real,—after the manner of nacre appearing to be silver,—it must be misconception: and how can this be the world's material cause? And, if it be a material cause, and if the world was made out of it, as a jar is made of clay, why are the name and form of the world said to be false? I reply, that the difficulty thus expressed is incapable of solution. The Vedántins are herein most inconsistent. In some respects their "ignorance" looks like misconception; and still they will not name it so, but the cause of misconception,† nay, of the whole world: for they describe it as being, like the Sánkhya "nature," a complex

"*There are* five parts *predicable:* is, appears, *is* delightsome, form, and name. The first three are of Brahma; the remaining two, of illusion."

This couplet is cited anonymously in the *Vedánta-paribháshá*, p. 36. *Jagad-rúpam* is there given, erroneously, for *máyá-rúpam.*

* The, Vedántins, when they speak of existence and joy as appearing in external things, are intelligible; since those things are apprehended as existent, and are supposed to minister delight. But how can intelligence be said to appear in all external things, as in a jar, for instance? The explanation of our philosophers is, that, inasmuch as such things appear, their appearing is a sign that they are connected with intelligence. Thus: घटः सन् घटो भाति घट इष्ट इत्यादिलौकिकव्यपदेशोऽपि सच्चिदानन्दरूपब्रह्माध्यासात् । *Vedánta-paribháshá* p. 35. "The conventional expressions 'A jar is,' 'A jar appears,' 'A jar is desirable,' &c., are also from imagining oneness, *with the jar,* of Brahma,—existent, intelligence, and joy."

† This will be shown in the seventh chapter.

of the three *guṇas*, and the world's material cause.* Furthermore, they denominate it the power of Íśwara.† These assertions of theirs have little congruity with each other.

Another perplexity is offered to the reader, in their comparison of Brahma and the world to nacre and to nacrine silver severally. That comparison, he must of necessity think, could not be intended, by the Vedántins, to be taken in its strict literality. For they cannot mean, he will say, that the ignorant mistake Brahma for the world, just as a man labouring under misapprehension mistakes nacre for silver. Brahma, he will object, is invisible: how, then, can he become an object of vision, and be mistaken for the world? Moreover, though a man who takes nacre for silver misconceives, yet the form before his eyes is not a false form, but that of nacre, or, rather, nacre itself. Similarly, if it be held, that "ignorant" men take Brahma to be the world, though their so taking him would be a mistake, it must likewise be believed, that this world, visible, tangible, unintelligent, and changeable, is Brahma; in other words, that Brahma has those qualities. Let it be granted, that the name of the world is false; still, how can its form be so?

Difficulties such as these would certainly suggest themselves to a person of discrimination; and they are insoluble. At the same time it is true, that the comparison lately mentioned is adduced in Vedánta treatises of the highest credit, and with the design that its literal import should be accepted.‡ We find it asserted there, that, when a man mistakes

---

* इमानि भूतानि त्रिगुणमायाकार्यत्वेनत्रिगुणात्मकानि ।
Vedánta-paribháshá, p. 36. "These elements are composed of the three *guṇas*, because effects of illusion, *itself* composed of the three *guṇas*."

† See the *Vedánta-sára*, p. 4; where, in a citation from some Upanishad, illusion (*máyá*)—termed *ajnána* in the text-book—is denominated *devátmasakti*, "the proper power of Deva, or I″śwara."

‡ To the objection, that Brahma, not being an object of vision, cannot be mistaken for the visible world, this reply is returned by the Vedántin: न च

nacre for silver, false silver is actually produced over the nacre. The nacre is the substrate of the silver, and is called its illusory-material cause; while ignorance is said to be its material cause. Analogously, in the estimation of the Vedántins, Brahma is universally diffused; and over portions of him, the world, a thing of falsity, is actually produced:* Brahma is

नीरूपस्य ब्रह्मणः कथं चाक्षुषादिज्ञानविषयतेति वाच्यम् । नीरूपस्यापि रूपादेः प्रत्यक्षविषयत्वात् । *Vedánta-paribháshá*, p, 18.

"' How can Brahma, the colourless, be the object of visual or other perception?' Let not this be asked: for colour and such other *things*, though colourless, are objects of perception."

It is a maxim of all the Hindu schools, that qualities have themselves no qualities; and hence colour is colourless. Therefore, implies the writer here cited, if the possession of colour were a condition indispensable to perceptibility, colour would be invisible. Sophistry such as this could scarcely be matched. But the objector, probably a Naiyáyika, who is thus answered, maintains, that the condition specified holds only in respect of substance, not in respect of quality; for quality is perceived through substance. To this it is rejoined, that Brahma is denied to be substantial, and that, consequently, the condition does not apply to him. And again, though it were granted, that Brahma is substantial, still, like time, which also wants colour, he could be the object of visual and other perception. How time can be such an object, the Vedántin only knows.

* In the *Vedánta-paribháshá*, p. 6, we read, that, in perception, the object perceived becomes non-different from the subject of right notion; but that, in inference, &c., the object does not become so. The author's explanation is this. Non-difference from the subject of right notion does not here mean oneness with it, but the non-possession of an existence distinct from that of such subject. To exemplify: since a jar is imagined in the intelligence which is appropriated to it, the very existence of the jar-appropriated intelligence,—technically called the object-intelligence,—is the existence of the jar. For it is not admitted, that the existence of an imagined thing differs from that of its substrate: तथाहि । घटादेः स्वावच्छिन्नचैतन्येऽध्यस्ततया विषयचैतन्यसत्तैव घटादिसत्ता अधिष्ठानसत्तातिरिक्तारोपितसत्ताया अनङ्गीकारात् । Thus it is shown how the object of perception is non-different from the object-intelligence. It remains to show how that object becomes non-different from the intelligence which is the

its substrate, and its illusory-material cause; and ignorance is its material cause. The world, thus, is false; and, there-

subject of right notion. Intelligence appropriated to the internal organ is called the subject of right notion. When an organ of sense, as the eye, impinges upon an object, the internal organ is said to evolve, to be emitted through the eye, to betake itself to the object, and to be transformed into its shape. This transformed portion of the internal organ is known as an affection. *Vide ut supra*, p. 4. Along with the internal organ the intelligence thereto appropriated is produced to the object perceived; that is to say, as the dimensions of that organ are amplified by the evolution, which remains continuous with the source of evolution, so increase the limits of the intelligence appropriated to the organ in question: for intelligence being assumed as all-pervading, it cannot be said, literally, to have motion. On a jar being brought within a house, the jar-appropriated ether and the house-appropriated ether become one; they being supposed distinct, so long as the jar was outside of the house. Similarly, when the internal organ reaches its object, the intelligence appropriated to that organ becomes one with the object-intelligence; and, since the object is non-different from the object-intelligence, it becomes one with the intelligence appropriated to the internal organ, which intelligence is the subject of right notion. This does not, however, take place in inference; for, inasmuch as, there, the object does not come into contact with an organ of sense, the internal organ is not thought to be drawn out to that object through an organ of sense. Consequently, as the intelligence appropriated to the internal organ does not reach the spot occupied by the object-intelligence, the two do not become one; nor does the object of inference become non-different from the subject of right notion.

From this it is plain, that a portion of Brahma, a portion designated as object-intelligence, is considered, by the Vedántins, to be external to the beholder, and to take up a determinate space; in which portion of Brahma a jar, for instance, is imagined, through ignorance, to exist. In this exemplification, Brahma and the jar are precisely analogous to nacre and the silver for which it is mistaken.

Corresponding language will be found in the *Vedánta-paribháshá*, p. 11; where it is expressed, that it is not the whole of intelligence that serves as substrate to apparent silver, but only so much of it as is appropriated to the present nacre.

Though nacre is, in a certain sense, viewed as the substrate of nacrine silver, yet Brahma also, the substrate of everything practical and apparent, is so, and in a truer sense, by virtue of his being the sole veritable entity.

It should never for a moment be forgotten, that, with the Vedántins, intelligence always means Brahma.

fore, so are its name and form. Its existence in one way is false, and, in another way, is true: the former, when it is viewed as the world; the latter, when it is viewed as Brahma.* Hence the Vedántins maintain, that the world is false; and, at the same time, that it is identical with Brahma, inasmuch as it is Brahma himself that, owing to ignorance, appears as the world.

As on all other topics, so on that of the nature of soul, the Vedánta doctrine presents a variety of opinions. The principal, of which all the rest are modifications, are these two.† Some say, that a portion of Brahma, or of the pure spirit, appropriated to the internal organ, constitutes the soul;‡ others, that it is a reflexion of Brahma in the internal organ.§ It will be made evident, in the sequel, that, on close examination, the internal organ, taken by itself, is found to possess, in the tenets of the Vedántins, those characteristics which are referrible to the soul, and by which we recognize the soul as such.

---

* If it be asked, whether the existence apprehended in such a cognition as "A jar is" be that which belongs to Brahma, and is true, or that which belongs to the world, and is false; the Vedántin's answer is twofold, according to two several theories. The first theory is, that it is Brahma's true existence which is there cognized; the second, that it is the world's false existence. See the two passages from the *Vedánta-paribháshá*, cited at p. 171.

† Named, respectively, *avachchhinna-váda* and *pratibimba-váda*.

‡ The Sanskrit is: जीवो नाम अन्तःकरणावच्छिन्नं चैतन्यम् । *Vedánta-paribháshá*, p. 8.

§ तस्य * * * अन्तःकरणेषु प्रतिबिम्बं जीवचैतन्यम् । *Vedánta-paribháshá*, p. 41. The *tasya*, "his," refers to the pure Brahma, mentioned just previously.

The theory of reflexion is to be understood in its strict material literality. This appears from the subjoined objection and its answer: न च रूप-हीनस्य ब्रह्मणो न प्रतिबिम्बसम्भवः रूपवत एव तथात्वदर्शनादिति वाच्यम् । नीरूपस्यापि रूपस्य प्रतिबिम्बदर्शनात् । *Ibid.*, p. 42.
"'A reflexion of Brahma, he being colourless, cannot be; for it, *a reflexion*, is seen of that only which has colour.' Let not this be asserted; since a reflexion is seen of colour, itself colourless."

The views in question, of what makes up the soul, are always inculcated as just described; and yet the importation into them of the Brahma-element, or reflexion of Brahma, is altogether deceptive. And this Brahma-element, or the reflexion of Brahma, it is taught, is not the adjective part of the soul, but its substantive part. This opinion the Vedántins, building on a maxim which will be cited in the fifth chapter, and recurred to in the seventh, believe themselves justified in entertaining.

When these theories, as has been said, are thoroughly scrutinized, the soul turns out to be the internal organ. And, if it be so, or even if it be a reflexion of Brahma, can it be one with him? The answer, in consonance with Vedánta notions, to this interrogatory will be seen in the seventh chapter.

With reference to the soul, the Vedántins hold, that, though it is Brahma, yet, being subject to illusion, or ignorance, it has forgotten its true nature, and, looking upon the internal organ and the body as real, and identifying itself with them, considers itself to be man, or the like. And, although all things in vicissitudinous life are false, from ignorance soul thinks them true, and calls some of them mine, and the rest others', and imagines that some things make it happy, and that others render it miserable. It being thus, there arise, in the soul, desire and aversion, in consequence of which it engages in good works and in bad. Afterwards, to receive the requital of those works, it has to pass to Elysium, or to Hell, and to take birth repeatedly. All these experiences and mutations are, to be sure, false:* but, nevertheless, they seem to it as true; and hence is all its wretchedness.

---

* शरीरं खगंनरकौ बन्धमोचौभयं तथा ।
कल्पनामाचमेवैतत् किं मे कार्यं चिदात्मनः ॥

"The body, Elysium, Hell, and so both bondage and liberation, are but mere imagination. What, *then*, have I, essentially intelligence, to do *with them?*"

Again, the Vedántins, like the other Systematists, maintain, that the soul has been, from all eternity, in the bondage of illusion. They do not say, that illusion, or ignorance, came into being at some particular period, and took the soul captive. For, if it thus had origin, it would be necessary to assign a cause of its origin; and, besides, even after being emancipated, it might, in consequence of the production of some new ignorance, incur jeopardy of being taken captive afresh. On this ground they allege, that illusion has existed from beyond all duration of time,* and that, coeternally with it, the soul has been enthralled, and will thus continue until emancipated. But how is this notion, that illusion has always existed, reconcilable with the position, that, besides Brahma, one without a second, nothing ever has been, or is, or is to be? What, further, becomes of the position, that Brahma is, in his nature, eternally pure, intelligent, and free? For the soul is Brahma, and yet, having been in bondage to illusion from all eternity, is impure and unintelligent. With a view to repel these objections, the Vedántins declare, that illusion is a thing of so peculiar a character, that at once neither does it exist nor does it not exist. It cannot be said to be, inasmuch as it does not possess true existence. On the other hand, it cannot be said not to be, inasmuch as it possesses the existence called apparent.† This is what they mean in

---

This couplet was supplied by a learned Vedántin, and was referred, by him, to the *Ashṭávakra-gítá*, second canto.

* See the first foot-note at p. 35.

† Practical and apparent existence, it has been shown, do not at all differ from each other, as regards reality, or falsity. Hence, it is all one, in effect, whether the Vedántius call a thing practical, or whether they call it apparent. The author confesses, that he has seen no passage to support him in classing illusion among apparent objects; nor would he spontaneously have thought of thus classing it. The authority of an eminent Vedántin led him to take the view here assumed as correct. The fact, that illusion never comes into play in practical transactions, may have induced the Vedántins to consider it as apparent.

saying, that "Illusion cannot be set forth as being either existent or non-existent."* By this device they would preserve intact the dogma of non-duality, and also make out Brahma to be, in his nature, ever pure, intelligent, and free, and at the same time would account for the thraldom of the soul, and its consequent round of trials. For illusion, though it has apparent existence, has not really real existence; and so the dogma of monism suffers no injury. Again, though illusion has not really real existence, yet it possesses apparent existence; and so it is capable of taking the soul captive. And again, the Vedántins say, that, as illusion is only apparent, so the soul's being fettered is practical; that is, as illusion is false, so the soul's being fettered is likewise false. Neither was the soul ever actually fettered, nor is it now fettered, nor has it to be emancipated.†

---

* अज्ञानं तु सदसद्भ्यामनिर्वचनीयम् । *Vedánta-sára*, p. 4.
नासद्रूपा न सद्रूपा माया नैवोभयात्मिका ।
सदसद्भ्यामनिर्वाच्या मिथ्याभूता सनातनी ॥

This couplet is cited, as from the A'ditya-purána, by Vijnána Bhikshu, in the *Yoga-várttika-bháshya* ; MS., *fol. 79, verso.*

"Illusion is, by nature, neither a nonentity, nor an entity, nor, indeed, both— *combined. It is* not describable either as existent or as non-existent: *it is* false, and *it is* eternal."

† बन्धं च मोक्षं च तथैव मूढा बुद्धेर्गुणान् वस्तुनि कल्पयन्ति ।
दृगावृतिं मेघकृतां रवौ यथा यतोऽद्वयासङ्ग चिदेतदच्चरम् ॥
* * * * * * * * * * *
न निरोधो न चोत्पत्तिर्नबद्धो न च साधकः ।
न मुमुक्षुर्वै मुक्त इत्येषा परमार्थता ।

These verses are from the *Viveka-chúdámani*, which is ascribed to S'ankara A'chárya.

"The foolish groundlessly imagine in the true entity, *i. e., Brahma,* bondage and emancipation, which appertain to the intellect, *or internal organ, here; as they attribute* the veil before the eyes, caused by clouds, to the sun *itself,*

Accordingly, I warn my readers against being misled by the notions, so prevalent among the vulgar, that, according to the Vedánta, Brahma was once void of qualities, and then, assuming them, made the world: and that some small portion of the pure Brahma parted from him, got deluded by illusion, and then became souls; which souls, when they free themselves from illusion, will be united to Brahma; &c. &c. The teachers of the Vedánta do not allege, that Brahma was once void of qualities, and subsequently, taking them upon him, formed the universe; but they allege, that to be without them has ever distinguished him, and ever will distinguish him.* Equally, his possession of qualities, and his operating the origin, continuance, destruction, &c. of the world, are from everlasting; for herein

---

under the idea, that the sun is darkened ; for that, Brahma, is intelligence secondless, unaffected by aught, and indefectible."

* * * * * * * * *

"Destruction is not, nor, again, origination; nor is any bound, or, yet, taking measures to be liberated; nor is there any aspirant after emancipation, or any one emancipated. Such is the truth."

The second of these couplets occurs, as of his own composition, in what passes for the commentary of Gauḍapáda on the Máṇḍúkya-upanishad. See the Bibliotheca Indica, Vol. VIII., p. 432.

सिद्धस्यैव ब्रह्मखरूपस्य मोच्यस्यासिद्धत्वभ्रमेण तत्साधने प्रवृत्त्यु-

पपत्ते: | Vedánta-paribháshá, p. 47. "Though emancipation, Brahma himself, already has place, yet the mistaking it for non-existent can account for taking action to bring it about."

Mark the fallacy of this. Spirit, ever emancipated, and free from bondage, is likewise ever warranted from misapprehension, an affection of the internal organ, which organ is unemancipated from eternity to eternity. In this misreasoning, and in the language in which it is couched, the Vedántins and the Sánkhyas are completely at unity.

* See the passage cited at p. 35. Among the six things there reckoned as beginningless, the pure Brahma is included. Often in most Vedánta writers, but with especial frequency in the works of S'ankara A'chárya, the epithet of "ever and essentially pure, intelligent, and free," nitya-s'uddha-buddha-mukta-swabhávam, is found applied to Brahma.

Buddha is here metonymical; since, in strictness, Brahma is held to be bodha, "intelligence,"—not "intelligent."

the Vedánta is consentient with the other Systems. But his having no qualities is true *(páramárthika)*, and his having qualities is practical. The former is really real : whereas the other is not so ; it arising simply from the imputation, by the ignorant, to Brahma, of what does not belong to him. Nor is it asserted, that, at some period, a part of Brahma was separated off, fell into the snare of illusion, and became soul. The accredited doctrine is, that neither Brahma nor any portion* of him can ever be truly beguiled by illusion.† And yet the soul has always been what it is, distinct from Brahma,‡ and has always been ensnared by illusion, or ignorance, coeval with itself. Nevertheless, the soul is Brahma, and

---

* Pure Brahma, it is maintained, is without parts. In the *Mándúkya-upanishad*, Brahma is spoken of as of four parts ; three, as the soul *(jivátman)*, which experiences three states, those of waking, dreaming, and sleeping insensibly ; and one, as pure Brahma. A'nanda Giri thus introduces two sentences of S'ankara A'chárya, where commenting on the passage adverted to.

आत्मनो निरवयवस्य पादद्वयमपि नोपपद्यते पादचतुष्टयं तु दूरो त्सादितमिति शङ्कते । कथमिति । परमार्थतश्चतुष्ट्यात्माभावेऽपि कल्पनिकमुपायोपेयभूतं पादचतुष्टयमविरुद्धमित्यभिप्रेत्याऽऽद्यं पादं व्युत्पादयति । आहेत्यादिना । *Bibliotheca Indica*, Vol. VIII., p. 340. "Of the impartite spirit not even two portions can be predicated ; still less, four. This is meant by ' How,' &c. Though, in truth, *it* has not four portions, still an imaginary quaternion of portions, consisting *partly* of means and *partly* of end, is not incongruous. With this in view, the first portion *of Brahma* is etymologized as follows : ' He says,' &c."

† Were it otherwise, Brahma would be changeable ; and, in the Vedánta, he is esteemed to be unchangeable.

‡ अयं चान्योन्याभावोऽधिकरणस्य सादिते सादिः यथा घटे पटभेदः । अधिकरणस्यानादित्वेऽनादिरेव यथा जीवे ब्रह्मभेदः ब्रह्मणि वा जीवभेदः । *Vedánta-paribháshá*, p. 32. "And this mutual non-existence, *or non-identity*, when its substrate is originated, is *itself* originated ; as the non-identity of cloth in a jar. If the substrate is beginningless, so *is the non-identity ;* as that of Brahma in the soul, or that of the soul in Brahma."

always has been so; and wherever it is found called a part of Brahma, such language is used only from the standing point of practical existence. Strictly speaking, the soul, in the sense in which it is Brahma, is not so merely as a part of him, but as the whole; and, in the sense in which it is not Brahma, it is no part of Brahma regarded as a whole, but is entirely distinct from him. Nay, rather than speak of it as being distinct from Brahma, it ought to be said, simply, that it is not Brahma. For, from the aspect from which it is not Brahma, Brahma does not exist at all: and how, then, can it be spoken of as distinct from Brahma? The case is like that of nacrine silver, when thought to be genuine silver: it not being, to the beholder, nacre at all; wherefore he will not say, that it is distinct from nacre. In the same way, pure Brahma, contemplated from the standing point of practical existence, has no existence whatever: there is no Brahma, except him that has qualities, or I's'wara, the maker of the world; to which are to be added the world and souls, all quite separate one from another. From that point of view it is, then, wrong to speak of the soul as being separate from the pure Brahma. Therefore, though the soul, from the standing point of practical existence, has always existed as soul, from the standing point of true existence, it has always been veritably Brahma. And, though the soul has always been Brahma, yet neither to Brahma, nor to any part of him, has there ever attached, or can there ever attach, in any way, the least ignorance or alterability. Evermore, in his nature, does he remain altogether pure, intelligent, and free.

From all this it will be patent to the reader, that the Vedántin not only holds the ignorance-imagined world, and its maker, I's'wara, to be practical and false, but maintains, also, that the imaginer of the world and of its maker, namely, ignorance, is apparent and false. The imagining the world and its maker is that which makes soul to be soul; and hence the soul, as soul, is practical and false: the one Brahma, in his nature ever pure, intelligent, and free, alone is true. If, then, it be asked, how it can be, that the soul has, from all eternity, been in captivity to ignorance, and yet is Brahma; he being, however, unchangeably pure: the answer is, that, assuredly, it cannot be; only the misguided Vedántins think that it can. Ignorance, by reason of which the soul, the world, and I's'wara appear, according to them, to exist, they believe to be false, that is, to be nothing; and, of course, there is nothing that can derive impurity or change to Brahma. This will be clearly explained, over and over again, in coming chapters; and so it is unnecessary to dwell on it further on this occasion. And it is highly material that the reader should take notice, that the tenet of the falseness of ignorance is the very key-stone of the Vedánta, and must never be lost from view for a single moment. In constantly recurring to it, as I do in this book, I may be supposed to lay myself open to the charge of tedious and useless repetition. The tenet referred to is, however, not only one of paramount moment, but also difficult to grasp and to retain; and, if it be not mastered, the Vedánta is impossible to be understood.

Further, I would beg the reader to believe, that the Vedánta, however perspicuously expounded, is most bewildering. Some of my own countrymen, and foreigners, in particular, if they read what I write, may conclude, as the result of a hasty glance, that I have set down many things without having grounds for them, and that I have spun enigmas out of my own brains. All such I entreat to avoid a hasty judgment, and to go through my volume patiently and attentively. They will then, I suspect, change their minds. If, in one place where it is looked for, my authority for a statement be found wanting, it will be seen produced elsewhere, and more appropriately; and, if I do not solve all objections as fast as they arise, still I trust, that a careful perusal of my entire treatise will leave few doubts undispelled.

And now I wish to mention one or two things that are very

likely to occur to foreigners who give their attention to the Vedánta and the other Hindu Systems. In the first place, there are many expressions, in the treatises on these systems, the precise sense of which they will not apprehend; and, in the second place, when they come upon glaring absurdities and incongruities, refusing to see them in their true light, they will give them such a turn as to render everything most reasonable and excellent. Whoso would acquaint himself with the philosophical opinions peculiar to a strange country, should by no means content himself with simply reading a book or two, whether by himself, or with aid, and then at once set to theorizing about them. If he wishes to understand those opinions really and thoroughly, he must apply himself perseveringly, for several years, to the study of works in which they are set forth; and he must mix familiarly with the people who profess them, until, by frequent converse, he learns how those people are affected and influenced by their views; and he must hear them speak about them without constraint, and spontaneously. In short, he must, as it were, become one of themselves; and then, and not till then, can he certify himself, that he has actually got at the true purport and import of their belief. Leaving this digression, I shall address myself to what remains to be said on the Vedánta doctrine of the soul.

According to the Vedántins, when the soul, bound by illusion, becomes convinced, that the world is false, and that itself is Brahma, existent, intelligence, and joy, it escapes from further vicissitude, and realizes Brahmahood. But, even after the acquisition of this knowledge, the soul has to tenant the body, till it exhausts the experience of its fructescent works; and so long it cannot evade happiness and misery. This experience exhausted, it obtains disembodied isolation, plenary emancipation. In thus determining, the Vedánta is in unison with all the other Systems; and also in prescribing purity of intellect as indispensable to emancipative knowledge. This purity is the fruit of good works, such as repetition of sacred names, austerities, and pilgrimage, kept up during several births.* In order to gaining emancipative knowledge, the practice of devotion likewise is prescribed. The accounts of I's'wara, found in the Puráṇas and other books, as that he assumed the forms of Vishṇu, S'iva, &c., and achieved various actions, are also respected by the Vedántins;† who, again, hold it proper to go through the sacrifices and other ceremonies enjoined in the Veda. They declare, however, like the other Systematists, that, if a man estranges himself from the world, and gives himself wholly to spiritual studies and exercises, and becomes an ascetic, he must desist from all ritualism. Still they do not impugn the ceremonial portion of the Veda as folly. Notwithstanding the ritual renunciation of the ascetic, as has been mentioned, it is not deemed improper for him to engage in mental devotion addressed to Vishṇu, Mahádeva, and other first-class deities, forms of I's'wara. Whoever, therefore, hearing, that the Vedántins believe in Brahma without qualities, infer, that they reject Vishṇu, S'iva, and the rest of the pantheon, and that they discountenance idolatry and such things,. and that they count the Puráṇas and similar writings false, labours under gross error.‡ Regarded from the standing point of practical

---

* तच् च ज्ञानं पापव्ययात् स च कर्मानुष्ठानादिति परम्परया कर्मणां विनियोगः । *Vedánta-paribháshá*, p. 49. "And this right apprehension *is obtainable* by one *after* elimination of sin; and this *elimination results* from performance of *good* works. Thus is the connexion, mediately, of works *with right apprehension.*"

† स च परमेश्वर एकोऽपि स्वोपाधिभूतमायानिष्ठसत्त्वरजस्तमोगुणभेदेन ब्रह्मविष्णुमहेश्वरादिशब्दवाच्यतां भजते । *Vedántaparibháshá*, p. 9. "And this supreme I's'wara, though one, yet, because of the difference between the *guṇas*,—goodness, passion, and darkness,—belonging to illusion, his, *I's'wara's*, associate, receives the appellations of Brahmá, Vishṇu, Mahes'wara, &c."

‡ S'ankara A'chárya, while engaged in refuting the Bhágavatas, confines

existence, these are all real and authoritative. From the standing point of true existence, all things, including even the Upanishads, the source of the Vedánta faith, are looked upon as false. Such are the leading dogmas of the Vedánta.

CHAPTER 3.

Examination of the Vedánta Views concerning the Supreme Spirit.

The first article of the Vedánta creed, as it has been given, is, that "Brahma is true." However, the Vedantins, in denying all qualities to him, render him such, that it is impossible to

himself to the doctrinal moiety of their system, where that moiety is discrepant from the Vedánta, and acknowledges as commendable the whole of its ritualism. His words are these: तन् यत् तावदुच्यते योऽसौ नारायणः परोऽव्यक्तात् प्रसिद्धः परमात्मा सर्वात्मा स आत्मनाऽऽत्मानमनेकधा व्यूह्य अवस्थित इति तन् न निराक्रियते । स एकधा भवति द्विधा भवतीत्यादिश्रुतिभ्यः परमात्मनोऽनेकधाभावस्याऽधिगतत्वात् । यदपि तस्य भगवतोऽभिगमनादिलक्षणमाराधनमजस्रमनन्यचित्ततयाऽभिप्रेयते तदपि न प्रतिषिध्यते श्रुतिस्मृत्योरीश्वरप्रणिधानस्य प्रसिद्धत्वात् ।
Brahma-sútra-bháshya, II., 2. MS.: on the aphorism उत्पत्त्यसम्भवात् ।
"What you *Bhágavatas* here allege, *to-wit*, that Náráyaṇa,—known to transcend the unmanifested, *nature;* the supreme Spirit; one with all,—has of himself exhibited himself in various divisions, is not controverted. For, from 'He becomes one, he becomes two-fold,' and other scriptures, the manifoldness *of manifestation* of the supreme Spirit is gathered. Moreover, the religious service, *prosecuted* incessantly, and with undistracted attention, of that adorable one, consisting in pious resort, &c., which is inculcated *by you*, is not objected to; by reason, as is well known, that *there is injunction of* devotion to I'swara in the Veda and the Smṛitis."

The reader, if curious about the particulars of the mode of worship in vogue among the Bhágavatas, may consult Colebrooke's *Miscellaneous Essays*, Vol. I., p. 416. Elucidations will there be seen of the terms *abhigamana, upádána, ijyá, swádhyáya,* and *yoga,* as employed by those sectaries.

prove his existence. When they hear us ascribe to the Supreme Spirit intelligence, will, power, and other attributes, and speak of Him as Maker of the world, they silently deride us, in the conviction, that we are lamentably ignorant: for our views, to their thinking, impute imperfection to Him, in giving Him qualities; and they suppose, that we, at the best and furthest, stop short at I's'wara, and make no approach to the pure Brahma beyond. But they do not consider, that such a supreme Spirit as they contend for cannot be proved to exist. From the world, an effect, it must be inferred, that it had an efficient cause: hence God, its Maker. By what argumentation can one establish the existence of a being transcending Him, a being not a maker? Moreover, I would ask the Vedántin in what sort we charge imperfection on the Supreme Spirit, in ascribing to Him such attributes as omnipotence and omniscience? And, if Brahma be void of all qualities, on what ground is he supposed to be ulterior to the Creator? For a being without qualities, if conceivable, cannot be deemed either excellent or otherwise. But, waiving this, it is certain, as was said, that Brahma without qualities cannot be proved an entity. Preception tells us nothing of him; and inference teaches us no more; since he has no relation with anything. For, agreeably to the Vedántin's definition, Brahma is related to nothing, either as cause, or in any other way.

It might be supposed, by some, that, since the Vedántins call Brahma the substrate of the world, it is wrong to say, that they deny his relativity. I reply, that the sublime conception, that God is the stay of the world, is, indeed, most true. But neither true nor sublime is the notion of the Vedántins, that Brahma is the world's substrate. They mean, that he is so, just as nacre is the substrate of fancied silver. As nacre is mistaken for silver, so is Brahma mistaken for the world. Again, let it be ever kept in mind, that, by the Brahma whom the Vedántins call the world's substrate, or illusory-material cause, is ordinarily meant, not the pure Brahma, now under discussion, but Brahma the illusion-appropriated, or illusion-associated,* Is'wara, who is ignorance-imagined and false.

The Vedántins are, however, forced to look upon the pure Brahma also as the ultimate substrate of all. Since Brahma the illusion-associated, and likewise the illusion which is his associate, are ignorance-imagined and false, a substrate must be found for them; and it can be found, we are told, in the pure Brahma,† and nowhere else. But this pure Brahma is not held to be, consciously, and by virtue of his will and power, the cause of the universe to which he stands in the relation of substrate.‡ So well-known, in fact, is it, that Brahma

---

* ब्रह्मैव घटाद्युपादानं तस्य मायोपहितस्य चैतन्यस्य सकल-घटाद्यन्वयित्वात् । *Vedánta-paribháshá*, p. 44. "Brahma himself is the material cause, *i. e., the illusory-material cause*, of a jar, or the like; for this illusion-associated intelligence extends to all jars, and so forth."

† See the second extract from A'nanda Giri at p. 158.

‡ As is stated in the text, the Vedántins ordinarily speak of the illusion-associated Brahma, I's'wara, as the world's illusory-material cause; but, it must be understood, it is his pure-Brahma portion that is held to be so. The illusory-material cause of the world—which world is reckoned false—must be a true entity; and, inasmuch as the illusion-associated Brahma, as such, is false, and so the world likewise, he cannot, as associated with illusion, be its illusory-material cause. The Vedántins are compelled to maintain, that his pure-Brahma portion is, here, alone to be taken account of. On other occasions, however, all that is predicated of this being, I's'wara, is referred to his illusion-portion; as, for instance, the conscious and efficient causativity of the world, omniscience, omnipotence, &c. &c. अविद्या नाम विद्यानिवर्त्यानिर्वचनीयानादिभावरूपेति वक्ष्यते । तद्विलासस्य तज्जनितो वृत्तिविशेषः परमेश्वरस्येच्छासङ्कल्पप्रयत्नरूपः । *Vedánta-s'ikhámaṇi*, MS., *fol.* 2, *verso.* "'Nescience,' as will be declared, is a beginningless entity, not to be described *as true*, *or as unreal*, *and* eliminable by science, *i. e., right apprehension*. And its 'play' is a certain affection, therefrom produced, in the shape of the supreme Is'wara's beholding, *or apprehension*, will, and activity; *by which three Is'wara makes the world*."

Similarly, the limited apprehension, will, activity, &c. of Brahma appropriated to the internal organ, in other words, of soul, are referred to the soul's internal-organ portion, not to its Brahma-portion.

has no activity, will, and other qualities, that it ought not to be expected of me to adduce authority for what I assert. However, I will quote a passage in proof. The author of the *Sankshepa-s'áríraka*, after battling long with the Vais'eshikas on the point in question, thus delivers his own doctrine: "Moreover, from the son of A'nakadundubhi,—announced in the Veda; outreaching speech and thought; unalloyed intelligence, without rise or disappearance; lord,—this entire universe was produced unconsciously."*   And how was the world

---

Hence, when the Vedántins ascribe illusory-material causativity to the illusion-associated Brahma, they consider him as indeed a conscious and efficient cause: but, since, only as illusion-associated, he is such a cause,—*viz.*, since conscious and efficient causativity appertains to his illusion-portion only,—as a conscious and efficient cause, he is false.

Again, the Vedántins, as mentioned above, ultimately ascribe illusory-material causativity to the pure Brahma, whom they indeed count a true entity: only he is, avowedly, devoid of all that constitutes a conscious and efficient cause.

The reason why the Vedántins generally refer to the illusion-associated Brahma the illusory-material causativity of the world, is this. Brahma, it is laid down, possesses such causativity, in the sight of the ignorant only, by whom the world is reputed to be real. To such, the material cause of the world, or illusion, is likewise real; and, in like manner, Brahma is, to them, necessarily associated with illusion. Consequently, when Brahma the illusion-associated is spoken of as the illusory-material cause of the world, it is not intended, that he, as such, is such a cause, but solely as pure Brahma: and yet, to the ignorant, he is not, in fact, unassociated Brahma, but Brahma associated with illusion.

* अपि च वैदिकवाङ्मनसातिगानुदितलुप्तचिदेकरसात् प्रभोः ।
अभवदानकदुन्दुभिनन्दनादमतिपूर्वमिदं सकलं जगत् ॥

No MS. of the *Sankshepa-s'áríraka* is just now accessible for reference.

By "son of A'nakadundubhi" is meant Krishna.

The earlier Vedántins, S'ankara A'chárya and his proximate followers, were—as will be seen in a coming note,—Vaishnavas, and held Vishnu, or Krishna, to be the supreme Spirit himself. They use the word Vásudeva, a name of Krishna, as a synonym of Brahma.

Thus, S'ankara, commenting on the *Katha-upanishad*, says: विष्णो-
व्यापनशीलस्य ब्रह्मणः परमात्मनो वासुदेवाख्यस्य । *Bibliotheca In-*

produced unconsciously from the son of A'nakadundubhi? The answer is, precisely as silver is produced from nacre; not as an effect owes its origin to a conscious agent. Hence I maintain, that, if Brahma be not conscious creator of the world, or its stay, otherwise than as nacre is to silver, that is to say, in spite of himself, to establish that such a substrate exists is not to make out, that Brahma, as essentially existence, intelligence, and joy, is an entity. To prove, that any being is such a stay of the world as the Vedántins talk of, it must first of all be shown, that the world is illusory. And, though the world be so considered, how is it determined, that its stay, or substrate, which is mistaken for the world, a visible and material thing, is void of qualities, impassible, without form, immutable, essentially existence, intelligence, and joy, as the Vedántins describe Brahma?

Now, the Supreme Spirit, God, whom the Bible calls the Upholder of the world, is not so as nacre is to silver, or as the ground is to a jar, or as a thing qualified is to its qualities, or

---

dica, Vol. VIII, p. 114 "Of ' Vishṇu,' known as Vásudeva,—pervader *of all*, Brahma, the supreme Spirit."

Vásudeva, as a word, means "son of Vasudeva." The Vedántins, however, try to force from it, etymologically, various senses available for epithets of Brahma. The author of the *Sankshepa-s'aríraka*, one of the older Vedántin doctors, expresses and implies, throughout his book, that Vishṇu is the supreme Brahma of his own school. But S'iva, he says, is the I's'wara of the Vais'eshika and other anti-vaidika denominations:

मतिमतां प्रवरो ऋषभध्वजः
कशभुगादिमुनिप्रवरप्रभुः ।

In the stanza at the beginning of this note, he puts "son of A'nakadundubhi" for Vásudeva, because the latter word was refractory to his prosody. A'nakadundubhi, otherwise called Vasudeva, was father of Vásudeva, that is to say, Kṛishṇa.

By the application of the term *vaidika* to Vásudeva, it is intimated, that Kṛishṇa is the supreme Brahma of the Vedántins.

As, in the chapter here cited from, the Vedánta theory is set in opposition to the Vais'eshika, &c., so is Kṛishṇa set in opposition to S'iva.

as its threads are to a web. He is called the world's Upholder, because by His wondrous and inscrutable will and might the world is supported. As it did not originate spontaneously, so neither is it self-sustaining, but is upheld by the constant exercise of the Divine Will. To speak figuratively, the hand of His will holds up its existence. Let that hand be withdrawn but for a single instant, and it would at once fall into non-existence. Such is the exalted sense in which the Bible speaks of God as the Stay of the world; as where it says: "In Him we live, and move, and have our being." From other passages of Holy Writ, where God is mentioned as the Creator and Upholder of the world, it is evident what meaning we are to assign to the text just cited. How wide, then, is the difference between the Vedánta doctrine, on the point here discussed, and the doctrine of the Bible!

But, over and above all this, it should not be forgotten, that, in the estimation of the Vedántins, the pure Brahma's being even the unconscious substrate of the universe is not true *(páramárthika)*. For the ignorance by which he is imagined to be such a substrate, is itself maintained to be false :* a position necessary for the integrity of monism. Strictly speaking, then, there is not even so much of a connexion between the pure Brahma and the universe as seemed, a minute ago, to be promised. This is strange absurdity; but I am not responsible for it. I take the Vedánta as I find it, and trace its principles to their issues.

And let no one suppose, that the places in the Upanishads and other Vedánta works, where an omniscient or omnipotent being, or the conscious and efficient cause of the world, is spoken of, are claimed, by the Vedántins, as referring to their pure Brahma. On the contrary, they assert, that their I's'wara is there meant. Names which they give to him are, Brahma with qualities, Brahma adulterate, illusion-associated

---

* This will be shown in the eighth chapter.

Brahma, illusive Brahma,* and even supreme Brahma and Supreme Spirit. For—as should be distinctly kept in mind—it is the supreme Brahma himself, imagined, by ignorance, as associated with illusion, as creating the world, and as endowed with the attributes of omniscience, &c., that is I's'wara.

The case of the soul, and that of the world, are, however, precisely like that of I's'wara; for the soul and the world are nothing but Brahma mistaken for them. Why, then, is I's'wara, in a more special and eminent sense than the soul and the world, considered to be one with Brahma? The Vedántin would reply, that his system persuasively accommodates its language, when addressed to the vulgar, to their erroneous views. The vulgar are not conscious, that they call the supreme Spirit himself soul and the world; but they are conscious, that they believe him to be the omnipotent and omniscient creator. But what I think to be the true reason is this; that, though the Vedántin, in order to save monism, is forced upon the invention, that Brahma is void of qualities, yet his inner consciousness does not acquiesce in this position. Hence he is involuntarily led to speak of Brahma and I's'wara promiscuously, as if they were the same.

The first of the Vedánta Aphorisms, to be sure, professes to enquire about Brahma; and the second defines him to be author of the world's origin, subsistence, and end. Yet it must not be inferred, from this, that the Vedántins really so conceive of their pure Brahma. It is not, that the essential nature of the pure Brahma is there defined; but a false character is imputed to him, with intent to point out his true nature from afar.†

---

* See the second extract from A'nanda Giri, cited at p. 158. "Brahma adulterate" translates *s'abala-brahman*.

† The Vedántins have two sorts of definitions of Brahma. The first, *swarúpa-lakshaṇa*, describes his true nature, and is worded; "existent, intelligence, and joy." The other definition, that in question, is called *taṭastha-lakshaṇa*. *Taṭastha* signifies "standing on the shore." True to the metaphor,

It may be asked, whether the Vedántins consider their

such a definition denotes a characteristic which, though not in fact inhering in the thing defined, approximates to it, and indicates it. The ordinary illustration represents a man as pointing out the new moon to another, by directing him to look at a certain branch of a certain tree.

Rámánanda Saraswatí, expounding the commentary on the second aphorism of the *Brahma-sútra*, mentioned above, writes thus : ननु जिज्ञास्य-निर्गुणब्रह्मणः कारणत्वं कथं लक्षणमिति चेदुच्यते । यथा रजतं शुक्तेर्लक्ष्यां यद् रजतं सा शुक्तिरिति तथा यत् जगत्कारणं तद् ब्रह्मेति कल्पितंकारणत्वं तटस्थं सदेव ब्रह्मणो लक्षणमित्यनवद्यम् ।
Bibliotheca Indica, No. 64, p. 38. "But how can causativity be a characteristic of Brahma, destitute of qualities, the object of enquiry? If this be asked, the reply is: In like manner as silver is a characteristic of nacre, in the proposition 'That which is *mistaken for* silver is nacre,' so, in the proposition, 'That which is *mistaken for* the cause of the world is Brahma,' imaginary causativity is a merely suggestive characteristic of Brahma. Thus *is all* unimpeachable."

Thus it is declared, that Brahma is held to be author of the world's origin, continuance, and end, just as nacre is nacrine silver.

The description of the *taṭastha-lakshaṇa* given by the author of the *Vedánta-paribháshá*, pp. 34, 35, may appear, to a hurried reader, to make against the above : तटस्थलक्षणं नाम यावल्लक्ष्यकालमनवस्थितत्वे सति यद् व्यावर्तकं तदेव । यथा गन्धवत्त्वं पृथिवीलक्षणं महाप्रलये परमाणुषु उत्पत्तिकाले घटादिषु च गन्धाभावात् । प्रज्ञते च जगज्जन्मादिकारणत्वम् । "A suggestive characteristic is that which does not correspond temporally to the object characterized, and which *yet* distinguishes *it from other things*. Thus, the having odour is a suggestive characteristic of earth; for, at the great consummation, there is no odour in the *terrene* atoms; nor *is there any* in jars and the like, at the time of *their* production. And, in the case in hand, *i. e., of Brahma*, the being the cause of the origin, &c. of the universe *is the suggestive characteristic*."

It might be thought, from this, that, however the causativity of the universe does not always appertain to Brahma, still it appertains to him at some particular period or periods; as odour, to the earth. But the reader cannot be too often cautioned, that the expressions of the Vedántins are frequently most deceptive. What has just been stated is, suitably to the Vedánta, true as far as it goes: only it is not the whole truth. Brahma's causativity of the world's origin, &c. is, to be sure, non-eternal, even as the developed universe itself is

I's'wara to be altogether false. They regard illusion-appro-

non-eternal. Both the causativity and the universe are, however, not only non-eternal, but false. They are only ignorance-imagined; and, immediately on the acceding of right apprehension, they are falsified, or proved to be nothing. For this very reason they are called transitory : तादृशमधिकरण
यदि चैतन्यव्यतिरिक्तं तदा तस्य नित्यत्वमसिद्धं । ब्रह्मव्यतिरिक्तस्य
सर्वस्य ब्रह्मज्ञाननिवर्त्यतायाः वच्यमाणत्वात् । *Ibid.*, p. 32. "If such substrate is other than intelligence, *i. e., Brahma,* its eternalness is not established. For, as will be declared, all but Brahma is falsifiable by right apprehension of Brahma."

The ensuing passage will clear up the meaning of Dharmarája : ननु
वेदान्तेर्ब्रह्मणि जगत्कारणत्वेन प्रतिपाद्यमाने सति सप्रपञ्चं ब्रह्म
स्यात् अन्यथा सृष्टिवाक्यानामप्रामाण्यापत्तिरिति चेन् न । न हि
सृष्टिवाक्यानां सृष्टौ तात्पर्यं किन्त्वद्वये ब्रह्मण्येव । तत्प्रतिपत्तौ
कथं सृष्टेरुपयोगः । इत्थम् । यदि सृष्टिमनुपन्यस्य प्रपञ्चस्य
निषेधो ब्रह्मणि प्रतिपाद्येत तदा ब्रह्मणि प्रतिविद्धस्य प्रपञ्चस्य वायौ
प्रतिविद्धस्य रूपस्येव ब्रह्मणोऽन्यत्रावस्थानशङ्कायां न निर्विचिकि-
त्समद्वितीयत्वं प्रतिपादितं स्यात् । ततः सृष्टिवाक्याद् ब्रह्मोपादे-
यत्वज्ञाने सति उपादानं विना कार्यस्यान्यत्र सत्त्वशङ्कायां निर-
स्तायां नेति नेतीत्यादिना ब्रह्मण्यपि तस्यासत्त्वोपादनेन प्रपञ्चस्य
तुच्छत्वावगमे निरस्तनिखिलद्वैतविभ्रममखण्डं सच्चिदानन्दैकरसं ब्रह्म
सिध्यतीति परम्परया सृष्टिवाक्यानामप्यद्वितीये ब्रह्मण्येव तात्पर्यम् ।
उपासनाप्रकरणपठितसगुणब्रह्मवाक्यानान्तु उपासनाविधिपेक्षितगु-
णारोपमात्रपरत्वं न सगुणपरत्वम् । निर्गुणप्रकरणपठितानां सगुण-
वाक्यानां तु निषेधवाक्यापेक्षितनिषेध्यसमर्पकत्वेन विनियोग इति
न किञ्चिदपि वाक्यमद्वितीयब्रह्मप्रतिपादनेन विरुध्यते । *Ibid.*, pp
40, 41. "'If Brahma is set forth, by the Vedántas, *i. e., the Upanishads,* to be the cause of the world, he must be in relation with the world ; *and the consequence is duality.* Else, the *scriptural* declarations of creation come to be 'alsified.' Not so. The passages which speak of creation do not aim to teach *the verity of* creation, but *to impart a knowledge of* the secondless Brahma. How is *the description of* creation subservient to the knowledge of him ? In

priated Brahma as I's'wara.* A part of him may be false; but how can that other part of him, which is Brahma, be

this wise. If *the existence of* the universe in Brahma were denied, and creation were not mentioned, the surmise might arise, that the universe, denied *to exist* in Brahma, exists somewhere else; even as colour, *though* denied to exist in the air, *exists in other things:* and thus an indubitable account of non-duality would not have been given. Hence, when it is ascertained, from the passages concerned with creation, that *the universe* is a material effect, *viz.*, *an illusory-material effect*, of Brahma, the surmise, that *the universe*, the *material* effect, could exist elsewhere *than in Brahma*, the material cause, is dispelled. Then, by the statement, in 'Not it, not it,' and other *scriptural passages*, of the non-existence of it, *the universe*, in Brahma also, the utter nihility of the universe being ascertained, Brahma,—freed from all suspicion of duality; impartite; the existent intelligence and joy, unalloyed *with aught else*,—is established. Thus, the aim of even the passages relating to creation is, to set forth, indirectly, Brahma as without a second. The object of the passages read in the devotional sections *of the Upanishads*, which announce Brahma with qualities, is, simply to impute qualities falsely *to Brahma*, *which qualities are* demanded by the injunctions to devotion; *and their object is not to teach that he is* possessed of qualities. As for the use of the passages read in sections *of the Upanishads* taken up with *Brahma* without qualities, *which passages* speak of *him as* having qualities, it is, to indicate, supplementarily. the object denied, *viz.*, *qualities, which object is* demanded by the passages denying qualities, to Brahma. Thus no passage whatever is inconsistent with the declaration of Brahma as secondless."

The Vedántins, accordingly, discourse of Brahma's causativity, and other qualities, simply with intent to confirm the idea of their entire nonentity.

It will be sufficiently clear, from what precedes, how essentially Dr. J. R. Ballantyne has misapprehended the purport of the Vedánta system. "So far," he says, "is the conception of *Brahm* from being reduced to that of a nonentity by the Vedántic tenet of his being *nirguṇa*, that, according to one of Vyása's aphorisms, as rendered by Mr. Colebrooke (*Essays*, p. 352), 'Every attribute of a first cause (omniscience, omnipotence, etc.), exists in *Brahme*, who is devoid of qualities.' It is rather strange, that the occurrence of this passage in Mr. Colebrooke's well-known essay should not have sufficed to awaken a suspicion, that the term 'devoid of qualities' must be employed in a sense other than that of an empty substratum—a nonentity." *Christianity contrasted*, &c., p. 46.

* मायावच्छिन्नं चैतन्यं च परमेश्वरः । *Vedánta-paribháshá*, p. 9. "Intelligence appropriated to illusion is I's'wara, supreme."

so? In reply, I ask, whether they do not maintain, that Brahma as appropriated to the internal organ constitutes the soul? And why do they call the soul false? The reason is this. They assert, that Brahma, as appropriated to the internal organ, or else as reflected in it, constitutes the soul; and yet they deny, that Brahma is truly so appropriated, or reflected; there being, according to them, no true contact between Brahma and the internal organ, but only an erroneously imputed contact; since, like the rest of the world, the internal organ is false. Hence, though the soul is called Brahma appropriated to the internal organ, still, since his appropriation to the internal organ is false, the soul as soul is false. Similarly, though they call Brahma appropriated to illusion I's'wara, they declare, that the contact of illusion with Brahma is not true, but merely imagined. Hence, with them, I's'wara is Brahma appropriated to illusion; and yet they believe their I's'wara's appropriation to illusion to be imaginary; and, therefore, their I's'wara is imaginary, namely, imagined by ignorance. According to their opinion, even the false I's'warahood of this illusion-appropriated I's'wara belongs to his illusion-portion, not to his Brahma-portion; in like manner as the false activity, experience of happiness and misery, and other qualities of the imagined internal-organ-appropriated soul, reside in its internal-organ portion, not in its Brahma-portion. When, therefore, they call I's'wara maker of the world, and omnipotent, it must be understood, that they deny activity and other qualities to his Brahma-portion.

Sometimes the Vedántins give to illusion the appellation of power of I's'wara. Still, it does not inhere in the true nature of I's'wara, his Brahma-portion, in the way we hold, that power inheres in one who is powerful. For we regard this connexion as true; but the connexion between Brahma and illusion is false. It is distinctly stated, in the *Vedántasára*, that, as a snake is erroneously surmised in a cord, just so the entire universe, beginning with ignorance, is erroneously surmised in Brahma.* Here, it should be observed, ignorance itself is comprehended in the universe, the object of erroneous surmise. By ignorance, as will be seen by the reader of the *Vedánta-sára*, illusion—which is the material cause of the world, often denominated the power of Ís'wara,—is here intended.

Not except by apprehending these mysterious matters of the Vedánta, can one be preserved from being misled by its language. To make good this assertion, I produce a passage on the subject of ignorance-associated intelligence, or Ís'wara. It is this: "Intelligence associated with ignorance, when the former is chiefly considered, is the efficient cause; and, when its associate is so considered, the material cause: as the spider, when itself is chiefly considered, is the efficient cause, and, when its body, *whence its web is derived*, is so considered, the material cause, as regards its thread, the effect."† On reading this, one of the uninitiated will express himself in this wise. " Here, plainly enough, two statements are put forth touching Ís'wara. His body—ignorance, or illusion,—is called the material cause of the world; and himself, the efficient cause of the world, or its maker. And what is he, in distinction from ignorance, his body, but pure Brahma? And does it not follow, that this pure Brahma is accounted maker of the world?" I reply, that no one who has fathomed the Vedánta doctrine can come to such a conclusion

---

* असर्पभूतायां रज्जौ सर्पारोपवत् वस्तुन्यवस्त्वारोपोऽध्यारोपः । वस्तु सच्चिदानन्दाद्वयं ब्रह्म । अज्ञानादिसकलजडसमूहोऽवस्तु । p. 4.

† अज्ञानोपहितचैतन्यं स्वप्रधानतया निमित्तं स्वोपाधिप्रधान-तयोपादानं च भवति । यथा लूता तन्तुकार्यं प्रति स्वप्रधानतया निमित्तं स्वशरीरप्रधानतयोपादानं च भवति । *Vedánta-sára*, p. 7. Ís'wara is sometimes called *máyávachchhinna*, and, sometimes, *ajnánopahita*; or "illusion-appropriated" and "ignorance-associated."

as is thus implied. By way of explanation, I will first show how, according to the Vedántin, the case stands, in its fulness, as regards the spider; and then, how the illustration of the spider and his web is applicable, according to the Vedántin, in respect of Ís'wara. It must be understood, that, in the view of the Vedántins, as the human soul is, in fact, ever pure, intelligent, and free Brahma, precisely so is the self, or soul, of the spider. Hence, as activity and other qualities belong to the human soul only by erroneous imputation,* only thus do they belong to the soul of the spider: there being no true connexion between those qualities and soul; for those qualities are properties of the internal organ. How, then, are we to explain, that the spider, *i. e.*, the spider's soul, is called an efficient cause? The answer is, that its causativity is accounted for by erroneous imputation. Then, an objector may urge, the efficient causativity and material causativity of the spider both appertain to its body: for the internal organ is called the subtile body, and it must, therefore, be regarded as body; and, this being the case, why is a distinction taken between the spider and its body, and the former called efficient cause, and the latter, material cause? My reply is, that, in the passage of the *Vedánta-sára* under discussion, the exoteric notion

---

* शीतस्यैव जलस्यौपाधिकौष्ण्याश्रयत्ववत् स्वभावतो निर्गुण-
स्यैव जीवस्यासक्तकरणाद्युपाधिवशात् कर्तृत्वाद्यध्यवप्रतिभासो-
पपत्तेः । यदि जलादावौष्ण्यमारोपितं तदा प्रकृतेऽपि तुल्यम् ।

Vedánta-paribháshá, p. 45. "For, as water, assuredly cold *in its proper nature*, is *erroneously taken to be* the subject of heat which appears, in consequence of *the water's* proximity to its associate, *fire*, to inhere *in the water;* so, it may be explained, the soul, by essence truly void of qualities, is *wrongly* supposed, by reason of *its being taken to be identical with* the internal organ and others of its associates, *the true subjects of activity &c.*, to be the subject of activity and the like. If *it is admitted, that* the heat in water and other *cold substances* is falsely ascribed, *i. e.*, *misapprehendingly referred to them*, then *be it known, that* similar *wrongness of ascription has place* as regards what is in discussion, *viz., the soul*."

is adopted. For, when the Vedántins speak of the origin of the world, for instance, they do not believe its origin to be true. This mode of expression they call false imputation. It consists in holding for true that which is false, in accommodation to the intelligence of the uninitiated. At a further stage of instruction, when the time has arrived for propounding the esoteric view, the false imputation is gainsaid: and this gainsaying is termed rescission.* The soul of the spider has no true efficient causativity; and yet everybody considers the spider as possessing it. Hence, with reference to common opinion, such causativity is falsely imputed to him, and he is called an efficient cause. The qualities of his external and gross corporeal frame are, however, never attributed to his soul: his body being regarded, by all, as distinct from his soul.† Hence, when the author of the *Vedánta-sára* treats the body of the spider as a thing distinct from his soul, and calls the former the material cause of his web, he goes along with other men. All that has here been said about the spider is applied, by the Vedántins, to their I's'wara.

The Naiyáyikas, and many others, hold I's'wara, regarded, by them, as mere spirit, to be the maker of the world. But these poor men, as a Vedántin would say, are unaware of the esoteric fact, that in truth, the maker of the world is not his spirit,—that is, his Brahma-portion, to which I's'warahood is falsely imputed,—but his associate, which is his subtile body, or internal organ.‡ On this point, the Vedántins,

---

* "False imputation" and "rescission" have been selected to represent *adhyáropa* and *apaváda*.

† As for the Chárvákas, and the profoundly ignorant, who take the gross body itself to be the soul, they are scarcely worthy of the notice of the Vedántin, who especially shapes his instruction to meet the supposed wants of the Naiyáyikas and similar philosophers. These, the Vedántin says, though wise enough to distinguish the soul from the gross body, are, nevertheless, unable to distinguish it from the internal organ, and attribute to the soul the qualities which belong exclusively to that organ, *viz.*, apprehension, will, activity, &c. See, further, what Vijnána Bhikshu says in the last extract at p. 52.

‡ For, with the Vedántins, I's'wara, no less than the soul, requires a sort of

condescending to avail themselves of the language of the, to them, parcel-blind Naiyáyikas, and many others, falsely impute efficient causativity to I's'wara, and denominate him efficient cause. But none of these short-sighted folk take I's'wara to be the material cause of the world. This cause some of them find in atoms; others, in something else material. What, then, would the Vedántins offer as a material cause? Nay, as the very world is, to them, nothing, what need of a material cause at all? Nevertheless, seeing what the vulgar way of thinking is, one must be enunciated; and they find it in

subtile body, or internal organ. It is called his causal body. Neither can do anything without one. The aggregate of the causal bodies of all souls, that is to say, distributive ignorances, make up I's'wara's causal body, which is illusion. See the *Vedánta-sára*. Strange to say, the ignorance of a single soul renders that soul subject to misapprehension, and keeps it parviscient, parvipotent, &c.; but the aggregation of these individual ignorances, or illusion, allows I's'wara to be exempt from misapprehension, and communicates to him such attributes as omniscience and omnipotence.

"In the furthest distance of the chamber sate an old dim-eyed man, poring with a microscope over the torso of a statue, which had neither base, nor feet, nor head; but on its breast was carved Nature. To this he continually applied his glass, and seemed enraptured with the various inequalities which it rendered visible on the seemingly polished surface of the marble. Yet evermore was this delight and triumph followed by expressions of hatred, and vehement railing against a being, who yet, he assured us, had no existence. This mystery suddenly recalled to me what I had read in the holiest recess of the temple of Superstition. The old man spoke in divers tongues, and continued to utter other and most strange mysteries. Among the rest he talked much and vehemently concerning an infinite series of causes and effects, which he explained to be—a string of blind men, the last of whom caught hold of the skirt of the one before him, he of the next, and so on till they were all out of sight; and that they all walked infallibly straight, without making one false step, though all were alike blind. Methought I borrowed courage from surprise, and asked him,—' Who, then, is at the head to guide them?' He looked at me with ineffable contempt, not unmixed with an angry suspicion, and then replied, 'No one;—the string of blind men goes on for ever without any beginning: for, *although one blind man cannot move without stumbling, yet infinite blindness supplies the want of sight.*'" Coleridge's *Lay Sermons*, pp. 149, 150.

This passage bears upon more than one Hindu philosopheme. The Italics are not Coleridge's.

ignorance, or illusion, which invents the world. Let the Naiyáyikas take this, in place of their atoms, and the Sánkhyas, instead of their "nature," and so gratify their insensate craving. One may be perfectly sure, that, when the Vedántins speak as I have represented, they express themselves, by way of "false imputation," to bring themselves down to the level of common minds. In truth, agreeably to their views, Brahma has neither creatorship, nor omniscience, nor omnipotence; and, for this reason, he is not, in truth, Ís'wara.

It may be asked, whether the Vedántins really consider Ís'wara to be nothing; whether the long accounts of him, which are found in the Upanishads and other books, are all to no purpose; and whether his characteristics, and those of the soul,—as that he is omniscient, and the soul is parviscient,—which are laid down, and the laboured discussions about these matters, are merely vain prattle. The Vedántins, I reply, declare, that equally are the world and Ís'wara simply practical, *i. e.*, imagined by ignorance, and false; and the long accounts just now spoken of are only statements of the suppositions of the uninitiated, propounded by way of false assumption. This they declare; and there is no doubt, that, in congruity with their doctrines, they are obliged so to declare. Still, they have not the assent, to it, of their innermost convictions. In their hearts, they have an unshaken confidence, that there is an Ís'wara, omnipotent, omniscient, omnipresent, and maker of the world. But it has been shown, that, strangely enough, they ascribe a real existence to those things even which they call false, to-wit, the practical and the apparent. They look upon Ís'wara as practical; and, therefore, their inward belief in his existence does not surprize them; nor do they find any difficulty in reconciling this belief with their capital dogma, that nothing but the secondless Brahma is true.*

---

* There are two sorts of Vedántins. Some have no taste for worship, while others are devoted to it. The former doubtless believe, equally with

CHAPTER 4.

Proof that the Existence of Brahma cannot be deduced from the Position of the Vedánta, that the Internal Organ requires an Illuminator.

I have asserted, in the last chapter, that the Vedántins' Brahma without qualities is not to be established, by any argument, as existing; he having no connexion with anything, either as efficient cause, or otherwise. To this the Vedántins may reply, that there is an argument for their purpose, as yet unproduced. It is, that the mental affection "This is a jar,", or "This is a web," for example, stands in need of an illuminator: for the internal organ is unintelligent; and, therefore, its affections cannot cognize a jar, a web, or similar object.

---

the latter, that I's'wara really exists; and these, to the best of their knowledge, worship with earnest faith, sincerity, and love. Of the true God, and of His attributes, which Holy Writ alone can teach, they are ignorant; but their devotion is fervent to Ráma, Krishna, and others, whom their books represent as God. Sarvajnátma Muni, author of the *Sankshepa-s'ariraka,* and Madhusúdana Saraswatí, author of the *Adwaita-siddhi,*—to take examples from among renowned Vedánta doctors,—were ardent devotees of Vishnu. And there are, to this day, among the Vedántins, thousands of men equally religious.

In passing, the error may be noted,—so generally prevalent, now-a-days, both here and abroad: see Professor Wilson's translation of the *Vishnu-purána,* Preface, p. x.,—of supposing, that S'ankara A'chárya, the celebrated Vedántin, was a follower of S'iva. Of this opinion are many of his own adherents, the Gosains in particular. But it appears otherwise from books undoubtedly of his composition, such as the *Sútra-bháshya,* &c.; in which Vishnu is, again and again, especially, and all but exclusively, magnified. Another argument may be drawn from the fact, that he enjoined upon his disciples to salute each other with names of Vishnu. Of two *dandins,* a younger and an elder, the first uses "Harih," and the other replies "Náráyana." On these grounds, the author is strongly disposed to believe, that S'ankara was a Vaishnava.

See, likewise, the notes at p. 195 and p. 199. S'ankara, where he writes against the Pás'upatas, a famous sect of S'aivas, is silent on the subject of their devotion; but, on coming to refute the peculiar tenets of the Bhágavatas, he dwells with unction and admiration on their religious exercises and service.

Hence, something is indispensable, by whose contiguity the unintelligent internal organ is to be illuminated: and that something is the intelligent spirit, or Brahma.* In reply, I ask, whether, in maintaining, that Brahma, or spirit, is intelligent and illuminating, it is meant, that he himself, through the medium of the internal organ, cognizes such an object as a jar, or a web: in other words, does he apprehend, that "This is a jar," "This is a web," &c.? And, when the internal organ is called the cognizer of a jar, or the like, is it intended to call it so only metonymically? For I too talk, by way of metonymy, of the eye as cognizing colour, and of the ear as cognizing sound; I really understanding, however, that the eye and the ear are not themselves cognizers, but merely media of cognition. What is said above about Brahma is not to be interpreted in like manner; since, by such an interpretation, the Vedántin would not prove the existence of his Brahma,—over pure, intelligent, and free, unchangeable, essentially existence, intelligence, and joy,—but the existence of souls, impure, ignorant, and wretched. The Vedántins do not hold, that the pure spirit, Brahma, really cognizes objects; that is to say, they do not allege, that the pure spirit cognizes objects in this manner— "This is a jar," "This is a web," &c.† For, if they allowed this sort of cognition to him, they would have to allow to him

---

* Spirit, universally, is held to be one with Brahma. The soul *(jivátman)* of any thing, or body, is a synthesis of spirit *(átman)* and internal organ. This organ abstracted, the residuum is, in all cases, pure Brahma. Compare the note at p. 2.

The tenet stated in the text is thus expressed in S'ankara A'chárya's Commentary on the *Kena-upanishad*: न ह्यन्तःकरणमन्तरेण चैतन्यज्योतिषा दीपितं स्वविषयसङ्ख्याध्यवसायादिसमर्थं स्यात् । *Bibliotheca Indica*, Vol. VIII., pp. 36, 37. "For the internal organ, unless illuminated by the light of intelligence, would be incapable of willing and apprehending its object."

† Proofs of all the statements in the present chapter will be found in the chapter following.

will, activity, happiness, misery, and so forth; and, as a consequence, he would be a doer of good and of evil works, and an heir of Elysium, or of Hell, and a partaker of threefold pain. And all this is at variance with the Vedánta economy; which asserts, that spirit is Brahma, neither doer, nor experiencer, neither sinful, nor virtuous, &c. &c. Since, then, you deny, that the pure spirit, Brahma, really cognizes things,—and yet they are cognized, and there is a cognizer,—what does so cognize them? It is the internal organ, after all. And, whatever it is that cognizes objects,—as "This is a jar," "This is a web,"—whether you call it internal organ, or anything else, what necessity has it of an illuminator?* Nobody

---

* Of course we owe to the Deity our original and continued possession of the faculty of apprehension. But, since we are endued with this faculty, we need, in order to our apprehending objects, nothing further than the use of our senses and other appointed means. Different, however, is the notion of the Vedántin; which is, that it is our internal organs, not our real selves, that are concerned in apprehension. The assertion, that Brahma, or spirit, is required to illuminate the internal organ, does not signify, that we stand in need of God's help to aid us to apprehend. It is not meant, that Brahma, by a voluntary exercise of his power, illuminates that organ: for Brahma has no such power. The idea intended is, that the internal organ, simply by reason of its proximity to Brahma, who is unconscious, becomes illuminated; just as iron moves, when brought near the magnet. In fact, Brahma's influence, of whatever description, in the production of effects, is exerted in this way only.

निश्चिले संस्थिते रत्ने यथा लोहः प्रवर्तते ।
सत्तामात्रेण देवेन तथैवायं जगद्रूहः ॥
अत आत्मनि कर्तृत्वमकर्तृत्वं च संस्थितम् ।
निश्चलवादकर्तासौ कर्ता सन्निधिमात्रतः ॥

"As the iron moves, when the precious stone, void of will, is apposed to it; precisely so the aggregate of worlds *is moved, without exercise of volition,* by Deva, sheer existence. Hence there exists, in spirit, agentship and non-agentship. As having no will, it is not an agent: *and* it is an agent, because of mere proximity."

These verses are from the *Yoga-vásishṭha*. See the Calcutta edition of

feels that it has any. In the kinds of cognition known as perception, inference, &c., there is need, respectively, of a sense, of perception of invariable attendedness,* &c., but there is no need of any aid other than one of these; nor are we conscious of any such. The Vedántins, however, contend, that another is indispensably desiderated; the cognizer of objects, the internal organ, being unintelligent, and so devoid

---

1851, p. 390. A bad reading, यथाऽऽस्तोक्तः, has been discarded on authority. Vijnána Bhikshu cites these lines in the *Sánkhya-pravachana-bháshya*, p. 71.

सन्निधिमात्रेणाऽधिष्ठातृत्वात् कर्त्तृत्वमुदासीनत्वं चाऽविरुद्धमिति भावः। S'rídhara Swámin's *Subodhiní*, Bombay edition, *fol.* 45, *verso*.

"Since *Brahma* is superintendent solely by virtue of juxtaposition, his being an agent and his being neutral *as to agency* do not conflict."

On this point the Sánkhyas and the Vedántins are quite at unity. Witness Vijnána Bhikshu: चक्षआभिस्तु पुरुषस्य सन्निधानादेवाऽधिष्ठातृत्वं सत्त्वादिरूपमिष्यते मणिवत् । यथाऽयस्कान्तमणेः सान्निध्यमात्रेण चाल्यनिष्ठकर्त्तत्वं न सङ्कल्पादिना तथैवाऽऽदिपुरुषस्य संयोगमात्रेण प्रकृतेर्महत्तच्चकरूपेण परिणामनम् । *Sánkhya-pravachana-bháshya*, pp. 70, 71.

"We hold, that the soul's 'superintendentship,' in creatorship, &c., is 'from nearness' alone; 'after the manner of the precious stone.' As *this*, the magnet, merely from nearness, and not by will, &c., draws out an iron pin; so, by simple contact of the primal soul, *Hiranyagarbha, there takes place* an evolution of nature, in the shape of the great *principle*."

A little further on it is explicitly stated, that the superintendency of soul is only nominal; true superintendency belonging exclusively to the internal organ.

Referring to the illumination of the internal organ, Vijnána says, that the intellect becomes intelligent from the contiguity of soul: बुद्धेश्च या चित्ता सा पुरुषसान्निध्यात् । *Ibid.*, p. 109.

In opposition to the view in question, it is assumed, and will soon be proved, that it is one's self that apprehends, and that the illuminator desiderated by the Vedántins is superfluous.

* These are the instruments of right notion recognized in the Nyáya. The tenets and phraseology of that school of philosophy, so far as they are reasonable, are adopted, throughout this volume, in opposing the Sánkhya and the Vedánta.

of inherent power of cognition. Hence, they go on to say, that power is derived to it by the contiguity of the intelligent spirit, from which contiguity it becomes quasi-intelligent; just as iron moves, when brought near the loadstone. Spirit, or Brahma, as being that from contiguity of which the unintelligent becomes quasi-intelligent,—and solely on this account,—is affirmed to be intelligence and illuminating. "Similarly," the Vedántins would add, "it is declared, respecting their *purusha*, or 'soul,' by our younger brothers the Sánkhyas; and they are incomparably more perspicacious than you Christians, and the Naiyáyikas, and other thinkers of the cruder sort." To this I reply: "Good sirs, not till I accept the truth of your concatenation of groundless theories, can I grant that your illuminator is wanted. To be brought to your way of thinking, I must be convinced, first, that it is the internal organ which cognizes things; secondly, that a cognizer can be unintelligent; thirdly, that an unintelligent cognizer could be made quasi-intelligent by the mere juxtaposition of something else; and, lastly, that, becoming only as it were intelligent, and not positively so,* it could do that which is competent to

---

* The notions now under comment are equally those of the Vedántins and of the Sánkhyas. No passage, bearing on the point of doctrine implied in the words to which this note is appended, is at this moment producible from any Vedánta treatise. The following is from Vijnána Bhikshu: नन्वधि-ष्ठात्वं घटादिवद्चेतनस्य न युक्तं तत्राऽऽऽह । लौहवत् तदुव्यञ्जि-तत्वादिति । अन्तःकरणं हि तप्तलौहवच् चेतनोव्यञ्जितं भवति । यतस्तस्य चेतनायमानतयाऽधिष्ठात्वं घटादिष्वाप्तुमपपद्यत इत्यर्थः ।
Sánkhya-pravachana-bháshya, p. 72. "' It is not reasonable *to assert*, that this *internal organ, which is* unintelligent, like a jar, or similar thing, can be a superintendent.' With reference to this *objection*, it is said: ' Because *the internal organ is* illuminated by that, *viz., soul*, as iron *is heated to redness by fire*.' The internal organ becomes illuminated by the intelligent one, after the manner of heated iron. Therefore, since it becomes as it were intelligent, it can exercise superintendence, which a jar, or the like, cannot. Such is the sense."

The ninety-ninth Aphorism of Book I. is thus in part expounded.

none but one really intelligent. And all these notions are assumptions resting upon no proof. I ask you, why you call the cognizer of objects unintelligent? Why not intelligent?" "What!" you reply, "can the internal organ be intelligent? No; only the spirit can." Again I ask, why you call the cognizer internal organ? Why not call it spirit? To this you will say, that, if you did, you must yield the point, that spirit is, in its nature, ever pure and free. It comes, then, to this, that, in order to make good a favourite fancy, you are willing to contradict universal experience, and to transgress the limits of reason for the sake of mere dreams. These things I have dealt with in my examination of the Sánkhya; and so it is unnecessary to go into detail about them here. Still, if you will allow me, I will add a few words. What do you mean by spirit? Is it a thing different from yourself and myself? Or is it the same? You will reply: "How can we consider spirit to be anything different from ourselves? For the spirit is my true proper essence, and yours; and therefore it is called self." I rejoin, that, if you consider yourself and myself to be spirit, and, again, the cognizer of objects to be unintelligent, it follows, that you take spirit to be unintelligent; you and I being cognizers of objects. For, in canvassing the Sánkhya, I have shown, that our consciousness, that we cognize objects, and that we will, &c., cannot be erroneous. Consequently, if the cognizer be unintelligent, you and I are so: and, if we are so, spirit likewise is so; since we, as you have said, are spirit. The reason why you err here is, that, to establish a favourite fancy, you call that unintelligent which really is intelligent; and, when you have made the intelligent unintelligent, you cast about for something else to hold for intelligent, to serve as illuminator of the unintelligent. For what are the characteristics of the intelligent but the qualities of cognizing, willing, and the like? To denote such qualities is the express purpose of the word intelligent. Whatever is competent to cognize or apprehend objects can require nothing more to be intelligent. Call it internal organ, or unintelligent, or thick darkness, or how you like; the thing is not altered by altering its name. Your own natural reason, too, tells you, that, to be able to cognize is to be intelligent. Listen how completely you and the Sánkhyas mistake on this point. You say, that the internal organ, being unintelligent, cannot cognize of itself. From this it is evident, that you hold the cognizing of objects to be the office of what is intelligent. If you acknowledge this, and also, that the internal organ cognizes, why do you call that organ unintelligent? Is it because you have given it the name of internal organ? How unreasonable a thing to do! You are aware, that cognizing is the function of what is intelligent; and you are, further, aware, that the internal organ cognizes. Still you gratuitously declare it to be unintelligent; and then you fabricate an illuminator to render it intelligent. But does that illuminator make it positively intelligent? No; only quasi-intelligent. At first it was not intelligent; and, for that reason, all was at a stand: but now, merely from its having been made as it were intelligent, it becomes operative. Just reflect, however. If a thing, not once only, but a thousand times, were made only quasi-intelligent, not positively intelligent, it would still be other than intelligent; and whatever is so is unintelligent; and nothing that is unintelligent can do the office of the intelligent. But why waste time in such discussion? In brief, I express it as my view, that the cognizer of objects, namely, that which apprehends, wills, and energizes, is one's self; as yourself, or myself. Name this self internal organ, or unintelligent, or whatever you choose: I shall not be alarmed; nor shall I go in search of an illuminator for it. The faculties of apprehending, &c., we are convinced, were given by God, Creator of the world and Almighty. And, since He has endowed us with them, and since we know, intuitively, that He has appointed the senses, the cognition of constant attendedness, and so on, to be our helpers, why should we take up with a fond invention?

CHAPTER 5.

Argument to show, that the Brahma of the Vedántins, as being quite Void of qualities, is reduced to nothing.

I have said, that the Vedántin's Brahma has no qualities: in other words, he does not possess the faculties of apprehending, willing, &c. &c.* Now, it is impossible to imagine the

---

* See the passage from the *Vedánta-paribháshá*, quoted at p. 176. Dharmarája, who is there writing against the Naiyáyikas, denies the possession of qualities, as by them understood,—namely, apprehension, will, activity, &c.,—to Brahma. A substance, says that author, is, with the Naiyáyikas, the substrate of qualities; and Brahma, as being *nirguṇa*, or " not possessed of qualities," is not a substance.

Indeed, the element *guṇa*, in the word *nirguṇa*, is generally to be taken as denoting what the Naiyáyikas mean by qualities. See, further, the extract from the *Vedánta-paribháshá* at p. 209.

But, even when *nirguṇa* points to the three *guṇas* termed *sattwa, rajas,* and *tamas,* it is not to be supposed, that the twenty-four qualities of the Naiyáyikas—adopted, almost all of them, by the Vedántins—are excepted. Among those qualities, one set, comprehending colour, taste, &c., belongs to external objects; while apprehension, will, activity, &c., appertain to the internal organ; and some, as number, dimension, &c., are predicable of both. But external objects and the internal organ are alike evolutions from goodness, passion, and darkness, the components of illusion, and the material cause of all but spirit. Dispossess Brahma of the three *guṇas* just enumerated, and he is dispossessed of consciousness and all similar attributes,—in short, of everything conceivable.

Dr. J. R. Ballantyne has written as follows: "The Vedántists are sometimes charged with holding, that the phenomenal *is* the real,—in other words, with material Pantheism. At the same time they are charged with the wildest extravagance, of an opposite description, in declaring, that the Supreme is *devoid of qualities,* or, in Sanskrit, *nirguṇa.* With regard to the relation of the real and the phenomenal, no point appears to have occasioned more perplexity to the European assailants of Vedántism than the employment of this term *nirguṇa,* so frequently connected, in the Vedántic writings, with the name of the Supreme *(Brahm).* We find, for example, a zealous writer against Vedántism declaring, that, ' In any sense, within the reach of human understanding, he *(Brahm)* is *nothing.* For the mind of man can form no notion of matter or spirit apart from its properties or attributes.' And the same writer calls upon his readers to admire the

existence of anything without qualities. To our understandings, whatever is such is nothing. The Vedántins, however,

> extravagant notion, that *Brahm* exists 'without intellect, without intelligence, without even the consciousness of his own existence!' Now, the reply to all this is, that the word *nirguṇ* ‡ is a technical term, and must be understood in its technical acceptation. It means 'devoid of whatever is meant by the term *guṇa* ;' and the term *guṇa* is employed * * * * to denote whatever is phenomenal. In denying that anything phenomenal belongs constitutively to the Supreme Being, the Vedántin speaks very much like Bishop Berkeley, and like other good Christians whom Milton's epic has not educated into a semiconscious Anthropomorphism. * * * * * In short, the Vedántin denies, that the Supreme either has or requires either senses or bodily organs ; and, holding that organs of sense or motion are made up of what he calls *guṇa*,—as we Europeans in general say they are made up of what we prefer to call *matter*,—he asserts, that the Supreme is *nirguṇa*, in very much the sense that we Europeans assert, that God is *immaterial*. We say, guardedly, 'in very much the sense,' and not simply 'in the sense ;' because the term *guṇa* denotes, strictly, not the *imperceptible* quiddity 'matter', but what Berkeley calls *the sensible*, or the sum of the objects of sense. Theologically, the Vedántin, asserting that the Deity is *nirguṇa*, and the Christian, asserting that God is *immaterial*, are asserting the very same fact in terms of separate theories ; just as two chemists might make each the same assertion in regard to some individual specimen, while the one spoke of it as destitute of chlorine, and the other spoke of it as destitute of oxymuriatic acid."
> *Christianity contrasted*, &c., pp. 43—45.

Besides that a most sublime conception of the Deity is groundlessly attributed to the Vedántins, in the passage just extracted, two totally different ideas are there confounded ; that of immateriality, and that of not possessing senses and bodily organs. It is first implied, that the Vedántin, by the word *nirguṇa*, denies to his Supreme all senses and bodily organs ; and then it is asserted, that *nirguṇa* denotes what we mean by immaterial : for that the Vedántin, like Berkeley, does not believe in the "imperceptible quiddity, matter." Now, supposing this assertion, which is not true, to be true, still the subtle tenet of repudiating matter can in nowise be suggested by the term *nirguṇa*, if used of Brahma, to express, for one thing,—as it has been inferred to do,—that he is destitute of senses and bodily organs. The word *guṇa* is sometimes applied indeed to the senses and bodily organs, but never to signify "the sensible," or quality involved in the ordinary *nirguṇa*. One of its several meanings is that of appliance, or instrument ; and it is in this acceptation that it denotes the senses and bodily organs. See Vijnána Bhikshu's explanation of *guṇa*, in the last extract from the *Sánkhya-pravachana-bháshya* given

though maintaining that Brahma has no qualities, deny that he is nothing: for, say they, on the score of excellence, he is surpassingly superior to all else that is; he being essentially existent—or, rather, as they explain the word, existence,—intelligence, and joy. My reply to this is, that the presence of what are called qualities is an indispensable condition of existing. As for those who, differing from the mass of mankind, refuse to take a distinction between corporate qualities and that of which they are predicated, and hold them to be identical, I have no dispute with them. This is a most difficult matter, besides that I am not here called upon to contest it. Qualities—whichever of the two views just intimated is held concerning them,—must, at all events, be maintained. Otherwise, nothing can be proved to exist. Brahma, the Vedántins allege, is essentially existence, intelligence, and joy; and, if his nature as intelligence deserved to be called so, and, similarly, his nature as joy, I should not say, as I do, that he is nothing. But, even if his intelligence and joy were so described, by the Vedántins, as to deserve to be called such, still it would be impossible to establish his existence: for he is neither the efficient nor the material cause of the world; and hence he is out of relation with the world; and how, then, can we arrive, by inference, at a conviction of his existence? I will show, however, that the hypothetical Brahma of the Vedántins, as they describe him, comes out to be a nonentity. They declare, that he is constitutively cognition, and yet cognizes nothing: for, according to the Vedánta, the cognizing anything, or cognition re-

---

at p. 43. The following words, from another work of the same author, plainly indicate, that the term *guṇa* is applied to the organs of sense, &c., solely to mark them as instruments: सत्त्वादित्रयं * * * द्रव्येऽपि पुरुषोपकरत्वात् पुरुषबन्धकत्वाच् च गुणशब्देनोच्यते इन्द्रियादिवत् ।
Sánkhya-sára, MS., fol. 7, verso. "The triad consisting of goodness, &c., though substantial, *and not qualities*, is called, like the organs of sense, by the appellation of *guṇa*, as being, *like them*, ministrant to the soul, and from binding the soul, *even as they do*."

lative to an object, is an affection of the internal organ;* and Brahma's constitutive cognition is not such.† An object abstracted, cognition is impracticable: for how can there be cognition where there is no cognizing an object?‡ If there can

---

* न खरूपभूता प्रज्ञा वस्तुतो बाह्यविषयेष्यते बुद्धिवृत्तिरूपा त्वसावज्ञानकल्पिता तद्विषया भवति । A'nanda Giri on S'ankara A'chárya's *Mándúkya-bháshya: Bibliotheca Indica*, Vol. VIII., p. 340. "In verity, it is not constitutive cognition that is held to have the external for its object, but that *cognition which is* an affection of the intellect, *i. e.*, *here, the internal organ,—and which is* ignorance-imagined,—has that, *the external*, for its object."

The emphasis must not be laid on the word "external," in this passage; for things external and internal—as will shortly be proved,—are objects of the same species of cognition. It happens to be the cognition of the external that is mentioned in the passage on which A'nanda Giri is annotating; and hence his importation of the epithet in question.

† चैतन्यलक्ष्या प्रज्ञा खरूपभूता न बाह्ये विषये प्रतिभासते तस्या विषयानपेच्चत्वात् । "It is not the cognition which is one with intelligence, and is constitutive *thereof*, that presents itself in respect of, *i. e., that apprehends*, external objects; for such *cognition* is irrelative to objects."

This extract just precedes the words cited in the last note. The reason for bringing in the word "external" is the same in both places. Where the word "objects" is last mentioned, it is unqualified. It applies to objects of whatever description.

The ensuing couplet occurs, it is said, in the *Ashṭávakragítá*:

ज्ञाता ज्ञानं तथा ज्ञेयं चित्तयं नास्ति वास्तवम् ।
अज्ञानाद् भाति यन्नेदं सोऽहमस्मि निरञ्जनः ॥

"These three, the cognizer, cognition, and the cognizable, are not true. He in whom, owing to ignorance, this *triad* appears *as true* am I, emotionless."

Since all these are false, Brahma, being postulated as true, is no cognizer, and, likewise, has no cognition of objects in his essence.

See, also, the passage from the *Yoga-vásishṭha*, at p. 177, in which that cognition which is of the essence of spirit is plainly taken to have no relation to objects, whether external or internal.

‡ Compare Coleridge's Thesis I. : "Truth is correlative to being. Knowledge without a correspondent reality is no knowledge; if we know, there

be, why not call the walls around us, and the roof overhead, forms of cognition? How have the Vedántins, by changing names, forgotten the genuine nature of things! By giving the titles of internal organ, unintelligent, &c., to that which is really intelligent, or the cognizer of objects, they have brought themselves to regard it as unintelligent. On the other hand, by applying to that which is unintelligent, and cognizes nothing, namely their "spirit," the epithets of essential cognition, self-illuminated, &c., they have passed to look upon it as intelligent. Can a pebble be transformed into a diamond by one's calling it so?

It can never be said of the pandits, whatever subject they may be handling, that they leave their views but partially explained. Cognition relative to an object they divide into memorial and non-memorial. The non-memorial the Vedántins discriminate into six sorts, and allot an instrument to each.* Among these sorts are included the cognition of Is'wara, and that of the soul.† On this topic the Vedántins discourse with great diffuseness, and lay down precisely how it is that Is'wara cognizes,‡ and how it is that the soul cognizes.

---

must be somewhat known by us. 'To know' is, in its very essence, a verb active." *Biographia Literaria*, Vol. I., p. 268.

* These instruments are thus specified in the *Veda'nta-paribháshà*, p. 2:

तानि च प्रमाणानि षट् प्रत्यक्षानुमानोपमानागमार्थापत्त्यपलब्धि-भेदात् ।

† Concerning perception, we read: तच् च प्रत्यक्षं पुनर्द्विविधं जीवसाक्षीश्वरसाक्षि चेति । *Vedánta-paribháshá*. p. 8. "And that perception, again, is of two kinds; that in which soul is the witness, and that in which I's'wara is so."

It is meant, that one sort is the soul's, and that the other is I's'wara's.

‡ यथा विषयेन्द्रियसन्निकर्षादिकारणवशेन जीवोपाधिन्तःकर-णस्य वृत्तिभेदा जायन्ते तथा खद्यमानप्राणिकर्मवशेन परमे-श्वरोपाधिभूतमायाया वृत्तिविशेषा इदमिदानीं षट्त्र्यमिदमि-

Besides the sorts of cognition here spoken of, memorial and non-memorial, none is recognized as relative to objects; and every one of these is defined as being an affection of the internal organ.*

With us, the eyes and other senses, to which the Naiyáyikas add the mind, are only media of cognition. Not so, however, with the Vedántins, is their internal organ: it is but the apprehender of objects, and the sole apprehender thereof;† though, from their perplexed style of expression, they seem to allot the function of apprehension to the soul, and that of a medium to the internal organ. Thus, they state distinctly, that "Perceptive right notion is intelligence itself,"‡ and that "The sub-

दानीं पाञ्चयितव्यमिदमिदानीं संहतंव्यमित्याद्याकारा जायन्ते ।
Vedánta-paribháshá, pp. 9, 10. "In like manner as, from connexion of an organ of sense with an object, or other cause, divers affections are produced in the internal organ, the soul's associate; so, from the desert of creatures destined to be brought forth, there arise, in illusion, the associate of supreme Is'wara, various affections, in the form of 'This is now to be created,' 'This is now to be cared for,' 'This is now to be done away,' &c."

Also see the passage from the *Vedánta-s'ikhámaṇi*, adduced at p. 198. I's'wara's apprehension, will, and activity are there said to be affections of the internal organ.

* In dreamless sleep even, maintain the Vedántins, a sort of cognition has place. This cognition is an exception, as to its origin. Still, it is an affection, one evolved from ignorance; and it is not of the essence of spirit. During dreamless sleep, the internal organ, the ordinary producer of cognition, is thought to be dissolved. See the *Vedánta-sára*, p. 6.

It is a momentous error to suppose, as has recently been done, that the cognition which the Naiyáyikas count for one of their four and twenty qualities is claimed, by the Vedántins, under the title of *chit*, as constitutive of Brahma. That cognition is, indeed, acknowledged by the Vedántins, but, being relative to objects, is an affection of the internal organ. The Naiyáyikas, on the other hand, consider it to be a property of the soul; and, on this very account, they are lightly reputed by the Vedántins and Sánkhyas. See *The Bible for the Pandits*, Introduction, pp. XLV.—LXIV., where the error referred to is committed.

† The Vedántin's internal organ has erroneously been called a medium of cognition, in a passage soon to be cited from *Christianity contrasted*, &c.

‡ प्रत्यक्षप्रमा चाज्ञन चैतन्यमेव । *Vedánta-paribháshá*, p. 2.

ject of right notion is intelligence appropriated to the internal organ;"* &c. &c. Lest my readers should here be in doubt,† I will first evince, that the cognition which we call so, the cognizing of objects, is, in the Vedánta, nothing but an affection of the internal organ; whence it follows, that only the internal organ is a cognizer. And then I intend to show what we are to understand by the Vedántins' applying the designations of right notion and subject of right notion to intelligence, that is to say, Brahma.

We find an object of perception defined as "non-difference from the subject of right notion."‡ Intelligence appropriated to the internal organ is meant by the expression "subject of right notion;" and it is said, that "Non-difference from the subject of right notion is not *here denotative of* oneness with it, but is the non-possession of an existence distinct from that of the subject of right notion."§ I explain. In the view of the Vedántins, as silver is imagined in nacre, so the world is imagined in Brahma; and, as the existence of the silver is one with that of the nacre, so is the existence of the world one with that of Brahma. The drift of this is, that the silver and the world, as such, are nothing, but, as nacre and as Brahma, severally, have true existence. It is further stated, that, on one's perceiving a jar, the jar becomes, in the following manner, non-different from the subject of right notion. When the jar is seen, an effluence from the internal organ passes through

---

* अन्तःकरणावच्छिन्नं चैतन्यं प्रमातृचैतन्यम् । *Vedánta-paribháshá*, p. 4.

† There is very much in this section, and especially in the present chapter and that immediately succeeding, which the author would have thought it quite unnecessary to write, but for his making acquaintance with Dr. J. R. Ballantyne's *Christianity contrasted with the Hindu Philosophy.*

‡ प्रमात्रभिन्नत्वम् । *Vedánta-paribháshá*, p. 6.

§ प्रमात्रभेदो नाम न तावदैक्यं किन्तु प्रमातृसत्तातिरिक्तसत्ताकत्वाभावः । *Vedánta-paribháshá*, p. 6.

2 G

the eye to it, and takes its form. This effluence of the internal organ is called an affection. When, therefore, the internal organ thus reaches the jar, at that place intelligence appropriated to the internal organ, namely the subject of right notion, and the jar-appropriated intelligence, in which the jar is imagined, become one; just as, if one brings a jar into the house, the jar-appropriated ether and the house-appropriated ether become one. In the way lately stated, the existence of the jar is not different from that of the jar-appropriated intelligence, one with the subject of right notion; and hence the jar becomes non-different from that subject. Thus, the definition of object of perception, cited just above, applies to a jar seen with the eye. In reply to an objection suggested to that definition, it is said, that the subject of right notion must be understood to be "associated with the affection which has taken the form of the given *object of perception.*"* To this, again, it is excepted, that, with such a qualification, the definition is inapplicable to an affection. As a jar is an object of perception, so is an affection; and, therefore, the definition of object of perception ought to cover affection also. The objection just mentioned is expressed thus: "In this case, there is the exclusion of affection; for, inasmuch as, from fear of an infinite regress, a *second* affection cognizing the *primary* affection cannot be acknowledged, the definition aforesaid, giving *to the subject of right notion the characteristic of* associatedness with the affection that has taken the form of it, *i. e.*, of its object, is not *inclusive* of that *affection, here considered as the object of perception, which ought to be comprehended by the definition.*"† To this it is rejoined: "Though, from fear of an

---

* तत्तदाकारवृत्त्युपहितत्वस्याऽपि प्रमातृविशेषणत्वात् ।   *Vedánta-paribháshá*, p. 6.

† नन्वेवं दत्तावयाप्तिः अनवस्थाभिया वृत्त्यगोचरवृत्त्यनङ्गी-कारेण तत्र साकारवृत्त्युपहितत्वघटितोल्लकणाभावादिति ।
Vedánta-paribháshá, p. 7.

infinite regress, *we do* not *acknowledge*, that the affection is cognized by a second affection, *still*, since it is acknowledged, that it is self-cognized, *the definition*, 'to possess an existence non-different from that of intelligence, the subject of right notion, associated with affection cognizing it, *viz.*, *the object of perception*,' is applicable to it, *namely, to the affection which is the object of perception.*"* This proves, that, in the account of the Vedántins, an "affection" is always a matter of consciousness. If, however, such an affection be not cognition itself, but, like the eye, or the ear, a medium of cognition, how can it be an object of immediate consciousness? Is any one conscious of an immediate consciousness of such a medium of cognition? Do the Naiyáyikas, who call the mind an internal organ only, in other words, simply a medium of cognition, like the eye, &c., ever declare, that it becomes an object of immediate consciousness?† Of our cognition of a jar, or the like, we are, indeed, conscious; and so it is certain, that such an affection of the internal organ as has here been dwelt on is nothing but what we call cognition. Moreover, as I made out, when discussing the Sánkhya, our consciousness of the qualities of

---

* अनवस्थाभिया त्तेर्देत्यन्तराविषयत्वेऽपि स्वविषयत्वाभ्युपगमेन स्वविषयदृच्चपहितप्रमातृचैतन्याभिन्नसत्ताकत्वस्य तत्रापि सम्भवात् । *Vedánta-paribháshá*, p. 7.

† If the Vedántins held the internal organ to be what its name promises, their tenet, that its affections are objects of consciousness, would be exposed to the following stricture, which is put into the mouth of an objector, and is answered by the simple denial, that the so-called internal organ is an organ: ननु अन्तःकरणस्येन्द्रियतया अतीन्द्रियत्वात् कथं प्रत्यक्षविषयतेति उच्यते न तावदन्तःकरणमिन्द्रियमित्यत्र मानमस्ति। *Vedántı-paribháshá*, p. 3. "' Since the internal organ is an organ of sense, and therefore is beyond cognition through the senses, how does it become an object of perception? The reply is, that there is no proof of the internal organ's being an organ of sense."

A good deal to the same effect follows this passage.

our souls, cognition, &c., is not distinct from those qualities; a notion which turns out to have the concurrence of the Vedántins: since, as we have seen, they do not hold, that an affection is cognized by a secondary affection, that is to say, in a distinct act of consciousness, but that it is self-cognized. In short, with them, the consciousness of cognition is not distinct from cognition itself.

That the Vedántins hold such an affection to be cognition, and that it is the internal organ which cognizes, appears, further, from this passage: "Affectional cognition is a property of the mind. Of this the scripture 'Desire, resolve, dubiety, trust, distrust, fixedness, unfixedness, shamefastness, understanding, fear,—all these are *of* mind alone,' is the proof. For cognition in the form of affection is intended by 'understanding.' Desire and the rest, as well, are, therefore, *proved to be* mental properties."* To this it is objected: "If desire and the rest be properties of the internal organ, how can the consciousness 'I desire,' 'I fear,' 'I cognize,' or the like, which cognizes them as properties of the soul, be accounted for?"† The answer given is: "As, though a *heated* iron ball does not possess the power of scorching, still, by *our* imagining the identity with it of fire, the possessor of that power, it is supposed, that the iron ball scorches; so, by imagining the identity *of the soul, i. e., of one's self*, with the internal organ, which evolves in the shape of happiness, &c., one supposes 'I

---

* वृत्तिरूपज्ञानस्य मनोधर्मत्वे च कामः सङ्कल्पो विचिकित्सा श्रद्धाश्रद्धा धृतिरधृतिर्ह्रीर्धीर्भीरित्येतत् सर्वं मन एवेतिश्रुतिः प्रमाणं धीशब्देन वृत्तिरूपज्ञानाभिधानात् । अतएव कामादेरपि मनोधर्मत्वम् । *Vedánta-paribháshá,* p. 3.

† ननु कामादेरन्तःकरणधर्मत्वे अहमिच्छामि अहं बिभेमि अहं जानामीत्याद्यनुभवः आत्मधर्मत्वमवगाहमानः कथमुपपद्यते । *Vedánta-paribháshá,* p. 3.

am happy,' ' I am miserable,' &c."* Now, we are certain, that " I cognize" denotes nothing but what we all call cognition ; and what is thus denoted, it is here laid down, is a property of the internal organ, and an affection of the same.

Not only cognitions of external things, but also cognitions with regard to one's self, or acts of consciousness, the Vedántins consider to be affections of the internal organ. For of the latter species are the cognitions " I cognize," " I desire," &c. ; since it is only with the aid of some quality, as cognition, desire, or suchlike, that we become conscious of our souls. We can never cognize the simple substance of the soul; as the Naiyáyikas, too, acknowledge.† And, though the Vedántin, like the Sánkhya, calls cognition, desire, &c., immediate objects of the witness himself, by which the soul is intended; still neither of them believes those qualities to be cognized by the soul unaccompanied by an affection of the internal organ.‡ In other words, those qualities are cognized by the internal organ itself;§ and the calling them immedi-

---

* अयःपिण्डस्य दग्धत्वाभावेऽपि दग्धत्वाश्रयवह्नितादात्म्याध्यासाद् यथा अयो दह्यतीति व्यवहारः तथा सुखाद्याकारपरिणाम्यन्तःकरणाध्यासादहं सुखी अहं दुःखीत्यादिव्यवहारः। *Vedánta-paribháshá*, p. 3.

† The soul becomes "an object of perception, from connexion with the specific qualities :" अभ्यक्तो विशेषगुणयोगतः। *Bháshá-parichchhedo*, forty-eighth stanza.

‡ न हि वृत्तिं विना साक्षिविषयत्वं केवलसाक्षिवेद्यत्वं किन्तु इन्द्रियानुमानादिप्रमाणमन्तरेण साक्षिविषयत्वम्। *Vedánta-paribháshá*, p. 7. "For, to be cognizable by the witness alone is not to become an object of the witness independently of an affection *of the internal organ*, but *it is* to be an object of the witness apart from *the aid of* an organ of sense, inference, or such other instrument of right notion."

§ तथा चान्तःकरणतद्धर्मादिषु केवलसाक्षिवेद्येषु इच्युपहितत्वघटितसाक्ष्यस्य सत्त्वान् नाऽव्याप्तिः। *Vedánta-paribháshá* p. 7.

ate objects of the witness is found, on scrutiny, to be deceptive.

Again, according to the Vedántins, the immediate cognition of the soul, which is said to result from listening to the Vedánta, and from consideration and meditation on it,—namely, the conviction, that one is void of cognition, will, and all other qualities, and of all mutation, and is the pure Brahma,—is itself an affection of the internal organ;* which affection is to be got rid of before emancipation is attainable.†

It must now be manifest, that the Vedántins' affection of the internal organ, which has thus been described, is what we mean by cognition, or the apprehension of things, be they external, or internal, *i. e.*, of the soul and its qualities. And all the divisions which those philosophers make of this cognition, or cognition relative to objects, are affections, as aforesaid. Consequently, the cognition which is given out as a constituent of Brahma, is irrelative to objects; that is to say, it is not cognition of anything, whether himself or aught else.

As we have seen, the Vedántins enunciate, that perceptive right notion is intelligence itself, and that the subject of right notion is intelligence appropriated to the internal organ. From this it seems as if, with them, intelligence itself were

---

"Thus, then, since the definition *of the object of perception*, as containing the words, 'associated with the affection,' &c., is applicable to the internal organ, its properties, &c., *which are* cognizable by the witness alone, there is no deficiency."

Hence, the properties of the internal organ, though said to be cognizable by the witness alone, are, in truth, cognized by an affection of that organ. Otherwise, the definition just given would be inapplicable to those properties.

For "associated with the affection," &c., see the first note at p. 228.

As the Vedántins allege, of the properties of the internal organ, that they are cognizable by the witness alone, so do they allege respecting apparent objects also. Yet, for the cognition of these, too, they contend, that an affection of the internal organ is indispensable. See the *Vedánta-paribháshá*, pp. 7 and 11.

* See the *Vedánta-sára*, p. 21.
† See the *Vedánta-sára*, p. 22.

both cognition and cognizer, and as if the internal organ, its affections, &c., were only media of cognition. Those declarations are to be understood as follows. The term cognition, as they apply it to Brahma, means, they say, not cognizing or apprehending, but illuminating; and it is the internal organ that is illuminated, or made capable of cognizing. Thus, in order that their unintelligent Brahma should be made out constitutively cognition, they have altered the sense of the word cognition to such an extent, that, in their employment, it signifies, primarily, to illuminate, and, only metonymically, to apprehend objects. That affection of the internal organ which—supposing such a thing to exist—ought to be veritable cognition, is, therefore, according to them, but metonymic cognition.* By asserting, then, that perceptive right notion is intelligence itself, they mean, that intelligence illuminates the affection. When an affection proceeds from the internal organ, and betakes itself to an object, a reflexion of intelligence falls on that affection; and so that affection is enabled to cognize the object. But for illumination from intelligence, it could cognize nothing; for it is pronounced, that "There, *namely, as for an affection and the reflexion of Brahma therein,* ignorance, *veiling the object of cognition, a jar, for instance,* is destroyed by the affection *which takes the form of that object;* and, by the reflexion, the jar is made to appear."† By this it is not to be understood, that the jar is made to appear to the reflexion of intelligence, that is to say, that the reflexion cognizes the jar; but, that the jar is made to appear to the affection, in other words, that the affection is rendered capable of cognizing the jar. In proof, that such is

---

* ज्ञानवच्छेदकत्वाच् च वृत्तौ ज्ञानत्वोपचारः । *Vedánta-paribháshá,* p. 2. " An affection *of the internal organ,* since it is that to which cognition, *i. e., Brahma,* is appropriated, is *itself* metonymically denominated cognition."

† This well-known passage, a half-couplet, runs thus;

तत्राज्ञानं धिया नश्येदाभासेन घटः स्फुरेत् ।

the meaning of the Vedántins, I cite this single passage, from among innumerable passages that might be produced: "For the internal organ, if it were not illuminated by the light of intelligence, would be incapable of willing and apprehending its object."* It is evident, from this, that it is the very internal organ, illuminated by intelligence, that cognizes things.

But, when they give to intelligence appropriated to the internal organ the name of subject of right notion, we are to understand, that the character which they ascribe to intelligence associated with the internal organ, really belongs to that organ. They have a maxim,—which all the other Systems subscribe to,—that "An affirmation, or a negation, when predicated of anything together with its associate, if debarred from the object substantive, is to be referred to the object adjective."† In their opinion, the quality of being a cognizer cannot be assigned to the soul, and, consequently, is debarred from it. For our cognition of objects is non-eternal; and, therefore, if it were regarded as constitutive of the soul, the soul would, to their thinking, be made out non-eternal and changeable.‡ And, again, if they held that cognition to belong to the soul, they must hold, that will, activity, happiness, misery &c., also belong to it; and the result would be, that the soul is indeed a doer of good and evil, and an ex-

---

* This passage, in Sanskrit and English, will be found at the foot of p. 213.

† सविप्रेषेवणो हि विधिनिषेधौ विप्रेष्ये बाधे सति विप्रेषवा-
मुपसङ्ग्रामतः ।

The maxim is integrated by these words: विप्रेष्ये बाधे सति
विप्रेष्यमुपसङ्ग्रामतः । "Debarred from the object adjective, it is to be referred to the object substantive."

‡ इन्द्रियजन्यज्ञानं चान्तःकरणवृत्तिः स्वरूपज्ञानस्यानादित्वात् ।
Vedánta-paribháshá, p. 42. "Cognition produced through the organs of sense is an affection of the internal organ; for constitutive cognition is beginningless."

But it must not be thought, that sensation only is an affection of the internal organ; for every kind of cognition of objects is so.

periencer of threefold misery: an issue most offensive to them; inasmuch as they would establish, that the soul is Brahma, eternally pure and free. Once more, their granting the soul to be a cognizer would involve the necessity of recognizing the relation of quality and subject as having place between it and its cognition: and even this much of an approach to duality they find unendurable.* On such grounds as these, the Vedántins would ascribe cognition and all other qualities to the internal organ, and keep the soul entirely a stranger thereto. And the soul, with them, is itself Brahma.†

I have seen it stated, that only the soul requires an internal organ; since, except for its aid, the soul cannot apprehend: but, as for Brahma, he can apprehend all things without its aid. And so it has been attempted to prove, that Brahma's cognition is real cognition.‡ All this is quite opposed to the

---

* No more are the Vedántins than the Naiyáyikas, or mankind at large, able to conceive, that either cognition, or any other quality, can subsist without a substrate. For that cognition, with them, which alone deserves to be thus designated, namely, an affection of the internal organ, has a substrate in that organ. See the first extract from p. 3 of the *Vedánta-paribháshá*, at p. 228. That cognition which is thought to be constitutive of Brahma is cognition only nominally, not properly, and hence is not a quality. It does not, therefore, stand in need of any substrate.

The Vedántins, and the Sánkhyas also, do not discriminate so sharply as the Naiyáyikas between substance and quality. The latter hold them to differ in their very essence; while the former consider them to be coessential. For, in the account of these, all things but spirit are evolutions from one root;—illusion with the Vedántins, and nature with the Sánkhyas. Still, they take thus much of distinction between substance and quality, as to regard them as being, severally, substrate and property.

† Spirit, one naturally supposes, is something intelligent. But the Vedántins and the Sánkhyas are necessitated, by their theories, to assign all the characteristics of what is intelligent to their internal organ. Hence, spirit is left, to them, unintelligent. Nevertheless, their inward consciousness shames them from professing, in terms, that it is so. That they are thus shamed is the real reason why they give to spirit the epithet of *jnána*, *chit*, *bodha*, &c. At the same time, they deprive these epithets, as thus employed, of their sole proper import.

‡ "Reverting to the charge of extravagance in the notion, that *Brahm*

Vedánta. I have shown, that it is wrong to regard the internal organ, in that system, as a medium of the soul's cognition; since, on examination, it is found to be no such medium, but itself the cognizer. That which lies beyond this organ is the soul, which never cognizes: and soul is Brahma. Of the soul there are two portions, Brahma and the internal organ. Hence, when the second is parted off, what remains is Brahma. This residue the Vedántins declare to be essentially existence, intelligence, and joy; and, as has been made evident, it is destitute of all faculty of knowledge and apprehension.

The opinion about Brahma, just now arraigned, is based on the error of supposing, that by him is meant I's'wara; the difference between the two, which the Vedántins inculcate, being overlooked.* But I's'wara, no less than the soul, has, they declare, in order to cognize, &c., need of an internal organ. I's'wara, they say, is Brahma associated with illusion; and they hold I's'wara to be omniscient, omnipotent, &c. &c. Yet the attributes of omniscience, omnipotence, &c., belong to I's'wara's causal body, which is illusion,† and not to the Brahma-portion of him. By consequence, all I's'wara's attributes, nay, he himself, are false, and imagined by ignorance.

Every doubt of the reader, as to the nature of Brahma's cognition, must, by this time, have been dispelled. Alike

---

exists 'without intellect, without intelligence, without even the consciousness of his own existence,' it may be well to repeat here what the Vedántin means by the terms thus rendered. By intellect (or mind) he means an internal organ which, in concert with the senses, brings the human soul into cognitive relation with the external. This, of course, he denies to *Brahm*, who, as Berkeley says of God, 'perceives nothing by sense as we do.'" *Christianity contrasted*, &c., p. 47.

* That this difference is overlooked in *Christianity contrasted*, &c., is evident from three things. First: the word Brahma is everywhere translated there by "God." Secondly: the attributes of omnipotence, omniscience, &c., are attributed to Brahma. Thirdly: no intimation even is put forth of any distinction, in the opinion of the Vedántins, between Brahma and I's'wara.

† See note at p. 210.

parviscience and omniscience, alike knowledge of himself and knowledge of what is not himself, are maintained, by the Vedántins, to be unworthy of Brahma. What sort of cognition, therefore, can that be which they consider as one of his constituents?

CHAPTER 6.

Strictures on the Position of the Vedántins, that the World is False; and a Reply to those who suppose, that the Vedántins' Views respecting External Things accord with those of Berkeley.

It is maintained, by the Vedántins, that " The world is false;" in other words, that it owes its origin to ignorance: the truth being, it is alleged, that it never has existed, and does not exist, and never will exist. To this effect the *S'iva-gítá* declares: " Just as the terrible snake *that is imagined* in the rope neither had origin, nor is, nor is to be destroyed; so the world, which has assumed an appearance simply by force of thy illusion, exists in thee, Nílakaṇṭha."*

I demand of the Vedántins, How is it that you assert falseness of the world, which is certified to us, by the senses, &c., to be true? Since you thus despise those proofs, what credit can be attached to anything that you advance? Proceeding in this way, you unsettle the foundations of everything, whether as regards this world, or as regards the next. And, on your own grounds, how can you refute the doctrines of others, or establish your own?

* रज्जौ भुजङ्गो भयदो यथैव
न जायते नास्ति न चैति नाशम् ।
त्वन्मायया केवलमात्ररूपं
तथैव विश्वं त्वयि नीलकण्ठ ॥

No manuscript of the *S'iva-gítá* is at this moment at hand; so that the chapter and verse where this stanza occurs cannot be stated.

Perhaps you will urge, that, since the senses, &c. often deceive us, they are totally unreliable. For instance, we are sure, that we see chariots, elephants, and other things, in our dreams; and yet they are proved to be false. I reply, that, if a seeming proof is made out, by a real proof, to be faulty, we reject it. But how can we contemn a proof which cannot be shown to be faulty? As for the things that we see in dreams, we call them false, because, on awaking, we find them to be so; and their falsity, as being matter of every-day experience, is indubitable. But who has ever found the external objects of nature to be false? Has not every man of all generations borne evidence to their truth?

If you say, that, to a man in dreamless sleep, the world disappears, and that his experience goes to disprove the truth of the world, I demur to the conclusion; since, a man's cognition being then suspended, he cannot be brought forward as witness for anything that then had place. It is the belief of the Vedántins, that, even in dreamless sleep, there subsists a sort of cognition.* Let this be granted: still, external things are not proved, thereby, to be false. To form any judgment whatever about them is not competent to his cognition; and, therefore, it cannot conclude their falsity. In like manner, a blind man is able to appreciate sound, touch, &c., but not colours; and so he can be no witness of their truth, or of their falseness.

I would also remind the reader of the argument I employed, when discussing the Sánkhya, to prove the existence of God. When we inspect the structure of the world, we become convinced, that it was planned, consciously, by some one, for a multiplicity of ends; and this consideration confutes your view, that the world is simply apparent,† and that eternal ignorance is the ground of its semblance.

---

* See a note at p. 224.

† It is true, that the Vedántins hold the world to be constructed by an intelligent designer, Iśwara; and such construction they believe, from the

Berkeley maintains, that objects of sense are only ideas, they having no existence in themselves and apart from perception. This is immaterialism. But he does not hold, that the things which we see, touch, &c., are false: his meaning is, that they are forms of perception. The perception of them constitutes, in his view, their existence; whereas the common opinion is, that they exist independently of perception. He does not say, however, they are imaginations of eternal ignorance; and, the Vedánta doctrine, that, on the removal of ignorance, and attainment of right apprehension, the whole world disappears, like a dream on awaking, he knows nothing of whatsoever. Whether his theory be tenable, or untenable, is a matter I am not here concerned with. My present purpose is, to show, that the doctrine of the Vedánta concerning the external world, besides being in conflict with the common opinion, has not so much as a resemblance to that of Berkeley. Yet a resemblance here has been asserted. It has been asserted, that the Vedántins, when they call sensible objects practical, do not mean, that they are false, but only that they do not exist apart from perception; and that the world is said, in the Vedánta, to be false, simply from ambiguousness of phraseology.*

But, for my part, I understand the Vedánta otherwise. First. According to Berkeley, objects of sense are forms of perception; but, according to the Vedántins, objects of sense are distinct from perception, and independent of it. The Vedántins, I have already shown, consider, that the cognition which apprehends external things is an affection of the inter-

---

standing point of practical existence, to have actually taken place. This view of theirs arises, however, from their taking practical things to be real, which things, at the same time, they would prove to be nothing,—only ignorance-imagined: a combination of incompatible notions ignored in the text, it being aimed at the latter of those notions; that which, with the Vedántins, is by much the more essential.

* See *Christianity contrasted, &c.*, pp. 38-42.

nal organ, let that cognition be perception, or inference, &c. ; and that the objects which that affection cognizes are distinct from the affection itself, and have existence independent of it.*

* यथा तडागोदकं छिद्रान् निर्गत्य कुल्यात्मना केदारान् प्रविश्य तद्देव चतुष्कोणाद्याकारं भवति तथा तैजसमन्तःकरणमपि चक्षुरादिद्वारा घटादिविषयदेशं गत्वा घटादिविषयाकारेण परिणमते । स एव परिणामो वृत्तिरित्युच्यते । अनुमित्यादिस्थले तु अन्तःकरणस्य न वह्न्यादिदेशगमनं वह्न्यादेश्चक्षुराद्यसन्निकर्षात् । तथा चायं घट इत्यादिप्रत्यक्षस्थले घटादेस्तदाकारवृत्तेश्च बहिरेकत्र देशे समवस्थानात् तदुभयावच्छिन्नं चैतन्यमेकमेव विभाजकयोरप्यन्तःकरणवृत्तिघटादिविषययोरेकदेशस्थितत्वेन भेदाजनकत्वात् । अतएव मठान्तर्वर्तिघटावच्छिन्नाकाशो न मठाकाशाद् भिद्यते ।

Vedânta-paribháshá, p. 4. "As the water of a reservoir, issuing through apertures, enters the fields rillwise, and becomes, like them, quadrangular, or of other shapes; so the passional internal organ, through the medium of the eye, or the like, extends itself to the place occupied by a jar, or other object, and is evolved in the form thereof. This same evolution is called an affection. But, in the case of inferential cognition, &c., there is no extension, on the part of the internal organ, to the locality of the fire, &c.; because these are not brought into connexion with the eye, &c. So, then, in the case of such a perception as 'This is a jar,' since the jar and the affection of like conformation thereto take up one and the same space, externally *to the body*, the intelligence appropriated to both, *viz.*, *the jar and the affection*, is but one: for, although the affection of the internal organ, and the object, as the jar, are two dividers *of intelligence, or Brahma;* still, since, *in the present instance*, they take up one and the same space, they do not operate to divide *the affection-appropriated intelligence from the jar-appropriated intelligence.* On this very account, the ether appropriated to a jar within the house does not differ from the ether of the house *itself*."

The purpose of all this is to show, that, in perception, affection-appropriated Brahma and object-appropriated Brahma are unified; for to show this is necessary, in the work cited, to explain its definition of perception.

We have seen it stated, that, in perception, the affection of the internal organ extends itself to the spot already occupied by the object perceived. In inferential or other cognition than perception, there is, however, no such extension of the affection; and it is, further, laid down, that the object and the

An affection is an evolution from the internal organ; but the objects which it cognizes are evolutions from ignorance, or illusion. And it must not be forgotten, that ignorance is not the reverse of right apprehension, mistake: for, in that case, it would itself be an affection of the internal organ; since both right apprehension and wrong apprehension are such affections. In the Vedánta, ignorance, like the "nature" of the Sánkhya, is an unintelligent substance. As the Sánkhyas take the visible world to be an evolution from nature, so do the Vedántins regard it as being an evolution from ignorance.* Of the confusion which besets this point I shall treat in the seventh and ninth chapters.

This, therefore, is certain, that the Vedántins concur with the generality of mankind as concerns the existence of external things apart from perception. Very little indeed have they of the philosophic profundity of a Berkeley.

---

affection are two several dividers of intelligence, or Brahma. In inferential cognition, &c., they serve as such; but not so in perception. From this it is clear, that an object is distinct from, and independent of, the affection, that is to say, the cognition, which apprehends it.

Had not an attempt been made to father Berkeleianism upon the Vedántins, it would have been most supererogatory to refer to any proof of the position, that the Vedántins take objects to exist irrespectively of their being perceived. From the standing point of true existence, not only objects, but the perception of them, are nothing; but, from that standing point whence perception is real, objects likewise are held to be so, and not to be dependent on perception.

Much too ready are learned foreigners to identify Indian notions with those of European speculators, ancient and modern. What are so hastily taken to be correspondencies will generally turn out, on further examination, to be mere fancied resemblances.

* Not simply practical things, but, strangely enough, apparent things also, are maintained, by the Vedántins, to exist separately from, and independently of, the apprehension of them. See a passage in the seventh page of the *Vedánta-paribháshá*, beginning अत एव प्रातिभासिकरजतस्थले । and the extract from the same work, cited at p. 169. To one aware, that the Vedántins hold notions such as that referred to, there must seem to be exceedingly slight grounds for comparing them, as to subtlety, with Berkeley.

Secondly. Though the Vedántins agree with the the bulk of men, as just stated, they take a line of their own, in saying, that objects of sense are imaginations of ignorance, or false. And herein they differ from Berkeley, too, who does not call such objects false, but forms of perception, and acknowledges them to be true, in the current sense of the term. The Vedántins compare the objects of the senses to a snake surmised in a rope, or to silver fancied in nacre, and hold them to be altogether false, and so our cognition of them to be erroneous. Hence, several of the great Vedántin doctors consider the world to be, in their technical language, apparent; and they add, that the regarding the world as belonging to another category than that of nacrine silver, i. e., the regarding it as practical, is prompted by a desire to assist the uninitiate.

Thirdly. In the Vedánta system, not only are objects of cognition imaginations of ignorance, and false, but cognition itself is so: for cognition is an affection of the internal organ; and, not being Brahma, it is to be classed with imaginations of ignorance, and falsities; just like a jar, or any other external thing. Objects and the cognizing them are, thus, held to be alike false.* How vast a gulf does this single point of difference place between the Vedánta and Berkeleianism!

Fourthly. In the theory of Berkeley, the world, birth, death, Heaven, Hell, and the happiness and misery arising therefrom,

---

* A'nanda Giri, discoursing about the affection cognition, observes:
न च साऽपि वस्तुतस्तद्विषयतामनुभवति वस्तुतः स्वयमभावाद् बाह्यस्य विषयस्य काल्पनिकत्वात् । स्वतस्तद्विषयत्वं प्रातिभासिक-मित्यर्थः । On S'ankara A'chárya's *Mándúkya-bháshya: Bibliotheca Indica*, Vol VIII., p. 340. "Not even does that *affection* veritably take cognizance of such *an external object;* because, in truth, it, *the affection*, does not itself exist, *and* because such an object is imaginary. By consequence, *an affection's* cognizing such *an object* is apparent. This is the sense."

See further, the couplet adduced from the *Ashtávakra-gítá* at p. 222.

though forms of perception, are true, and not of such a nature, that they vanish away on the supervening of right apprehension. On the other hand, agreeably to the Vedántins, when a man becomes convinced, that the objects which we cognize through our senses and other media of knowledge, are false, i. e., that they never existed, and do not now exist, and never will exist, and that Brahma alone, essentially existence, intellect, joy, is true, and that he is that man's self, all those objects dissolve into nothingness; as happens with nacrine silver, on our discerning nacre, mistaken for silver, to be nacre. Thus, it is said: "Like nacrine silver, the world appears true, so long as Brahma, the substrate of all, without a second, remains unknown."* When, therefore, the Vedántins declare, that this world, and the next, and all things thereto pertaining, are falsifiable by right apprehension, let no one explain their language to import, that, when a man acquires such apprehension, this world, and the next, &c., through God's grace, or from some other cause, become as nothing to him. It is not, the Vedantins themselves teach, that they become as nothing, but strictly nothing; they being recognized as illusive: and they become nothing in consequence of the acquisition of right apprehension, and from no other cause whatever. It is laid down, that there are two sorts of riddance of the products of ignorance. One, called cessation, takes place when, by the uprise of a new and opponent affection of the internal organ, or by getting quit of defects, an erroneous affection is destroyed, and, of course, its object. It is illustrated by the shattering a jar with a pestle. The other, known as falsification, is when the right perception of the nature of a thing dispels all ignorance, and the error regarding the

---

* तावत् सत्यं जगद् भाति शुक्तिकारजतं यथा ।
यावन् न ज्ञायते ब्रह्म सर्वाधिष्ठानमद्वयम् ॥

This is the seventh couplet of the *A'tma-bodha;* p. 4 of the Mirzapore edition of 1852.

thing, and the object of that error.* Thus it occurs in the case of nacre, so often mentioned;† and equally false with

---

* कार्यविनाशो हि द्विविधः कश्चिदुपादानेन सह कश्चित् तु विद्यमान एवोपादाने । आद्यो बाधः द्वितीयस्तु निवृत्तिः । आद्यस्य कारणमधिष्ठानतत्त्वसाक्षात्कारेण विनोपादानभूताया अविद्याया अनिवृत्तेः । द्वितीयस्य कारणं विरोधिप्रत्ययव्यक्तिर्दोषनिवृत्तिर्वा । तदिह ब्रह्मसाक्षात्काराभावात् स्वप्नप्रपञ्चो मा बाधिष्ठ मुसलप्रहारेण घटादेरिव विरोधिप्रत्ययान्तरोदयेन खञ्जनकीभूतनिद्रादिदोषनाशेन वा स्वप्नादिनिवृत्तौ को विरोधः । *Vedánta-paribháshá*, p 13.

"Destruction of the products *of ignorance* is twofold : the one, where the material cause, *viz., ignorance*, is included ; the other, where the material cause remains *untouched*. The first is *denominated* falsification ; the second, cessation. Of the former the cause is, the intuition of the true nature of the substrate *over which a false thing is imagined :* since, but for this *intuition*, nescience, *or ignorance*, the material cause, cannot be done away. Of the latter the cause is, the origination of an antagonistic affection, or else the abolition of defects. Hence, in the present instance, by reason of the non-existence of the intuition of Brahma, *the substrate of all imaginary objects*, however the world of dreams is not falsified, what incongruity is there *in supposing*, that, as a jar, or the like, *is destroyed* by the blow of a pestle, so, by the presentation of another and antagonistic conception, or by the discontinuance of sleep, or other defect, originative thereof, *i. e., of dreaming*, the chariot, or other thing *dreamt of*, ceases ?"

It is worth observing, that the Vedántins are not so accurate in the employment of their peculiar phraseology, as not frequently to use *nivṛitti*, "cessation," where they ought, agreeably to their own definitions, to use *bádha*, "falsification." Thus, in the extract from the *Vedánta-paribháshá*, p. 32, given at p. 204, Dharmarája would have done better, had he written, ब्रह्मज्ञानबाध्यतया. The translation supposes the required change to have been made.

† Two views, entertained touching the cause of things like nacrine silver, are referred to in the passage quoted below. It is according to the first only, that those things are held to be falsified by right apprehension of what is mistaken for them. According to the second view, such things, owing to the right apprehension in question, simply cease to exist. एवं च शुक्तिरूप्यस्य शुक्त्यवच्छिन्नचैतन्यनिष्ठाविद्याकार्यत्वपक्षे शुक्तिरितिज्ञानेन

nacrine silver become, according to the Vedánta, the whole world, and the ignorance which originates it, as soon as one has mastered the knowledge of Brahma.

CHAPTER VII.

The Soul, being subject to Ignorance, cannot, as the Vedántins hold, be One with the Supreme Spirit; a Description of Ignorance; and an Argument to show, that the Denial of the Soul's Identity with Brahma is not set aside by taking the Epithet of False, as applied to Ignorance, in the Acceptation of Perishable.

It is a maxim of the Vedánta, that "The soul is Brahma itself, and nothing other." How, I would ask the Vedántins, can this be? For they assert, that, on the one hand, soul errs by reason of ignorance; and that, on the other hand, Brahma is, in essence, ever pure, intelligent, and free, and can never for a moment be otherwise. Still they maintain, that the soul is Brahma; and, with intent to reconcile their contradiction, they resort to the most elaborate mystification. Some among them say, that the reflexion of Brahma in the

तद्ब्रानेन सह रजतस्य बाधः । मूषाविद्याकार्यत्वपच्छे तु मूषा-
विद्याया ब्रह्मसाचात्कारनिवर्त्त्यतया शुक्तितत्त्वज्ञानानिवर्त्त्यतया रज-
तस्य तच शुक्तिज्ञानान् निवृत्तिमार्च मुसलप्रहारेण घटस्येव ।

Vedánta-paribháshá, pp. 13, 14. "And so, on the opinion, that nacrine silver is a product of nescience residing in *and obscuring* nacre-appropriated intelligence, *there results,* from the cognition 'This is nacre,' falsification of silver, and of the ignorance pertaining to that *nacre.* But on the opinion, that *nacrine silver* is a product of radical nescience, *i. e., of the ignorance which resides in and obscures pure Brahma, and is the cause of the entire universe,* since such nescience, *the material cause of such silver,* is removable *solely* by intuition of Brahma, not by cognition of the true nature of nacre, *there ensues,* as the fruit of right apprehension of nacre, nothing more than the cessation of silver; in the same way as a jar *is destroyed* by the blow of a pestle."

internal organ is soul,* and that to the soul appertains all error; wherefore error has no connexion with Brahma.

Such as say thus, the reflexionists,† find no difficulty in maintaining, that the soul—a reflexion, with them,—is liable to error, and that Brahma is exempt therefrom. Other Vedántins, however,—those who hold the soul to be Brahma as appropriated to the internal organ,‡—the appropriationists,§ perceive, that, if the soul be simply as they allege, its defects must be participated by Brahma. In expatiating on this point, they disclose one of their mysteries. Though, in their view, the soul is Brahma as appropriated to the internal organ, and though it is said to err; yet, in truth, all its qualities, as cognition, will, &c., and error, likewise, belong not to its Brahma-portion, but to its associate, the internal organ; in accordance with the maxim " An affirmation, or a negation," &c. ‖

But the reader should be reminded, that the language of the reflexionists, no less than that of the appropriationists, is deceptive here. For, since, as has been shown, it is neither the reflexion of Brahma in the internal organ, nor Brahma as appropriated to that organ, to which the qualities of the soul truly appertain, but the internal organ, it is this that the Vedántins ought to consider to be soul.

None of those philosophers entertain the opinion, that the internal organ is the soul. When pressed with the question, how the soul, which is obnoxious to error, can be Brahma, they distinctly declare, that error affects the internal organ, not him. I tell the Vedántins, therefore, that, if that in which error resides is different from the Supreme Spirit, when you instruct it to regard itself as Brahma, you are practising deception. For who is it that you so instruct? Is it

---

* See the passage from the *Vedánta-paribháshá*, p. 41, cited at p. 186.

† In Sanskrit, *pratibimba-vádin*.

‡ See the passage from the *Vedánta-paribháshá*, p 8, cited at p. 186.

§ In Sanskrit, *avachchhinna-vádins*.

‖ This maxim is given in full at p. 232.

one who is in error? Or is it the pure, intelligent, free Brahma? If the former, you have declared, that it is different from Brahma; and, consequently, when you teach it, that itself is Brahma, you are misleading. If the latter, your labour is quite needless.

It is easy to perceive how the appropriationists satisfy themselves, that the soul is Brahma. Brahma, they argue, as appropriated to the internal organ, does not differ from the pure Brahma; just as the ether appropriated to a jar does not differ from the omnipresent ether. To be restored to Brahmahood, all that the soul has to do is, to get rid of the internal organ, which is false, and simply imagined by ignorance to exist: and it is right apprehension which abolishes that organ and all its qualities. But how do the reflexionists make out the soul to be one with Brahma? With them, as with all other Vedántins, reflexions of every description—whether of objects in a mirror, or the like, or that of Brahma in the internal organ,—are false, literally false, as nacrine silver is; not false as the Sánkhyas maintain them to be.* And yet they are false only as reflexions: in their identity with the things reflected, they are true. For, in the case of a reflexion, it is held, that what one beholds is the thing reflected; only that, through misapprehension, it appears to be different from it, and in a place where the thing is not actually located.†

---

* See the note at p. 52, and p. 92 of the text.

† मुखाभासको दर्पणे दृश्यमानो
मुखत्वात् पृथक्त्वेन नैवार्स्ति वस्तु ।
चिदाभासको धीषु जीवोऽपि तद्वत्
स नित्योपलब्धिस्वरूपोऽहमात्मा ॥

"I am that Spirit,—constitutively eternal apprehension,—*which manifests itself as soul*. For, similar to the reflexion of the face beheld in a mirror,—*which reflexion is* nothing whatever, *taken* apart from the face,—is the soul, the reflexion of intelligence, or *Spirit*, in intellects, or *internal organs*."

This is the fifth couplet of the *Hastámalaka*, which is credulously imputed to S'ankara A'chárya. The poem is in high esteem among the Vedántins.

Similar thereto is nacrine silver, which is nothing but nacre under the appearance of silver. It is false, as silver, but veritable, as nacre.

Of course, this statement will suggest doubts to the reader. First, there is the absurdity of comparing a reflexion and what is reflected to nacrine silver and nacre; and, again, if the soul, which is laid down as being a reflexion of Brahma, is, after all, nothing but Brahma, how can it be subject to error? If the soul be a reflexion, not when it is viewed as Brahma, but only when it is misapprehensively viewed as a reflexion, and as something different from Brahma, it comes out, that it is a nonentity.* Who, moreover, is it that sees the soul as a reflexion? For the soul itself is proved to be nothing; and Brahma is not liable to error: and, therefore, a third party is needed to make an error here possible.

But the reader must not allow himself to be perplexed or disheartened. If we have already reached what is clearly preposterous, there are more things of the same character awaiting us.

It is impossible for us to recognize as soul anything other than that which is endowed with apprehension, will, and other like qualities; and the Vedántins assign away these qualities to the internal organ. As for what they call ignorance, which they distinguish from error, or misapprehension, they are constrained to ascribe it to the pure Brahma, and not to the internal organ. If it were a reality, we should be obliged to

---

* Vijnána Bhikshu meets as follows the doctrine animadverted on in the text: प्रतिबिम्बस्य तुच्छत्वे प्रतिबिम्बरूपजीवस्य बिम्बरूपब्रह्मात्‌ सद्‌असद्‌भेदानुपपत्तिः सदसतोर्भेदानुपपत्तेः । अतुच्छत्वे चास्तनानात्वस्य भ्रष्टभेदेन स्वीकारापत्तिः अद्वैताद्यनुपपत्तिरिति । *Yoga-bháshya-várttika*, MS., *fol.* 28, *verso.* "If a reflexion be a nonentity, the soul, a reflexion, cannot be identical with Brahma, *the object* reflected: for there can be no identity of entity with nonentity. And, if *it be* not a nonentity, multeity of souls will be acknowledged in other terms *than direct terms*; and monism, &c. will go undemonstrated."

acknowledge, that, in the Vedánta, the soul is Brahma himself. But this ignorance, as we shall shortly discover, is wholly a thing of the imagination. A somewhat detailed account of it will now be given; and we shall learn what it is, and why the Vedántins are unable to refer it to the internal organ, and are forced to ascribe it to Brahma.

The word "ignorance" may mean absence of apprehension, and also misapprehension, or mistake. When the Vedántin says, that the world is imagined by ignorance, common sense supposes, that he intends, by ignorance, misapprehension; since the absence of apprehension cannot imagine. He contends, however, that he intends, by it, neither the one nor the other.* Nevertheless, he takes it to be the imaginer of false objects, and likewise to be eliminable by right apprehension. More than this, he accounts it a thing having an object; the object being, however, strange to say, not falsity, but verity. Accordingly, say what the Vedántins may, it seems to me, on taking account of the characteristics they attribute to ignorance, that it is a combination of two ideas, namely, the absence of apprehension whose object is verity, and error in mistaking a falsity for a verity: for those characteristics fit nothing save such a combination.

The Vedántins hold ignorance to have verity for its object; and this is not a characteristic of mistake: for mistake is cognition whose object is falsity; as, for instance, the cognition of nacrine silver. But ignorance, the Vedántins teach, has verity i. e., pure Brahma, for its object. The *Sankshepa-s'áríraka*

---

* अज्ञानं तु सदसद्भ्यामनिर्वचनीयं त्रिगुणात्मकं भावरूपं ज्ञानविरोधि यत्किञ्चिदिति वदन्ति । *Vedánta-sára*, p. 4. "Ignorance, it is declared, is a something that cannot be described as either existent or non-existent; constituted of the three *guṇas*; an entity; antagonistic to right apprehension."

The translation runs as if the original were सत्त्वासत्त्वाभ्यां, which it ought to have been.

says: "The impartite intellect alone is subject and object *of ignorance.*"* They declare, that ignorance of which the object is Brahma, is the cause of this world, a false thing; and so, that ignorance whose object is nacre†, is the cause of false silver. It appears, then, that ignorance, since verity is its object, is the absence of apprehension of the veritable. For, though the having verity for its object cannot be characteristic of absence of apprehension,—just as it cannot characterize mistake,—absence or negation not being an object-having thing; it is characteristic of apprehension. Hence, though it cannot be said, that the having verity for its object is characteristic of absence of apprehension, still, when the Vedántins assert, that ignorance has verity for its object, what there is of truth in their assertion—their confusion of ideas being rejected,—may be expressed by saying, that ignorance is the absence of apprehension whose object is verity, i. e., pure Brahma. And this absence of apprehension is, in my opinion, the power of concealment which they ascribe to ignorance; that is to say, its faculty of hiding verity.‡ For what can concealment of verity be but absence of the apprehension of it? But the Vedántins, instead of acknowledging this power of concealment to be one with ignorance, regard ignorance as an entity, of which concealment is a power.

* आश्रयत्वविषयत्वभागिनी
निर्विभागचितिरेव केवला ।

† See the extract from the *Vedánta-paribháshá*, p. 10, cited at p. 168.

‡ अस्याऽज्ञानस्याऽऽवरणविक्षेपनामकं शक्तिद्वयमस्ति । आवरणशक्तिस्तावत् * * * * * अज्ञान परिच्छिन्नमप्यस्मानमपरिच्छिन्नमसंसारिणमवलोकयितृबुद्धिपिधायकतयाऽऽच्छादयतीव तादृशं सामर्थ्यम् । *Vedánta-sára*, pp. 6, 7. "Of this ignorance there are two faculties, known as concealment and delusion. The faculty of concealment * * * * is a power such that, *by it,* ignorance, though limited, by veiling the mind of the beholder, as it were covers Spirit, unlimited and irrelate to the world."

If they said no more than this about ignorance, we might conclude it to mean simply absence of apprehension. They consider it, however, to be the imaginer of the false world; and to be such an imaginer is the work of mistake, not of absence of apprehension. Ignorance, then, since they make it to be the imaginer of the false world, must be misapprehension, or mistake. This mistake is, in my opinion, the Vedántins' second power of ignorance, its deluding power.* "Delusion" is when the false appears in place of the veritable; and this is mistake. But the Vedántins, instead of owning this power of delusion to be one with ignorance, hold it to be a power of ignorance.

I will show how the Vedántins here fall into error. Our cognition of the external world, *i. e.*, perception, inference, &c., is, to their thinking, misapprehension;† and, in order to keep Brahma pure from it, they appropriate it to the internal organ. But this wrong cognition they cannot identify with ignorance; since they are bent on making ignorance to be the cause of the whole world, so that it may be established as false. If they had said, that ignorance is mistake, an affection of the internal organ, then it might be, for them, the imaginer of the external world. But how could it imagine the internal organ? And, if it does not, the internal organ cannot be proved, as they would prove it, to be false. Therefore, with intent to make ignorance the imaginer of the internal

---

* विक्षेपशक्तिस्तु यथा रज्जुज्ञानं स्वावरणौ स्वशक्त्या सर्पादिक-मुद्भावयति एवमज्ञानमपि स्वावृतात्मनि स्वशक्त्या आकाशादिप्रपञ्चमुद्भा-वयति तादृशं सामर्थ्यम् । *Vedánta-sára*, p. 7. "The faculty of delusion is a power *thus illustrated*. As ignorance about a rope produces, by its own force, a *false* snake, or the like, in the rope which it conceals; so *radical* ignorance, *viz.*, *that concerning pure Brahma*, brings forth, by its own force, in the Spirit which itself conceals, the universe, made up of ether and the rest."

† See the couplet cited in the *Vedánta-paribháshá*, given at p. 173.

organ also,* they insist, that it is something different from mistake.† And here they are forced into fresh and greater absurdities.

> * तव चित्तात्मतमसा जनितं
> परिकल्पयत्यखिलमेव जगत् ।

"Thy mind, generated by thy ignorance, imagines the entire universe."
This half-couplet is from the *Sankshepa-sáríraka*.

† It is remarkable, that S'ankara A'chárya himself was unguarded in the language he employed regarding this doctrine. In the passage quoted below, he makes ignorance to be one with mistake : तमेतमेवंलक्षणमध्यासं पण्डिता अविद्येति मन्यन्ते । "Misapprehension of this description, *just before laid down*, the learned hold to be nescience." But Rámánanda, his commentator, redresses his laxity : अविद्याकार्यत्वादविद्येति मन्यन्त इत्यर्थः । "The import is, that they consider *misapprehension*, as being the product of nescience, to be *itself* nescience." See the *Bibliotheca Indica*, No. 64, p. 16.

Here it may be observed, once for all, that, alike as to the Vedánta, and as to the other systems of Hindu philosophy, the higher we ascend the stream of time, the more frequent do we find unphilosophical inexactness of phraseology. This inexactness is, of course, most frequent of all in the works of the inventors of those systems. Their care, it should seem, was well-nigh exclusively bestowed upon broad principles ; and the result was somewhat of vagueness, at least, in their modes of expression. Subsequent writers, as commentators and others, have, to be sure, amended the phraseology of their predecessors. But it has been with a view to remove the appearance of inconsistency in them ; it has not at all been with any intention of introducing new doctrines. These they have not introduced.

Of this assertion a justification is offered in the extract, and the annotation thereon, just adduced. With S'ankara, following the Upanishads, apprehension,—whether correct or erroneous,—will, activity, &c., are properties of the internal organ ; and, further, the whole universe, including the internal organ, is false, and imagined by ignorance, or nescience. How, then, in accordance with his views, could misapprehension and nescience be identical ?

It is desirable to keep ever before the mind the fact, that an uninitiated reader will come upon hundreds of terms and statements, in the expositions of S'ankara and other early Vedántins, which, though seeming, at first sight, contradictory of many things asserted in this volume, are, in fact, not so ; a right understanding of them requiring, that they should be understood with certain qualifications. In order to a full acquaintance with these qualifica-

When the Vedántins contend, that ignorance is something different from mistake, though they call it the imaginer of this false world, how can they say, that its imagining is like that of mistake? For mistake imagines by imputing existence to the non-existent: and hence its object is called false. The Vedántins, in calling the world imagined of ignorance, with a view to establish its falsity, ought to have taken the imagining of ignorance to be like that of mistake; but this was difficult for them to admit, since they had already erred in viewing ignorance as a thing different from mistake. And see the difficulty consequent to them. Their "ignorance," or illusion, like the "nature" of the Sánkhyas, now begins to appear to them an incognitive substance; and, as such, what sort of imagining can it possess? Like that of the "nature" of the Sánkhyas, and that of the atoms of the Naiyáyikas, it is no longer imagining, but positively the material cause of the whole world. And what now? Does the world turn out to be true, and does non-duality disappear, and duality supersede it? To this one would be brought, reasoning from their account of ignorance. Yet these results they utterly repudiate. The verity of the world they will never grant. If they did, all their toil would be to no purpose. Neither could the soul be Brahma, nor could emancipation come from right apprehension; as will be made clear in the ninth chapter. The belief, that the internal organ, &c., the whole world, are false, is the very life of the monistic doctrine. However, as has been shown, such is the waywardness of the Vedántins' intellect, that, though they consider a thing to be false, and call it practical and apparent, yet, as soon as they have called it so, it begins to look to them real. In like manner, since they call the world false, and give the name of ignorance to that which imagines it to be true, they ought not

---

tious, a thorough-going study of the whole scheme of the Vedánta is indispensable. No criticism that does not rest on a wide basis of Vedánta research, can be held satisfactory.

to regard this **ignorance as an unintelligent substance** : and yet, as they inconsistently regard the world to be, from one aspect, real, so they regard its cause, ignorance, or illusion, to be, like the "nature" of the Sánkhya, an unintelligent substance, and the world's material cause; and then it seems to them actually, after the manner of "nature," to bring forth the entire universe. Nevertheless, there is no question, that, to prove the world to be altogether false, is the vital principle and main point of the doctrine of non-duality. With this main point we should compare other points of the doctrine; and, if they are found not to harmonize, we should there leave the matter, and rest convinced of the weakness of the sages whose inconsistency we have detected. We are not to change that main point, thus taking away the essence of the doctrine, and foist a new theory upon the authors of the one in hand, in order that they may be made out to speculate reasonably.

Again, it should be borne in mind, that, as I have said before, the Vedántins believe the world to be falsifiable by right apprehension; whence it is manifest, that they hold the world to be veritably false. And another of their tenets is, that ignorance also, the imaginer of the world, is removable by right apprehension. This tenet supposes a third character of ignorance, which assimilates it both to mistake and to absence of apprehension. If ignorance be, like "nature," the material cause of the world, how is it removable by right apprehension? By right apprehension of a verity, the error committed in mistaking a falsity for it is undoubtedly removed, and the absence of apprehension of that verity is likewise terminated.

Whatever the confusion of the Vedántins on the subject of ignorance, since they make the pure Brahma himself to be the subject of it, and since, in their view, that which is ignorant is soul, I own, that, in this case, it follows, that the soul is one with Brahma. But now I ask, whether any one is conscious of such ignorance as has been described? And, if no one is, where are we to find a soul that is ignorant?* If the Vedántins reply, that whoever regards himself as other than Brahma, and the world to be true, &c., is a soul, I know that they mean one of us ordinary mortals. But so to consider—a misapprehension, in Vedánta phrase,—is not ignorance, but, in their language, an affection of the internal organ. Where, then, are we to look for ignorance and the ignorant? Nowhere, of a truth, but in the reveries of the Vedántins.

Waiving, however, all this, and taking the words of Vedántins as they deliver them, I urge, that, if the soul be ignorant, it cannot be identical with Brahma; for he, in their belief, is ever pure, intelligent, and free.†

---

* Universal consciousness is appealed to, by the Vedántins, in testimony, that this ignorance exists. Thus: अहमज्ञ इत्याद्यनुभवात् ।
Vedánta-sára, p 4. "From the consciousness 'I am ignorant,' &c."

But how can this be? For the ignorance which is the object of the consciousness "I am ignorant" is simply absence of knowledge, or, at most, misapprehension; and not the extraordinary invention which the Vedántins call ignorance.

† का पनरियमविद्या । किं भ्रान्तिज्ञानं किं वा भ्रान्तिज्ञान-कारणभूतं वस्त्वन्तरम् । यदि भ्रान्तिः सा कस्य । न ब्रह्मणः तस्य स्वच्छविद्यारूपत्वात् । न हि भास्करे तिमिरस्याऽवकाशः सम्भवति । न जीवानां तेषां ब्रह्मातिरेकिणामभावात् । भ्रान्त्य-भावादेव च तत्कारणं वस्त्वन्तरमप्यनुपपन्नमेव । ब्रह्मातिरेकेण भ्रान्तिज्ञानं तत्कारणं वाऽभ्युपगम्यतामद्वैतहानिः । किम्भूता च ब्रह्मणोऽविद्या । न हि कारणान्तरमस्ति । स्वाभाविकीति चेत् कथं विद्यास्वभावमविद्यास्वभावं स्यात् । *S'ástra-dípiká* MS., *fol.* 58, *recto*. "But what is this nescience? Is it misapprehension? Or something else, a cause of misapprehension? If misapprehension, whose? Not Brahma's; for he, *as you Vedántins hold*, is constitutively pure science. In the sun there can be no place for darkness. Nor *can it be* souls'; for these, *as you hold*, are not distinct from Brahma. And, since, *from your premisses*, misapprehension cannot exist, no more can a second thing, a cause thereof. Besides, for such as subscribe to misapprehension, or a cause of it, *as an entity* additional

But the Vedántins, though they are forced to locate ignorance in Brahma, still, in order to make him out to be essentially ever pure, intelligent, and free, maintain that ignorance itself is false. Most wonderful is this of all their wonders. And how is ignorance considered, by them, to be false? I must now address myself to answer this question.

On hearing, that the Vedántins regard ignorance as the cause of the world's appearing to be true, one would, of course, suppose, that this ignorance was understood, by them, to be itself true. For if ignorance did not actually exist, how could the world, which they hold to be a nonentity, have appearance? When a man mistakingly sees a snake in a rope, the snake is called false. At the same time, that man's misapprehension is not said to be false, but true. The Vedántins, however, maintain that ignorance is false. We ought, therefore, to enquire, how it is reckoned false, and what is gained to the Vedánta system by so reckoning it.

To the first enquiry we get two answers from the Vedántins. One is given by those whose mastery of their doctrine is not perfect; while the other is returned by such as have penetrated their system to its innermost arcana. The latter answer I shall speak of in the next chapter. The former, that which one hears from the bulk of Hindus now-a-days, I shall examine briefly at once.

This answer is, that ignorance is called false, inasmuch as it is eliminated by the supervening of right apprehension. But this is highly absurd. That is false which does not exist at all: but that which exists, and is destroyed at a given time, is not false, but uneternal and perishable.* If a Vedán-

---

to Brahma, monism evaporates. To continue, whence sprang Brahma's misapprehension? For there is no other cause, *with you ; Brahma being the sole entity.* If it be said, that it is natural *to him,* how, pray, can he whose nature is science be he whose nature is nescience?"

* Just as Párthasárathi says, in arguing against the Vedántins, with reference to the universe. His words are उत्पत्तिविनाश्यंगादनित्यता-

tin replies, that, in his technical language, false means uneternal, I have to say, that the fault of ignorance in the ignorant Brahma cannot be got rid of by thus denominating his ignorance; nor can you thus prove him to be essentially pure, intelligent, and free. The goodness or badness of a thing depends upon its nature, not upon the epithets applied to it. Suppose, that some one held in general esteem goes mad; whereat his friends are in great grief. A man comes and assures them, that he is not mad; his madness is false. And he adds, that, according to his own way of speaking, he only is really mad, who has been so from birth. The person miscalled mad was quite in his right mind for the first five and twenty years of his life; and, therefore, his madness is false. Would this speech be of any consolation to the friends of the respected maniac? Without doubt, the Supreme Spirit is essentially ever pure, intelligent, and free,—in the right sense of these terms; and He is so indefeasibly. Any so-called sacred book that asserts the contrary confutes, by its blasphemy, its pretensions to divine origin; and there can be no more certain mark of a false religion than such an assertion. In maintaining, that Brahma, as they describe him, is the Supreme Spirit, and in attributing to that Spirit unworthy and debasing attributes, the Vedántins, though unconsciously, do Him the foulest dishonour.

Ordinary Vedántins whom one meets, those who know their doctrine but superficially, though they speak as I have stated, about the falsity of ignorance, entertain, in their minds, a different view. They do not merely believe, as they say they do, that ignorance is perishable, and therefore false; for Brahma, they cannot but feel, would not thus be freed from all defect. They indeed believe, like their better-informed co-religionists, that ignorance is absolutely nothing whatsoever: only they are at a loss to explain themselves.

मानं स्यात् | *S'ástra-dípiká*, MS., *fol.* 58, *recto.* "From being originated and destroyed, it is simply *proved to be* non-eternal, *not false.*"

CHAPTER. VIII.

Criticism of the Vedánta Tenet of the Falseness of Ignorance, as set forth in Standard Treatises, and as held by Well-read Advocates of the Theory.

Vedántins who have attained to a thorough comprehension of their system, maintain, that ignorance is imagined by ignorance, and therefore is false. You will ask, imagined by what ignorance? The answer is, by itself. To this purpose the *Sankshepa-s'áríraka* says: "In the case of the ignorant one, ignorance is not of its essence: since, *for ignorance to be essential to it* would belie its nature,—intelligence, unchangeable, and without a second. Assuredly, ignorance is caused by ignorance exclusively. Nor may self-supportedness here be charged: for, as spirit proves the existence of everything knowable, and of itself also, from possessing the power of cognition; similarly, self-ignorance may imagine itself and other things. Thus there is no difficulty."* If, endeavouring

---

* अज्ञानमप्यविदुषोऽस्य न तु स्वतोऽस्ति
चैतन्यनिर्विकृततादय॰विरोधात् ।
अज्ञातताऽप्यनवबोधनिबन्धनैव
नाऽऽत्माश्रयत्वमपि चोदयितव्यमत्र ॥

आत्मा प्रसाधयति वेद्यपदार्थजातं
स्वात्मानमप्यवगतित्वमश्रुतियोगात् ।
स्वाज्ञानमेवमिदमात्मपरप्रकृतौ
प्रह्रं भवेदिति न किञ्चन दौस्थ्यमस्ति ॥

Sarvajnátman denies, as we have seen, that his position involves self-supportedness; but the author of the Sánkhya Aphorisms, and Vijnána Bhikshu, are of opinion, that the accusation is fairly brought home to the Vedántins.

नन्वविद्यावादेऽप्यविद्यायोगो वक्तव्यः तथा चाऽपारमार्थिकत्वान् न तया सङ्ग इति । तथाऽऽह ।
तद्योगे तन्निद्धावन्योन्याश्रयत्वम् ।

to establish such an impossibility as is here propounded, the Vedántins get confused, and plunge deeper than ever into error, small is the wonder. To illustrate the notion, that ignorance imagines itself, the author just cited instances the soul, which, through cognition, proves the existence of itself, no less than that of things external. But where is the parallelism? The illustration adduced is of no pertinence, except to decoy a man into a maze of words, and then to beguile him by a semblance of reasonableness. The author says, that the soul, by its cognition, proves, that external objects exist, and itself also. But, in proving their existence, does it imagine them? Not at all. They were already actually in being; and the soul does not invent them, either in imagination, or veritably. Hence, "to prove the existence of," as we find the phrase used above, means only "to apprehend," *i. e.*, "to certify as existent." A person resolved on finding the Vedánta rational, may here insist, that the author intends to show nothing more than what he said in the case of the soul, to-wit, that ignorance proves its own existence; in other words, that it, already existing, ascertains that it is so. If so, I reply, ignorance is made out to be a verity. As our rationalizer would interpret it, the extract is quite out of place. Further, on his showing, the contradiction which the author

---

अविद्यायोगादविद्यासिद्धौ चान्योन्याश्रयत्वमात्माश्रयत्वम् । चानवस्था वेतिप्रेष॥ *Sánkhyá-pravachaná-bháshya*, pp. 173, 174. "But, let the connexion of nescience *with spirit* be alleged to have place because of nescience itself. Then, since it, *nescience*, will be untrue, no contact thereof, *operative of change, will be wrought in spirit*. With reference to this, it is declared: 'If it, *nescience, by supposition* has place from the connexion of itself, there befals mutual dependence.' 'Mutual dependence,' *i. e.*, self-supportedness: or else, an infinite regress,—a supplementation *here* demanded."

It is because the case in question is one of "self-supportedness," that Vijnána thus explains "mutual dependence."

Aphorism 14 of Book V. is included in the above.

deprecates remains intact. Any one who is thoroughly conversant with the Vedánta will acknowledge, that, when its teachers discourse of ignorance after the manner of the verses I have cited, their purpose is, to prove, that ignorance is false,—just as nacrine silver is,—and, therefore, that the soul is essentially ever pure, intelligent, and free.

The *Sankshepa-s'áríraka* is an authority of the first rank; and it may be thought incredible, that it can be so weak as I have represented it to be. In anticipation of misgiving, I add, from the commentary of Purushottama Misra, the *Subodhiní*, his exposition of the verses in question:

" But, one may object, since ignorance, an eternal entity, is, like Brahma, impossible of elimination, how is emancipation, which consists in the elimination thereof, to be effected? Its being eliminable by right apprehension, on the ground of its falseness, is thus established: ' In the case of the ignorant one,' &c. To explain. Is the relation of ignorance to the ignorant one essential? Or is it imagined? It is not the former: ' not of its essence' Why? ' Since, *for ignorance to be essential*,' &c. If ignorance were in spirit essentially, it would be a true entity: but it cannot abide as true in a thing which is self-luminous intelligence, *as spirit is;* since light is repugnant to darkness. Again: if ignorance were a property of spirit, its being destroyed would alter the spirit, according to the maxim ' A property, acceding, or seceding, changes its subject.' Moreover: if ignorance were a true entity, the result would be duality. Hence, it is meant, there would be contradiction to the scripture which declares, *that spirit is* intelligence, unchangeable, and without a second. The latter is admitted: ' Assuredly, ignorance,' &c. The facts standing thus, there is no antagonism; even as there is none between the midday glare and the gloom for which the owl mistakes it. Such is the import."*

* नन्वनादिभावरूपस्याऽज्ञानस्य ब्रह्मवदेव निवर्त्तनासम्भवात्

As appears clearly from the words of the commentator himself, the author intends to establish, that ignorance is altogether false. That the commentator thus understands his intent is purged of all doubt by the illustration of the owl. The darkness which the bird is supposed to recognize, is purely fictitious. In like manner, ignorance, it is maintained, is nothing whatever, and yet imagines itself to exist.

I would ask, then, what resemblance there is between ignorance's imagining itself, and the soul's proving the existence of itself and of other objects? But observe, that the author's word *prasádhayati*, "proves as existent," is somewhat liable to mislead. In its connexion, it can signify only "certifies as existent." It looks, however, as if it had the sense of "makes," or "contrives;" and the transition from this to "invents," or "imagines," is not very violent. We now see how the author, beguiled by words, came to the conclusion, that the illustration produced by him was a valid proof that ignorance may imagine itself to exist. Deluded himself, he deludes others.

कुतस्तन्निवृत्तिरूपा मुक्तिः फलमित्यादृष्टङ्ग्य् तस्य मिथ्यात्वेन ज्ञान-
निवर्त्यत्वं साधयति अज्ञानमपीति । तथाहि अज्ञस्य खात्मन्य-
ज्ञानान्वयः किं खाभाविकः कल्पितो वा नाद्य इत्याद्द नविति ।
कुत इत्याद्द चैतन्येति । खभावत आत्मन्यज्ञानमस्ति चेद् वक्तु-
भूतं स्यान् न च खप्रकाशचिदात्मके वस्तुनि वस्तुतोऽज्ञानं वस्तितु-
महेति प्रकाशतमसोर्विरोधात् । तथाऽज्ञानमात्मधर्मश्चेत् तर्हि
खयं विनश्यदात्मानं विकुर्यात् ।

उपयन्नपयन् धर्मो विकरोति हि धर्मिणम् ।

इति न्यायात् । तथाऽज्ञानस्य वस्तुत्वे द्वैतापत्तिरिति चित्तनि-
र्विकारत्वादयश्रुतिविरोध इत्यर्थः । द्वितीयमञ्जीकरोतीति अज्ञा-
नताऽपीति । अमिष्ठ्वर्थः । तथात्वेऽहि मध्यन्दिनालोकमण्डले
कौशिकादिकल्पितान्धकारवदविरोधः स्यादिति भावः ।

Thus, in one respect, that illustration is inapposite. Still more so is it in another respect. As regards the soul, it exists, and therefore certifies as existent itself and other objects. On the other hand, how can ignorance, if it be nothing, imagine itself, or anything else? This is a sample of the gross absurdities which the Vedántins acquiesce in; and not only are they not abashed by them, but they are perfectly satisfied with them. For instance, Purushottama Mis'ra, near the words I have taken from him, says: "In this *system*, which maintains that *everything* transcends explanation, unreasonableness is no objection."* To accept such views as I have been treating of, supposes abolition of all right judgment. As I observed once before, there are many things pertaining to God, and to other spiritual matters, which our minds are incompetent to lay hold of, and which only bewilder us, the more we reflect on them. Still, if constraining evidence presents itself for believing those things, we are bound to believe them. But, if we receive as true, things which we cannot help perceiving to be false, what are we not to receive? Why are we not to hold, that Brahma is nothing, and that the soul is nothing? It is for the reason to decide these points; and we are not to imitate the Vedántins in abnegating reason, as they do, when it suits their purpose.

Utterances similar to that which I have extracted from the *Sankshepa-s'árīraka,* will be found in the *Siddhánta-les'a,* among other books. All those works lay it down, that, as the world is false, is imagined by ignorance, and appears only by reason of ignorance, so—the very pivot of the Vedánta system,—ignorance is imagined by ignorance, in other words, is nothing, and, from ignorance alone, seems to be something.†

---

* अनाऽनिर्वचनीयवादे नाऽनुपपत्तिदूषणम् ।

† This doctrine we may find in the *Vedánta-sára* even, though not enunciated very conspicuously. At p. 4 of that work we read : अमर्षभूतरज्जौ

Let us dwell upon this extraordinary and extravagant doctrine a little longer. I say to the Vedántins: If, in order to make out ignorance to be false, you assert, that it is imagined by ignorance, how does it not occur to you, that, on the supposition of its being nothing, it is impossible for it to imagine anything, either itself, or the world? And whence, if it be nothing, is the appearance of the false world? Your ready answer is, that you do not pronounce ignorance to be altogether nothing. I ask, what sort of thing is it, then? You reply, that it is an imagination of ignorance. To this I rejoin, that an imagination of ignorance is nothing: and, if it be considered to be something, your labour is all fruitless; since, in that case, the soul forfeits its character of being essentially ever pure, intelligent, and free. To this you say, that ignorance is not nothing; that its being self-imagined proves it to be unreal only from the standing point of true existence, and that it is not shown to be quite unreal. Ignorance is imagined by ignorance, and hence is called apparent;* and what is so is not entirely nothing, but possesses apparent ex-

---

सपरारोपवद् वस्तुन्यवस्तारोपोऽध्यारोपः । वस्तु सच्चिदानन्दाद्यं ब्रह्म । अज्ञानादिसकलजडसमूहोऽवस्तु । "False imputation is the imagining a false thing in a veritable thing; as a snake in a rope, *which, in fact, is not a snake. In what is now to be treated of,* the veritable thing is Brahma,—the existent, intelligence, and joy,—without a second: the false thing is the sum total of the inanimate, *viz.*, ignorance and so forth."

That whereby false things are here imagined in the veritable thing, Brahma, is ignorance. And ignorance itself is reckoned among those false things which are thus imagined. Clearly, therefore, ignorance is held to be self-imagined.

This is plainly the view touching ignorance taken by the author of the Sánkhya aphorisms, and by Vijnána Bhikshu, his expositor. See the note at p. 258.

* The author would here repeat, that he has not come across any passage in which ignorance is said to be apparent, and not practical. His authority, though good of its kind, is only oral. It is shown, however, at p. 188, that it matters nothing, in effect, in the Vedánta system, whether ignorance be of the one sort or of the other.

istence. For existence is of three kinds. That which is nothing whatsoever is known as non-existent; as the son of a barren woman, for example :* and ignorance, only if it were allowed to have true existence, would prove fatal to the character of spirit as being, by nature, ever pure, intelligent, and free.

But see to what the Vedántins thus come. On the one hand, they take ignorance to be nothing at all;—for, otherwise, Brahma could not be essentially ever pure, intelligent, and free;—and, to prove this very point, they assert, that ignorance is self-imagined. On the other hand, by giving to that ignorance the epithet of apparent, they at once begin to see a little existence in it,—just enough to avail for its self-imagination. They come to such a pass, that the term real, since they take it to signify both false and real, is useless towards distinguishing the one from the other. We ask them, whether, in their apprehension, that which they declare to be apparent really exists: for, if it does not, it can do nothing. Yes, it really exists, they tell us, but as apparent. What can be done for such reasoners? What words can we employ to convey our meaning to them, and to discover to them what is real and what is false, in other words, what is and what is not? Our only course, it seems to me, is, to discuss with them the subject of their three kinds of existence, the true, the practical, and the apparent, and to point out to them the error of those distinctions.

---

* See the second note in p. 163.

CHAPTER 9.

Examination of the Tenet of the Vedántins, that there are Three Kinds of Existence. Ignorance cannot be False; and, therefore, the Ignorant Soul cannot be one with the Supreme Spirit.

Before I criticize the doctrine of three kinds of existence, I would bespeak from the Vedántin the strictest attention. Without it, he will never be able to get at the truth. Let him lay aside his usual habits of thought for a short hour; and, while listening to what I have to offer, let him take account of his present consciousness.

When you, Vedántin, are assured, with respect to a given thing, that it indeed is, you have a conviction, that its existence is real. And did you ever feel, that the real existence of one thing, recognized by you as existing, was different from the real existence of any other thing so recognized? Do not all things which you perceive to exist at all, approve themselves to exist in one and the same manner? Again, when a thing appears to you to be non-existent, does it not appear to you to be simply and altogether so, and nothing more or less? It results, that whatever is is, and that whatever is not is altogether not,—with no room for a third condition. How, then, can you prove various sorts of existence?

But here the Vedántin's philosophical prejudice gets the better of him; and he declares, that he has a consciousness of sundry sorts of existence: for he says, that, when he mistakes a rope for a snake, he becomes conscious of apparent existence;[*] it appertaining to such a snake. When, however, you commit such a mistake, does the existence of the snake seem to you different from that of a jar, or the like? Does not the existence seem to be, in both instances, equally real? Undoubtedly, it does. How, then, is it made out, that, in mis-

---

[*] See pp. 167, etc.

taking a rope for a snake, you become conscious of a second kind of existence? You will reply, that, by reason of mistake, you look upon the snake's existence to be like that of a jar, or similar thing; but that they who know, that the object before you is a rope, call the snake, seen by you, apparent: and, on that account, to their apprehension, your consciousness concerns an apparent existence. Let them apprehend as they may, what do you apprehend? You are then conscious of the one sort of existence that you are habitually conscious of. As for the impression of the lookers-on, do they see any description of snake? Not at all. They are perfectly satisfied, that no snake is there. So, neither has a man labouring under mistake, nor one that does not so labour, any consciousness of apparent existence; nor can either of them prove such a thing to be. You will reply, that you are constrained to call such a thing apparent: "for, otherwise, how shall we name a thing that is not, and yet appears; as a snake surmised in a rope?" But how idle to trouble yourself about naming that which never had any being! That which is not, but only seems, through error, to be, is altogether non-existent; and why should you name it?

But the Vedántins say, that, when one mistakes a rope for a snake, the mistake is one of perception. Perception, however, cannot take place without the connexion of an object and an organ of sense. Hence, if, in the case instanced, you did not grant, that there was some sort of snake, there would be nothing for the eye to have connexion with, and there would be no mistake of perception.* My reply is, that the mistake in question is not perceptional, but inferential. Our senses can take cognizance of the qualities of things, as their colour, taste, length, &c. &c., but of nothing beyond these. When, therefore, a man mistakes a rope for a snake, he

---

* See the passages from the *Vedánta-paribháshá*, pp. 10 and 13, quoted at pp. 167 and 168.

merely cognizes, with his eye, something long; and there is no mistake in this. And then he infers, that the something long is a snake. But the fact of being a snake is not invariably concomitant* with length; for many things besides snakes are long. Hence, since the reason—the length—is fallacious, the inference—that a snake is present—is erroneous. The mistake of supposing a snake to be seen being, accordingly, not a mistake of perception, it is not necessary to hold that a snake is produced.

You, Vedántins, give to objects of mistake the designation of apparent. But mistake is where there is no object, and yet the notion of it. Consider, now, what are the requisites that make mistake to be mistake. In the first place, there is no object: in mistake an object is wanting. The notion of it is all that remains; and beyond this there is nothing. Whence, then, do you get an apparent object? Is it brought forth by a mere notion? Know, for a certainty, that, when a man mistakes a rope for a snake, there are only two things. One is the rope; and the other is, the man's mistake in surmising it to be a snake. There is nothing else; and there never was; and there never will be.

Hearing this, the Vedántin asks, in great astonishment, whether apparent things are altogether non-existent. He wishes to know, what difference there is left between such objects and the son of a barren woman.† Why do you think, I ask, that there is any?‡ But there is, he insists, an immense difference; for that apparent things are, once in a while, surmised by people, whereas no one ever surmises the son of a barren woman. My reply is, that the difference is merely one of surmise, not of object. The son of a barren woman

---

* This phraseology is that of the Nyáya.
† See the second note in p. 163.
‡ See near the end of the passage from Párthasárathi Miśra, at the foot of pp. 164, 165.

2 M

is not surmised, for the obvious reason, that, whoever knows what is meant when a barren woman is spoken of, is aware that she is a woman without a son. What wonder, if no one surmises such a son! And so, can one who knows a given thing to be a rope ever mistake it for a snake? He alone who does not know it to be a rope, so mistakes. Similarly, one who does not know what is intended by a barren woman, may take her to be a mother. How you encumber a simple matter with difficulties!

Let it be, the Vedántin here concedes, that a rope mistaken for a snake, and nacre mistaken for silver, and like things, have been shown to be quite unreal. But he will still maintain, that the things of the world cannot be so. For, he will say, we have dealings with them; and for this reason—though, like apparent things, they are imagined by ignorance, and our learned men believe them to be apparent,—for the readier apprehension of the uninformed, they are called practical. If they were altogether unreal, how could we deal with them? In reply, I ask, whether the dealing is real, or unreal. The Vedántin answers, that it is practically real, and yet not indeed real. And does he not call it ignorance-imagined? He does, he says. And what does he mean by that term, which he applies to practical dealing and to things practical? Does he mean appearing, by reason of ignorance, to exist? Or, derived from a substance termed ignorance, after the manner of a germ from a seed? To this interrogatory he may return one or other of the following answers. If he speaks from the promptings of common sense, he may say, that "ignorance-imagined" means "appearing, by reason of ignorance, to have existence." On the other hand, should he be thoroughly ensnared by the phraseology of the Vedánta, he will probably say, that it signifies "derived from ignorance," or illusion,—an unintelligent substance, and the material cause of the world, like the "nature" of the Sánkhya scheme. If such, I say to him, be the case, the existence of ignorance and of ignorance-imagined things does not differ from that of Brahma. And why, then, do you not call practical dealing and things practical indeed real? If you reply, that things sprung from illusion are denominated, in your peculiar language, practical only, and that the distinction of true is restricted to Brahma, I have to say, that, by these terms, you discriminate by class, not by existence; and thus your divisions of existence fall to the ground. In like manner the Naiyáyikas style some things limited in dimension, and others, unlimited; and, again, some, terrene, and others, igneous, &c.: and is difference as to existence thereby implied respecting them? And do you mark any difference as to existence, by calling, technically, and so only, one object true, and another, practical? Both are alike real. And, since both are real, what becomes of the dogma of monism, or non-duality? Can monism be established by simply showing, that two things are different in kind? If so, the Naiyáyikas, no less than you, are monists; for they hold, that Is'wara differs, in very many respects, from everything else.

Further, if ignorance does not mean mistake, how is this world got rid of by knowledge? For nothing except what is mistaken is falsified thereby. But, if the world be made out of ignorance, as a jar is made out of clay, knowledge can never do away with the world. When I find out, that what I mistook for a snake is a rope, the supposed snake is dispelled: but what knowledge is such that it can do away with a jar which stands before me? Take a club and break it, and it is destroyed, to be sure. Knowledge, however, cannot destroy it. And, as the world is not falsifiable by knowledge, so your material cause of the world, illusion, if it be not one with mistake, is not to be got rid of by knowledge; and then the soul's connexion with the world, and remaining in bondage, are real; and, therefore, the soul cannot be Brahma. The sense of the term ignorance being paltered with, everything, with you, is inverted. The authors of your system must, by "ignorance," originally have intended "mistake,"* when they spoke of the world as being ignorance-imagined; and by this epithet they meant to mark things as seeming, by reason of mistake, to have existence. Subsequently, entrapped by sophistry, they began to take a different view of those expressions. Had they not understood them in the way I have shown, the falseness of the world, and monism, and the removableness of ignorance by knowledge, &c., would never have been suggested to them. By this time, indeed, it will be conceded, that the phrase "ignorance-imagined" can endure no sense but that which I attach to it. Accordingly, since it means "appearing, because of ignorance, to exist," how can a thing so called exist? That which is not, but appears to be, can be said to seem, from ignorance, to exist. As for what is, and appears to be, it does not seem, from ignorance, but from knowledge, to have existence. How can a thing of the former description have existence? Does ignorance bring it forth, as a snake produces eggs? As, in discussing the subject of the apparent, I remarked, so now I repeat, that, when one says a thing is not, but is cognized, one denies its existence and affirms only the cognition of it; beyond which there is nothing. How, then, can your practical be established? And, as you call practical things ignorance-imagined, so you call practical dealing likewise; whence it follows, that the latter also is unreal. Then, in order to account for such practical dealing,—unreal, and seeming, because of ignorance, to exist,—what necessity is there for supposing any kind of real existence in that with which it is concerned? If a man has dreamed, that he mounted a horse, is there any need of his attributing any kind of existence to such horse? In short, to be consistent, you ought to regard the things of

---

* Such being the only natural and intelligible conception of *ajnána*, "ignorance," regarded as the imaginer of false objects. S'ankara A'chárya, not entirely disengaged from this conception, could, as we have seen, speak of "ignorance" as one with "mistake," though in the teeth of his own doctrine.

the world as altogether non-existent, just like nacrine silver and the son of a barren woman.

According to your notions, the difference between your three species of objects turns on cognition. There is invariable cognition, occasional cognition, and the absence of cognition. Such are the characteristics of those three species. To the first belong the things of this world; to the second, nacrine silver and the like; and, to the third, the son of a barren woman. But do not suppose, that these objects therefore differ among themselves. It is true, that, even to objects purely imaginary we are obliged to give names; and, if the cognition of one such object differs from the cognition of another, it is permissible, on account of that difference, to attach different names to those objects. Hence, if you only denominated one class of nonentities practical, and another class, apparent, I should not blame you. What I find fault with you for is this, that the terms practical and apparent suggest to you two separate kinds of real existence.

Now I wish to explain the nature of existence briefly, and to point out how you err concerning it. Consider, that, when you affirm, as regards what you call a true, a practical, or an apparent, object, that it is; in so affirming, you acknowledge, that its existence is, in all three cases, of the same description. What, then, becomes of their difference as to existence, which you affirm? If you say to yourself, that those objects themselves are of different sorts, namely, true, practical, and apparent, and that, therefore, they differ with respect to existence, I assure you, that this is a mistake. Let it be granted, that they are different, of different species: this fact does not concern their existing, any more than does the fact, that the Naiyáyikas divide certain things into limited and unlimited, establish, that those things have various sorts of existence. If the difference you contend for were a reality, it would be based on mental premisses. Thus, when we say, that salt water is different from sweet, we can both conceive the ground of the difference, and we can express it in words. But, when you say, concerning objects of three kinds, true, &c., that they are, do you picture to yourself any foundation for their existing diversely? Do not say, that there are some objects which really differ, but yet the grounds of their differing are not to be known; and that, in like manner, the ground of the difference between the existences belonging to true and other things is so subtle as to be impossible of discovery. It is only those things that you are not fully acquainted with, of which you can allege, that you are unacquainted with the ground of their differing. Of whatever thing you are certain, whether from perception, from inference, or otherwise, that it is, you know the existence of that thing already. It may be, that you are ignorant of its nature; still you are not ignorant of its existence. However you came by your information, as soon as you know, that a thing is, you are fully aware of its existence. Similarly, if you are sure, that what you style true things, and practical, and apparent, are, you are fully informed of their existence; and, if they are discrepant as to existence, you must know how they differ. If you do not know how they differ, but if it is clear, from your applying "is" to each of them, that they all appear to exist in one and the same way, what reason have you for speaking of three species of existence?

If you have understood me hitherto, listen a little further. You said, that you believe in different existences of true, practical, and apparent objects, because those objects themselves differ mutually; and you remember my reply, based on a concession.* But now I protest against your classification of objects, heretofore granted for argument's sake. Unlike the Naiyáyika division of things into limited and unlimited, it is grounded simply on your supposed difference in the nature of the existence of the aforesaid objects; and it falls to the ground with the fall of that difference.

---

* See p. 267.

I have now to say, that, even though you proved the world to be imagined by ignorance, and false, still you should not call that ignorance false. When, to make out ignorance to be false, you style it ignorance-imagined, does it not occur to you, that, if it were false, that is to say, no entity, it could not exercise imagination? In evasion of this question, you lay down, that ignorance, though ignorance-imagined, and, therefore, not real from the standing point of true existence, is not altogether nothing; it being apparent. What can be replied to such an absurdity? Whatever is ignorance-imagined, and, by consequence, not indeed real, is a sheer nonentity, and can imagine nothing.

Sometimes, the Vedántins declare, even things that owe their origin entirely to mistake, and are false, are able to produce effects. For instance, what is seen in dreams foreshows, it is said, good and evil.* Here, too, in my opinion, the Vedántins, from want of right consideration, are wide of the truth. Things that we see in dreams do not foreshow, as they allege they do; for such things are nonentities. Dreams themselves may foreshow; and these are entities. The object of a misconception is false; but the conception itself is true. When a man mistakes a rope for a snake, and is put in bodily fear, we are not to understand, as the Vedántins do,† that the snake,—for that is nothing,—but that the

---

* तथाऽपि खप्रदृष्टं तु वस्तु खर्गनिवासिनः ।
सूचकं हि भवत्येव जाग्रत्त्वर्थसिद्धये ॥

" Nevertheless, ye dwellers in Elysium, a thing seen in a dream certainly becomes indicative, that something real, belonging to the waking state, will be accomplished."

This couplet is from the *Brahma-gítá*, a part of the *Súta-sanhitá*. No MS. of it is at present accessible to the writer.

† परिकल्पितोऽपि सकलत्त्वया
गुरुरेव पूर्णमवबोधयति ।

man's misconception, which is entitative, is the cause of his fear.

By all these considerations it is proved, that, if, as the Vedántins maintain, the regarding the world as true, and the believing oneself to be a soul, are the result of ignorance, then that ignorance cannot be false, but must be true; and hence, we are indeed ignorant, and, consequently, we cannot be the Supreme Spirit.

And just as true are our sinfulness and misery. For there is sin in one's desiring or doing anything which one counts to be wrong: and there are many things which, though we so count them, we all desire and do; and we are, likewise, all conscious of misery. In treating of the Sánkhya system, I have shown, that our consciousness of cognition, will, activity, misery, &c., cannot be an error. Since, then, our souls are sinful, and subject to misery, for this further reason, they cannot be the Supreme Spirit; which, as the Vedántins confess, is ever pure, and essentially joy.

After adverting to a single topic more, I shall bring this chapter to a close. When I was discussing the Sánkhya,

परिकल्पितोऽपि मरणाय भवेत्
उरगो यथा न तु नभो मलिनम् ॥

"The preceptor alone, albeit imaginary, because all-sapient, gives instruction to the full; as it is the snake, albeit imaginary, and not the befouled ether, that operates for death."

The sense is this. Among things imagined, some may produce effects which are beyond the power of other things. Thus, a man may be fatally terrified by a rope mistaken for a snake; whereas the foul ether, an object equally chimerical, cannot work to the same end. Just so, an instructor, no less than all other men, is imaginary and false; and yet he is able to instruct, which other men are not.

In Hindu opinion, the ether is always essentially colourless and pure, and only from error is supposed to possess hue. See the note on ákása, at p. 120. The ignorant, it is said, think the blueness of the sky to be the befoulment of ether.

The couplet cited above is from the Sankshepa-sáriraka.

I set down what would be enough to refute the Vedánta as well. I said, that our consciousness of cognition, will, &c.,—however we may err as to other things,—cannot be erroneous. Consequently, even were I to allow the correctness of the Vedántins' allegation, that to regard the world as true is a misconception, yet so to regard it cannot be false; since we are conscious, that we have a cognition of the world's truth: a cognition which the Vedántins call erroneous. I repeat, that, if such a misconception as that just spoken of actually infects us, we cannot be the Supreme Spirit. Thus, also, am I able to answer the Vedántins. It was necessary, however, to examine and to expose, from various aspects, the arguments they produce to prove the falsity of ignorance; for therein, as I have before said, consists the whole strength of the Vedánta doctrine. It was of main importance, also, to refute their errors touching the subject of existence; those errors being most prejudicial to them in several ways. The labour I have expended on this head should not, then, be viewed as uncalled for.

CHAPTER 10.

Examination of the Vedántin's Emancipation; Proof, that the Vedánta does not deserve to be called Theistic; and a few Words on the Faculty of Judgment, its Power, and its Use.

When the notion is refuted, that the soul is identical with Brahma, the refutation follows, by implication, of the notion, that, when the soul attains to right apprehension, viz., the regarding itself as one with Brahma, it becomes liberated from all error, and, being Brahma realized,* is emancipated. For,

---

* This word is a makeshift; and so is "restored," used at p. 246, and elsewhere. It is impossible to express in rational language what becomes of the soul, when Vedantically emancipated. From all eternity it has been Brahma, and therefore has not to become Brahma, or, again, to be restored to Brahma-since the soul is not at all Brahma, its thinking itself to be so is not right apprehension, but the extreme of misapprehension; and, for thus thinking, instead of deserving to be emancipated, it deserves severe punishment.

Again, the emancipation of the Vedántins is punctually like that of the Nyáya and others among the Systems. In these, as I have said before, emancipation is, to be delivered from all pain, and to remain like a stone, utterly void of intelligence. And in this there is no experience of happiness. Precisely such is the condition of emancipation according to the Vedántins; however it may seem, from their language, that it is attended by happiness: for they describe Brahma as being intelligence and bliss. To be emancipated is, with them, realization of Brahmahood; and from this it should seem, that the emancipated must be happy. I have shown, however, that their Brahma is only nominally intelligence and bliss. He is intelligence that cognizes nothing, and bliss without fruition of happiness. What hope is there, that the soul would be happy, if it came to such a state as this?

We know, that all their doctrines concerning Brahma and the soul are most absurd; but, accepting them as set forth, we can even show, that their emancipation amounts to annihilation. They say, that the soul is false. If so, it can never actually be restored to Brahmahood. For a false thing cannot become true. So long as misapprehension endures, such a thing exists as a semblance; and, when right apprehension accedes, it vanishes away. To disappear into nothingness is, then, all that the hapless soul could attain to by acquiring right apprehension.

---

hood. Nor does it realize Brahmahood; inasmuch as, in the state of emancipation, it is void of all consciousness. A Vedántin does not hesitate to say: ब्रह्मैव सन् ब्रह्मैव भवति and विमुक्तस्य विमुच्यते । "Being already Brahma himself, it becomes Brahma himself," and "Free already, it is freed."

Hitherto I have been taken up with the leading doctrines of the Vedánta; and I have passed by nothing of main import. And now I venture to ask any thoughtful man, whether this scheme deserves to be called theistic. Viewed superficially, it has, I allow, a guise of theism; and yet, when investigated critically, I cannot see, that it is anything but a sort of atheism.

The distinctive article of theism is, the belief in a God: but God is eliminated from the Vedánta. Its Brahma is neither creator of the world, nor its preserver, nor its lord: in short, the world is out of relation to him. Let the Vedántins give to such an object the title of Brahma, or that of Supreme Spirit; still their doing so does not make them theists. Greatness does not consist in bearing a great name; but he that does mighty deeds, and is endowed with extraordinary excellencies, is great, and he alone. Why is God spoken of as supremely great? Because He created all, and regulates and governs all, and because He is omnipotent and omniscient, and endowed with divine attributes. Again, why is it proper for us, and incumbent on us, to honour and to love Him? Because He made us, and because we are His, and because He is our benefactor, and because, by reason of His adorable perfections, He claims the homage of our hearts. The religion which does not recognize in the Supreme the characteristics thus enumerated, does not really recognize God; and the worship which it teaches is not the worship of God. To devise a strange imagination, and to denominate it Brahma and Supreme spirit, will in nowise benefit the Vedántins.

Moreover, as, to a theistic religion, God and the adoration of Him are essential, so likewise is discrimination between sin and virtue: and this discrimination is ignored by the Vedánta. Sin and virtue are acknowledged, indeed, from the standing point of practical existence; but, nevertheless, they come to be, in truth, nothing. The ignorant man, consistently with these views, may dread sin, and follow after virtue:

but the rightly apprehending man should spurn at both.* He has no reason to fear the one, nor any motive for pursuing the other. Wherein, on this score, does the Vedánta differ from atheism? And can any one hope to be advantaged by such a belief?

The Vedántin would fain make out, by his sophistical arguments, that I's'wara, the world, and so forth are what he calls false. But, for all that, he is unable to rid himself entirely of the conviction of their self-evident and undeniable realness. Hence, as I have said, they present themselves to him as verities. To do away with the incongruity involved herein, the Vedántins have set up their theory of various sorts of existence. The objects above mentioned, I's'wara, &c., which show themselves as real, they allege to belong to the practical, not to the true; and so, by fallacies, they solace their mental disquietude.

My view, that the Vedánta does not merit a place among theistic religions, is based on a sifting of its leading and fundamental tenets. Its advocates, of course, here take issue with me. According to them, their system countenances the worship of God, and distinguishes between sin and virtue, &c. &c.; and such is their inconsistency, that they teach conformably. The harm they do is, therefore, less than would be done by inculcating overt atheism. Still, any scheme must be most pernicious, which is, in truth, repugnant to theism, even though its maintainers do not clearly perceive such repugnance. Those Vedántins, I have observed, who are naturally least inclined to evil, are least injured by their system. But its effect on

---

* यस्य नाऽहङ्कृतो भावो बुद्धिर्यस्य न लिप्यते ।
हत्वाऽपि स इमाँल् लोकान् न हन्ति न निबध्यते ॥

" He who has not the notion, that he is a doer, *and* whose intellect is not involved *by works*, though he were to slay *all* these denizens *of earth*, would not, *in fact*, slay, or be compromised. "

So runs the *Bhagavad-gítá*, XVIII., 17.

This is a perfectly legitimate deduction from Vedánta premisses.

those persons who have a strong bias to vice, is, I have likewise observed, such, that no excess of wickedness seems to them wrong. As for the former class, it is, I think, owing to their addiction to devotional exercises, rather than to matters of doctrine, that they are not equally depraved. But let a man give himself up to the Vedánta, and dwell constantly on such thoughts as that he is Brahma, and pure, and that sin and virtue are falsities; be his natural disposition however favourable, his reverence for God must become less, and his desire to discriminate good and evil must grow cold and languid. And the detection of his sins, and humility and grief because of them, how can these and suchlike, which are most necessary and beneficial to man, be possible to him? Indeed, it is unavoidable but that the Vedánta should work only prejudice to all whom it influences; in a lesser degree, certainly, to some than to others: but it cannot improve the fallen nature of any single mortal.

Reason admonishes us, that the true religion is that which meliorates our natural condition; which, surely, with every one of us, stands in great need of amendment. The best of men must be, in the eyes of God, grievously imperfect and sinful. Even they require the remedy of the true Faith. Moreover, no man can love God as he ought. One proof of due love to God is, the avoidance of all sin of whatever description: for sin is that which is opposed to the divine commands, and abhorrent to God. Yet there is no one who has not committed sins innumerable; and the natural man has turned from God, and is on the way to perdition. He wants, then, a religion to instruct him in the knowledge of God, and to lead him to worship and honour Him; and to show the exceeding heinousness of sin, and its terrible consequences, and how, by repentance and prayer, to free himself from its fetters. That religion from which we learn these things must be, we feel, from God. And, for philosophers—themselves corrupt, as being human,—to exhort their fellow-men, in contrariety to the teachings of that religion, to regard God as false, to think themselves one with Brahma, and to count sin, and virtue, and their fruits, nonentities, is to administer to a sick man poison, not medicine. Cease, I entreat you, my beloved countrymen, to consider as true a religion which contains such things as these.

I shall conclude with a few words on the faculty of judgment. God has given this to mankind in general; and, by reason of it, men believe, that there is a God, maker of the world; and they know, that it is good to practise virtue, and wrong to do evil, and what is the fruit of each; and that they should worship God, and secure His favour; and that from His favour springs true happiness. In most cases, such is its force, that, when a man sins, he at once condemns himself for his sin. But, now that man has lapsed from his original condition, his judgment is not so perfect, or so sure, as it was at the beginning of the world. As concerns things of a primary character, it speaks the same language to almost all; but, immediately on arriving at particulars, we mark a great discrepancy. Hence the origin of so many religions and sects. And the judgment of a man who accepts a false religion becomes more depraved than it would be otherwise. Nevertheless, let a man's religion be ever so far from the truth, and let his reason be ever so perverted by the lessons he has heard from his youth up, there are certain things in respect of which that man's better judgment will belie his doctrines. Thus is it with the Vedántins. There is no doubt, that the fundamental dogmas of the Vedánta are opposed to all godliness, and are subversive of the principles of morality. It is perfectly certain, that, according to them, one is not called upon to fear and to adore God, to detest sin, and to love virtue. Inconsistently enough, however, there are Vedántins who are earnestly devoted to the worship of what they take to be God. This comes from their following the dictates of their better judgment, the voice of God, rather than their own chief tenets. For the same reason it is, that, in the opinion of the Vedántins, even he who has acquired what they call right apprehension is not to do as he lists, but must eschew vice. In several other particulars, too, the Vedántins are seen to follow common sense, in contravention of their system. For instance: since they profess to regard the soul and the Supreme Spirit as one, why should they hesitate to allow, that the latter is changeable and impure? But not only do they hesitate here, but they refuse to admit, that the Supreme Spirit is other than ever pure, intelligent, and free. To seem to reconcile this position with the rest of their scheme, costs them great labour. Powerful indeed must be the natural instinct of truth, if, in spite of the causes tending to debilitate it, which I have lately spoken of, it still asserts its prerogative, with some effect, among very misbelievers. Even through their mouths it bears witness against false doctrine, and in behalf of God and the truth.

God be praised, that He has suffered us to retain thus much of this illumination; it being this alone that serves as a safeguard and moral guide to such men as are ignorant of the true religion. Except for it, no one can tell to what depth the human race would not have become degraded; so surcharged are false religions with error, so far do they militate against the majesty and purity of God, and so confused and imperfect are their principles of right and wrong. The reason, as we now find it, is, however, inadequate to lead us to the way of salvation, or to purify our corrupt nature. For these ends we must have recourse to the Word of God. And, as regards this Word, when presented, the reason, once more, is of great use, in enabling us to test it, and to recognize it for what it professes to be. Moreover, such is the efficacy of the Word of God, that, as an enquirer goes on studying it, provided he brings to that study due perseverance, impartiality, humbleness, and abnegation of self, his judgment daily becomes more and more defecated; and it enables him to distinguish clearly between what is true and what is false in matters of religious belief. But the result will not be thus, unless he applies himself to the search of Holy Writ in the way I have specified. For there are many truths which, though at the first blush they revolt the mind, are seen, after patient investigation, to be quite in accord with all that is reasonable and right.

The true religion is now accessible to the people of India. May God, in His infinite mercy, grant, my dear countrymen, that you quench not the divine light which He has lighted in your breasts; that, on the contrary, you may follow its leading; that you meekly and patiently try, by it, the Christian Scriptures; that you take hold on their priceless promises; and that, in the end, you may inherit, as your everlasting portion, the joy of the Heavenly Kingdom.

LIST OF THE PRINCIPAL SANSKRIT BOOKS QUOTED IN
THIS VOLUME.

Nyáya-sútra-vritti, by Vis'wanátha Bhattáchárya. Calcutta edition of 1828.

Bháshá-parichchheda, by Vis'wanátha Panchánana Tarkálankára Bhattáchárya. Edition in the *Bibliotheca Indica.*

Siddhánta-muktávali, by the same; a commentary on the *Bháshá-parichchheda,* and printed with it.

Tarkámrita, by Jagadís'a Tarkálankára Bhattáchárya. MS.

Tarka-sangraha, by Annam Bhatta. MS.

Tarka-dípiká, by the same; a commentary on the *Tarka-sangraha.* MS.

Vais'eshika-sútropaskára, by S'ankara Mis'ra. MS.

Dinakarí, by Bálakrishna and his son Mahádeva Bhatta Dinakara. MS.

Tattwa-kaumudí,—containing the *Sánkhya-káriká,*-by Váchaspati Mis'ra. Calcutta edition of *Samvat* 1905.

Sánkhya-pravachana- bháshya, by Vijnána Bhikshu. The Translator's edition, in the *Bibliotheca Indica.*

Sánkhya-sára,* by Vijnána Bhikshu. MS.

Pátanjala-bháshya-várttika, or *Yoga-bháshya-várttika,* by Vijnána Bhikshu. MS.

S'ástra-dípiká, by Párthasárathi Mis'ra. MS.

Púrva-mímánsártha-sangraha, by Laugákshi Bháskara. MS.

Bhátta-dípiká, by Khanda Deva. MS.

---

* The first edition is now passing through the press. The passages of the *Sánkhya-sára* quoted in this volume will be found there as below :

That cited at page 31,   at page   1.
————————————35,————————————22.
————————————36,————————————do.
————————————54,————————————23.
————————————do,————————————37.
————————————55,————————————40.
————————————59,————————————43.
————————————80,————————————15.
————————————222,————————————12.

S'ankara Achàrya's commentaries on the leading Upanishads, with A'nandajnana's—or A'nanda Giri's—annotations thereon. Edition in the *Bibliotheca Indica*.

Brahma-sútra-bháshya, or *S'áríraka-sútra-bháshya*, and the commentary on it ; by S'ankara A'chárya and Rámánanda Saraswatí respectively. Unfinished edition in the *Bibliotheca Indica*, and MS.

Bhagavad-gítá, or *I's'wara-gítá*, with S'rídhara Swámin's commentary, the *Subodhiní*. Bombay lithographed edition.

Ashtávakra-gítá, attributed to Ashtávakra the *Muni*. MS.

Brahma-gítá, a section of the *Súta-sanhitá*.

S'iva-gítá, an episode in the *Padma-purána*. MS.

Yoga-vásishtha, attributed to Válmíki. Calcutta edition of 1851. See p. 177.

Sankshepa-s'áríraka, by Sarvajnátma Muni. MS.

Subodhiní, by Purushottama Miśra ; a commentary on the *Sankshepa-s'áríraka*, MS.

Vedánta-paribháshá, by Dharmarája Díkshita. Calcutta edition of S'aka 1769.

Vedánta-s'ikhámani, a commentary on the *Vedánta-paribháshá*, by Rámakrishna Díkshita. MS.

Vedánta-sára, by Sadánanda Yogíndra. Calcutta edition of 1829.

Viveka-chúdámani, attributed to S'ankara A'chárya. MS.

A'tma-bodha, attributed to S'ankara A'chárya. The Translator's edition. Mirzapore : 1852.

Tattwa-bodha, anonymous ; printed at the end of the *A'tma-bodha*.

Hastámalaka, imputed to S'ankara A'chárya. It is printed at the end of the *Vedánta-sára*, &c., Calcutta edition of S'aka 1771.

Jívan-mukti-viveka, by Mádhava A'chárya. See p. 29.

Siddhánta-ratnamálá. See p. 35.

Krishnálankára, by Achyutakrishna A'nanda Tírtha. See p. 160.

Bhágavata-purána. Bombay lithographed edition.

Vidwan-moda-tarangini, by Chiranjíva Bhattáchárya.

Most of the MSS. used for this volume belong to the Translator. Accounts of almost all the works referred to are given in *A contribution towards an Index to the Bibliography of the Indian Philosophical Systems*. Calcutta : 1859.

EMENDATIONS AND ADDITIONS.

P. 2, note, l. 2, For "Divine Spirit" read "Brahma and Iśwara."

P. 5, l. 13. For "Deity" read "Brahma."

P. 7, note, ll. 9 etc. Strike out "presumed." By "sole" cause is meant "irrespectively of the works of souls."

P. 8, notes, l. 2 *ab infra*. Read साङ्ख्यशास्त्रस्य.

P. 9, note, l. 5. Read चेतो:.

P. 12, note, l. 2. Read व्यवक्रीयते. L. 15. Read बुड्ढा.°

P. 13, l. 2, Read "arise." Note, l. 4 *ab infra*. Read "son."

P. 14, note, l. 11. Read प्रकाश्य.°

P. 16, note, l. 9 *ab infra*. Read तत्त्व.° Read "*Brahma-sútra.*,"

P. 17, note, l. 5. Read ज्ञानपूर्वकं.

P. 21, note, l. 7 *ab infra*. Read दुःखभोग.

P. 30, notes, l. 3 *ab infra*. Strike out "generally".

P. 37, note, l. 11 *ab infra*. Read पुनर्दुः.° L. 4. "impelling," should not have been italicized.

P. 44, notes, l. 1. Put a comma after "*intellect.*"

P. 45, l. 3. Supply a comma after "discriminatively." Note, ll. 9 and 3 *ab infra*, and elsewhere. For "indifference" read "non-difference."

P. 60, l. 9 For "affection" read "evolution."

P. 64, note, ll. 9 and 6 *ab infra*. For "soul" read "spirit."

P. 71, note, l. 6. Vijnána Bhikshu says, at p. 23 of the *Sánkhya-pravachana-bháshya*: संसृप्तिस्त्वाऽविद्या मिथ्याज्ञानाख्या. *Sámvrittika* is, then, equivalent to *a'vidyaka*; and this scarcely differs in import from *máyika*. "Illusory," though an experimental rendering, may, therefore, be allowed.

P. 77, notes, l. 6. Read—मुख्यानम्

P. 80, notes, l. 5 *ab infra*. Read तत्त्वादि.°

P. 87, note l l. 12. and 21. For "Pandit" read "author."

P. 104, note, l. 3. Read "Vedas."

P. 110, l. 15. Read "as a jar, clay."

P. 111, l, 17. Put a comma after "body."

P. 120, notes, l 12. Read $\frac{7}{16}$

P. 172, l. 4. Read "a thing, they say, really produced."

P. 185, note, l. 4. For " betake" read " protend."
P. 205, notes, l. 22   Italicize " to Brahma."
P. 224, l. 7. Strike out "but," note, l. 3. read " diverse."
P. 231, l. 16. For " betakes" read " protends."
P. 235, l. 5. Important as is the doctrine of the objectlessness of Brahma's so-called cognition, and though it is acknowledged by every Vedántin, no express statement of it, in any regular Vedánta treatise, has yet fallen in the way of the author. The words about to be cited from Ratnagarbha are more directly enunciative of the doctrine adverted to than anything quoted in the body of this volume. Ratnagarbha is commenting on the *Vishṇu-Puraṇa*, I., 9, 41 :

विशुद्धं बोधनं नित्यमजमच्च्यमव्ययम् ।
अव्यक्तमविकारं यत् तद् विष्णोः परमं पदम् ॥

On this he says : विशुद्धं बोधनं विशुद्धज्ञानं दृत्तिज्ञानं व्यावर्तयति । विशुद्धत्वं दर्शयति अव्यक्तमिति यस्य विषयस्तदृच्चितम् ।

Bodhana is here explained by *jna'na*, " cognition ;" and it is stated, that its epithet *viśuddha*, " pure," is intended to severalize it from " modificational cognition ;" and that *avyakta*, in the sense of " objectless,"—since *vyakta* signifies " object,"—is added, in the original, by way of elucidating *viśuddha*.

The commentator, a learned Vedántin, is here writing of Brahma. That, in his exposition of *avyakta*, he unwarrantably Vedantizes the text he is explicating, is quite possible. At the same time, it is clear, that he regards Brahma's cognition as void of object.

P. 253, notes, l. 8. Read पुनः°

*** Numerous errors of accentuation, punctuation, &c., but of a sort not likely to cause any perplexity, have been left unnoticed in the preceding list. The translator, when the book was printing, was at such a distance from the press, that it was impracticable to furnish him with revises, or second proof-sheets.

www.ingramcontent.com/pod-product-compliance
Lightning Source LLC
Chambersburg PA
CBHW032057220426
43664CB00008B/1042